Teach Yourself
Microsoft® PowerPoint 2000
VISUALLY™

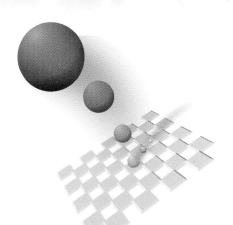

IDG's **3-D Visual™** Series

IDG BOOKS · *From* **maranGraphics™**

IDG Books Worldwide, Inc.
An International Data Group Company
Foster City, CA • Indianapolis • Chicago • New York

Teach Yourself Microsoft® PowerPoint 2000 VISUALLY™

Published by
IDG Books Worldwide, Inc.
An International Data Group Company
919 E. Hillsdale Blvd., Suite 400
Foster City, CA 94404

Library of Congress Catalog Card No.: 99-65044
ISBN: 0-7645-6060-3
Printed in the United States of America
10 9 8 7 6 5 4

Distributed in the United States by IDG Books Worldwide, Inc.
Distributed by CDG Books Canada Inc. for Canada; by Transworld Publishers Limited in the United Kingdom; by IDG Norge Books for Norway; by IDG Sweden Books for Sweden; by Woodslane Pty. Ltd. for Australia; by Woodslane (NZ) Ltd. for New Zealand; by TransQuest Publishers Pte Ltd. for Singapore, Malaysia, Thailand, Indonesia, and Hong Kong; by ICG Muse, Inc. for Japan; by Norma Comunicaciones S.A. for Colombia; by Intersoft for South Africa; by Le Monde en Tique for France; by International Thomson Publishing for Germany, Austria and Switzerland; by Distribuidora Cuspide for Argentina; by Livraria Cultura for Brazil; by Ediciones ZETA S.C.R. Ltda. for Peru; by WS Computer Publishing Corporation, Inc., for the Philippines; by Contemporanea de Ediciones for Venezuela; by Express Computer Distributors for the Caribbean and West Indies; by Micronesia Media Distributor, Inc. for Micronesia; by Grupo Editorial Norma S.A. for Guatemala; by Chips Computadoras S.A. de C.V. for Mexico; by Editorial Norma de Panama S.A. for Panama; by American Bookshops for Finland. Authorized Sales Agent: Anthony Rudkin Associates for the Middle East and North Africa.
For corporate orders, please call maranGraphics at 800-469-6616.
For general information on IDG Books Worldwide's books in the U.S., please call our Consumer Customer Service department at 800-762-2974.
For reseller information, including discounts and premium sales, please call our Reseller Customer Service department at 800-434-3422.
For information on where to purchase IDG Books Worldwide's books outside the U.S., please contact our International Sales department at 317-596-5530 or fax 317-596-5692.
For consumer information on foreign language translations, please contact our Customer Service department at 1-800-434-3422, fax 317-596-5692, or e-mail rights@idgbooks.com.
For information on licensing foreign or domestic rights, please phone 1-650-655-3109.
For sales inquiries and special prices for bulk quantities, please contact our Sales department at 650-655-3200.
For information on using IDG Books Worldwide's books in the classroom or for ordering examination copies, please contact our Educational Sales department at 800-434-2086 or fax 317-596-5499.
For press review copies, author interviews, or other publicity information, please contact our Public Relations department at 650-655-3000 or fax 650-655-3299.
For authorization to photocopy items for corporate, personal, or educational use, please contact maranGraphics at 800-469-6616.
Screen shots displayed in this book are based on pre-release software and are subject to change.

Trademark Acknowledgments

Permissions

The 3-D illustrations are the copyright of maranGraphics, Inc.

U.S. Corporate Sales	**U.S. Trade Sales**
Contact maranGraphics at (800) 469-6616 or Fax (905) 890-9434.	Contact IDG Books at (800) 434-3422 or (650) 655-3000.

ABOUT IDG BOOKS WORLDWIDE

Welcome to the world of IDG Books Worldwide.

IDG Books Worldwide, Inc., is a subsidiary of International Data Group, the world's largest publisher of computer-related information and the leading global provider of information services on information technology. IDG was founded more than 30 years ago by Patrick J. McGovern and now employs more than 9,000 people worldwide. IDG publishes more than 290 computer publications in over 75 countries. More than 90 million people read one or more IDG publications each month.

Launched in 1990, IDG Books Worldwide is today the #1 publisher of best-selling computer books in the United States. We are proud to have received eight awards from the Computer Press Association in recognition of editorial excellence and three from Computer Currents' First Annual Readers' Choice Awards. Our best-selling ...For Dummies® series has more than 50 million copies in print with translations in 31 languages. IDG Books Worldwide, through a joint venture with IDG's Hi-Tech Beijing, became the first U.S. publisher to publish a computer book in the People's Republic of China. In record time, IDG Books Worldwide has become the first choice for millions of readers around the world who want to learn how to better manage their businesses.

Our mission is simple: Every one of our books is designed to bring extra value and skill-building instructions to the reader. Our books are written by experts who understand and care about our readers. The knowledge base of our editorial staff comes from years of experience in publishing, education, and journalism — experience we use to produce books to carry us into the new millennium. In short, we care about books, so we attract the best people. We devote special attention to details such as audience, interior design, use of icons, and illustrations. And because we use an efficient process of authoring, editing, and desktop publishing our books electronically, we can spend more time ensuring superior content and less time on the technicalities of making books.

You can count on our commitment to deliver high-quality books at competitive prices on topics you want to read about. At IDG Books Worldwide, we continue in the IDG tradition of delivering quality for more than 30 years. You'll find no better book on a subject than one from IDG Books Worldwide.

John Kilcullen
Chairman and CEO
IDG Books Worldwide, Inc.

Steven Berkowitz
President and Publisher
IDG Books Worldwide, Inc.

WINNER
Eighth Annual
Computer Press
Awards ≥1992

WINNER
Ninth Annual
Computer Press
Awards ≥1993

WINNER
Tenth Annual
Computer Press
Awards ≥1994

WINNER
Eleventh Annual
Computer Press
Awards ≥1995

maranGraphics is a family-run business
located near Toronto, Canada.

At **maranGraphics**, we believe in producing great computer books–one book at a time.

Each maranGraphics book uses the award-winning communication process that we have been developing over the last 25 years. Using this process, we organize screen shots, text and illustrations in a way that makes it easy for you to learn new concepts and tasks.

We spend hours deciding the best way to perform each task, so you don't have to! Our clear, easy-to-follow screen shots and instructions walk you through each task from beginning to end.

Our detailed illustrations go hand-in-hand with the text to help reinforce the information. Each illustration is a labor of love–some take up to a week to draw!

We want to thank you for purchasing what we feel are the best computer books money can buy. We hope you enjoy using this book as much as we enjoyed creating it!

Sincerely,

The Maran Family

Please visit us on the web at:
www.maran.com

CREDITS

Authors:
Kelleigh Wing & Ruth Maran

Copy Editor:
Roxanne Van Damme

Project Manager:
Judy Maran

**Editing &
Screen Captures:**
Roxanne Van Damme
Raquel Scott
Janice Boyer
Michelle Kirchner
James Menzies
Frances Lea
Stacey Morrison

Layout & Illustrations:
Treena Lees

Illustrators:
Russ Marini
Jamie Bell
Peter Grecco
Sean Johannesen
Steven Schaerer
Roben Ponce

Screens & Illustrations:
Jimmy Tam

Permissions Coordinator:
Jenn Hillman

Indexer:
Raquel Scott

Post Production:
Robert Maran

Editorial Support:
Michael Roney

ACKNOWLEDGMENTS

Thanks to the dedicated staff of maranGraphics, including
Jamie Bell, Cathy Benn, Janice Boyer, Francisco Ferreira,
Peter Grecco, Jenn Hillman, Sean Johannesen, Michelle Kirchner,
Wanda Lawrie, Frances Lea, Treena Lees, Jill Maran, Judy Maran,
Robert Maran, Sherry Maran, Russ Marini, James Menzies,
Stacey Morrison, Roben Ponce, Steven Schaerer, Raquel Scott,
Jimmy Tam, Roxanne Van Damme, Paul Whitehead
and Kelleigh Wing.

Finally, to Richard Maran who originated the easy-to-use
graphic format of this guide. Thank you for your
inspiration and guidance.

TABLE OF CONTENTS

Chapter 1

Getting Started

Chapter 2

PowerPoint Basics

Chapter 3

Edit Text

Chapter 4

Format Text

TABLE OF CONTENTS

Chapter 5

Change Appearance of Slides

Chapter 6

Add Simple Objects

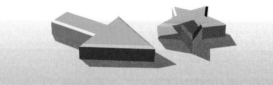

Chapter 7

Add Charts

Chapter 8

Add Tables

Chapter 9

Work With Objects

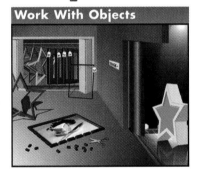

Chapter 10

Add Multimedia

TABLE OF CONTENTS

Chapter 11

Add Special Effects

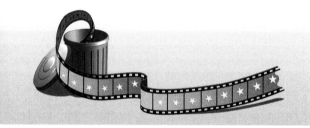

Chapter 12

Fine-Tune a Presentation

Chapter 13

Deliver a Presentation

Chapter 14

PowerPoint and the Internet

Playground Purchases

- Swings
- Slides
- Teeter-totters
- Baseball Backstop
- Basketball Court

CHAPTER 1

Getting Started

Wondering where to start with Microsoft PowerPoint 2000? This chapter will show you the way.

INTRODUCTION TO POWERPOINT

PowerPoint helps you plan, organize, design and deliver professional presentations.

Create Presentations

You can use PowerPoint to create presentations that you will deliver using a computer screen, overheads or 35mm slides. You can also save a presentation as a Web page and then publish the presentation on the Web. PowerPoint includes a wizard and pre-designed templates to help you create presentations.

Edit Text

PowerPoint offers many features to help you work with the text in your presentation. You can add, delete and move text, as well as change the importance of text on your slides. You can also check for spelling mistakes, find and replace text and insert symbols.

Format Slides

There are many ways you can change the appearance of text in your presentation. For example, you can change the font, color and alignment of the text. You can also change the slide design, color scheme and background of slides to enhance the overall appearance of your presentation.

Add Objects to Slides

You can add objects to slides to illustrate important concepts and make your slides more interesting. You can add objects such as simple shapes, clip art images, pictures, text effects, charts and tables.

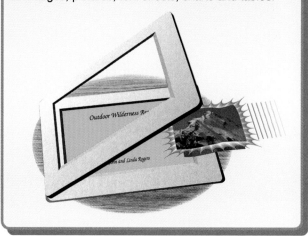

Add Multimedia to Slides

Adding multimedia to slides can make your presentation more entertaining. You can add sounds, movies and voice narration to slides. You can also play a music CD during your presentation to add background music to the slides.

Add Special Effects to Slides

PowerPoint includes special effects you can use to enhance your presentation and help direct the audience's attention to important information. You can add transitions to help introduce slides in your presentation. You can also add movement and sound effects to objects on the slides.

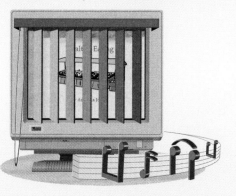

Deliver Presentations

You can rehearse and deliver a presentation on your computer screen. During your presentation, you can take notes, called meeting minutes, and refer to speaker notes that contain the ideas you want to discuss. PowerPoint also helps you create handouts that you can distribute to the audience.

CREATING GREAT PRESENTATIONS

Consider the Audience

You should consider your audience when developing the content and tone of your presentation. For example, a presentation for the engineering department of a company should be different than a presentation for the sales department.

Organize the Text

- Use uppercase and lowercase text, not ALL UPPERCASE.
- Discuss only one concept per slide.
- Include only main ideas on each slide.
- Do not include more than six points on a slide.
- Each point or slide title should be no more than two lines long.
- Spell check your presentation.

Choose Colors and Fonts

- Choose colors that match the mood of your presentation. For example, use bright colors to convey good news.
- Choose colors and fonts that make your text easy to read.
- Avoid using more than five colors per slide and three fonts per slide.

Add Visuals

Add visuals, such as pictures, charts, tables or movies, to your slides. Visuals can help enhance your presentation, but you should try to avoid cluttering your slides with visuals that have no purpose.

TIPS FOR DELIVERING A GREAT PRESENTATION

Rehearse the Presentation

Make sure you rehearse your presentation before you deliver it in front of an audience. This will help your presentation flow smoothly and can help ensure that you will complete the presentation in the time provided. If possible, practice your presentation in front of a friend or colleague.

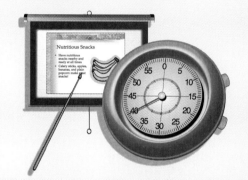

Check the Hardware

Before you deliver your presentation, check all the hardware you plan to use. Make sure you know how to operate the hardware and you have all the parts you need, such as spare bulbs or an extension cord. In case of a hardware failure, you should always have a paper copy of your presentation with you.

Check the Presentation Room

You should check the room you will be presenting in before the presentation. Make sure the slides are readable from all areas of the room. If necessary, determine the location of electrical outlets and light switches.

Check Your Body Language

When delivering a presentation, your posture should convey a relaxed and confident manner. Make eye contact with your audience while presenting and avoid hiding or clasping your hands.

CREATING GREAT PRESENTATIONS

View on a Computer Screen

You can deliver your presentation on a computer screen. This method is ideal for delivering a presentation to a small audience and allows you to add multimedia such as sounds, movies or animations, to your slides.

View on Two Monitors

You can present a slide show to an audience using one monitor while you view the presentation on another monitor. This allows you to see your speaker notes and the outline of your presentation while the audience views only the slides.

Use a Slide Projector

You can use a slide projector to deliver a presentation on 35mm slides. 35mm slides offer better color and crisper images than a presentation shown on a computer screen. A service bureau can output your presentation to 35mm slides.

Use a Computer Projector

You can connect a computer to a projector to display your presentation on a screen or wall. Computer projectors are available at many computer stores.

Use an Overhead Projector

You can use an overhead projector to display your presentation on a screen or wall. Many office supply stores sell overhead transparencies that you can print your presentation on. A service bureau can also print your presentation on overhead transparencies.

Use an LCD Panel

You can connect an LCD (Liquid Crystal Display) panel to your computer and then place the LCD panel on an overhead projector to display your presentation. The presentation will appear on a screen or wall as it would appear on a computer screen.

View at a Kiosk

You can create a self-running presentation that people can view at a kiosk. Kiosks are often found at trade shows and shopping malls.

View on the Internet

You can save your presentation as a Web page. You can then publish the presentation on the Internet to make the presentation available to people around the world.

USING THE MOUSE

A mouse is a handheld device that lets you select and move items on your screen.

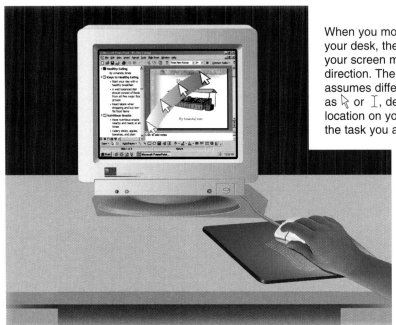

When you move the mouse on your desk, the mouse pointer on your screen moves in the same direction. The mouse pointer assumes different shapes, such as ⃗ or I, depending on its location on your screen and the task you are performing.

Resting your hand on the mouse, use your thumb and two rightmost fingers to move the mouse on your desk. Use your two remaining fingers to press the mouse buttons.

MOUSE ACTIONS

Click

Press and release the left mouse button.

Double-click

Quickly press and release the left mouse button twice.

Right-click

Press and release the right mouse button.

Drag

Position the mouse pointer over an object on your screen and then press and hold down the left mouse button. Still holding down the button, move the mouse to where you want to place the object and then release the button.

START POWERPOINT

You can start
PowerPoint to create
a new presentation
or work with a
presentation you
previously created.

START POWERPOINT

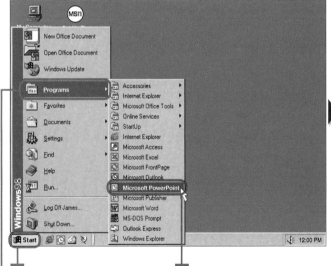

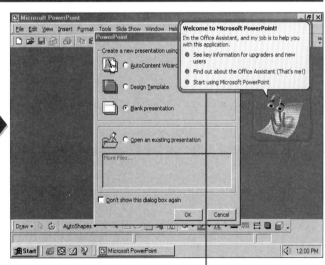

1 Click **Start**.

2 Click **Programs**.

3 Click **Microsoft PowerPoint**.

■ The Microsoft
PowerPoint window
appears.

■ The PowerPoint dialog
box appears each time you
start PowerPoint, allowing
you to create or open a
presentation.

*Note: To create a presentation,
see page 16, 20 or 22. To open
a presentation, see page 28.*

■ The Office Assistant
welcome appears the
first time you start
PowerPoint.

*Note: For information on the
Office Assistant, see page 34.*

THE POWERPOINT SCREEN

The PowerPoint screen
displays several items
to help you perform
tasks efficiently.

Menu Bar

Provides access to lists
of commands available
in PowerPoint.

Formatting Toolbar

Contains buttons to help you
select formatting commands,
such as Font and Font Size.

Standard Toolbar

Contains buttons
to help you select
commands, such
as Save and Open.

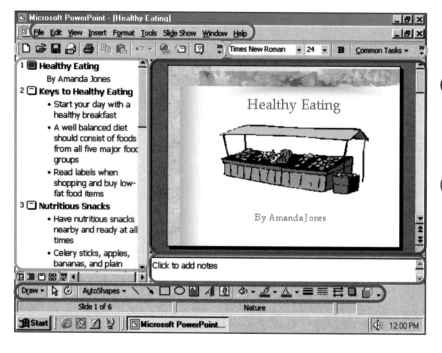

Slide Pane

Displays the
current slide.

Notes Pane

Displays the
speaker notes for
the current slide.

Outline Pane

Displays all the text
in your presentation.

View Buttons

Allow you to quickly
change the way
your presentation
is displayed on the
screen.

Drawing Toolbar

Contains buttons
to help you work
with objects in your
presentation.

SELECT COMMANDS USING TOOLBARS

A toolbar contains buttons that you can use to select commands. Each button allows you to perform a different task.

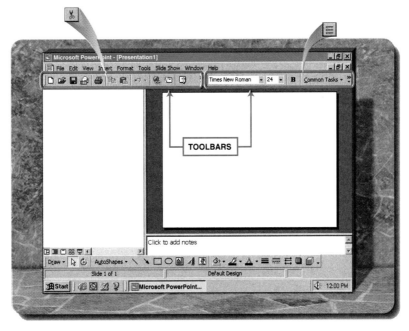

TOOLBARS

When you first start PowerPoint, the most commonly used buttons appear on each toolbar. As you work with PowerPoint, the toolbars automatically change to remove buttons you rarely use and display the buttons you use most often.

SELECT COMMANDS USING TOOLBARS

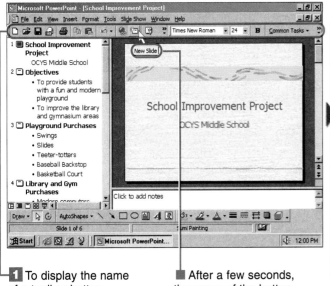

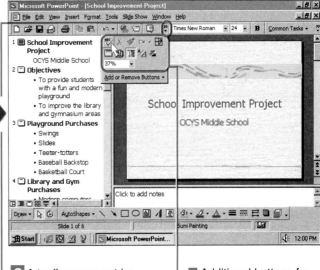

1 To display the name of a toolbar button, position the mouse ⌖ over the button.

■ After a few seconds, the name of the button appears in a yellow box. The button name can help you determine the task the button performs.

2 A toolbar may not be able to display all of its buttons. Click ⌖ to display additional buttons for the toolbar.

■ Additional buttons for the toolbar appear.

3 To use a toolbar button to select a command, click the button.

SELECT COMMANDS USING MENUS

You can select a command from a menu to perform a task. Each command performs a different task.

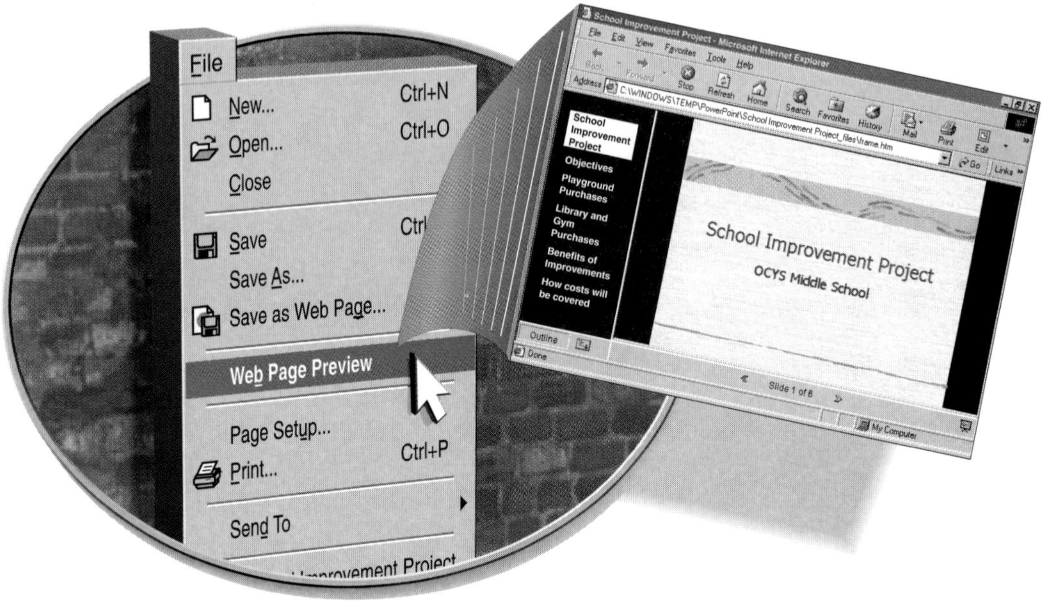

SELECT COMMANDS USING MENUS

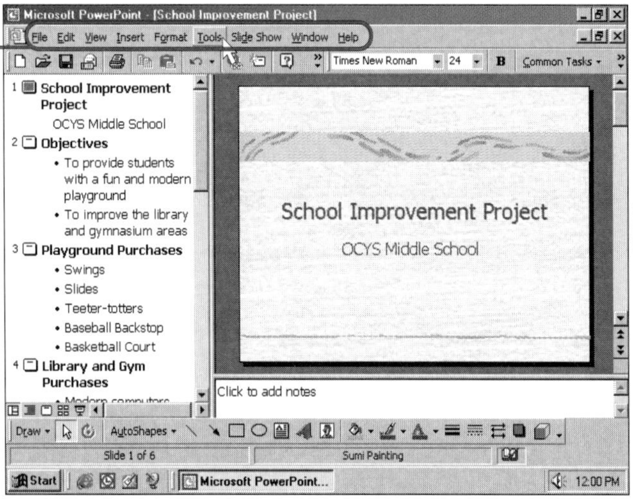

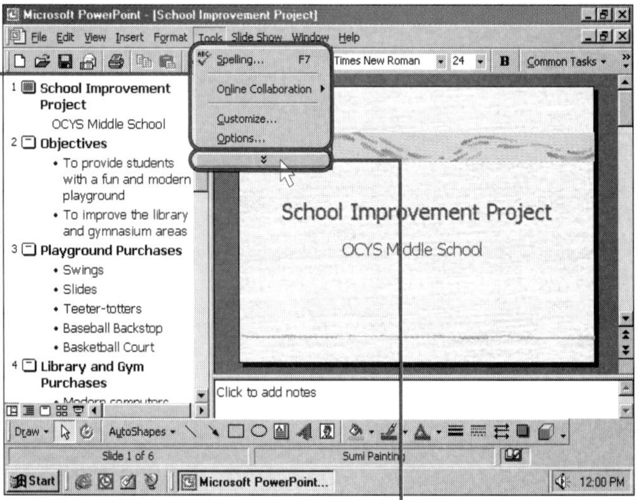

1 Click the name of the menu you want to display.

■ A short version of the menu appears, displaying the most commonly used commands.

2 To expand the menu and display all the commands, position the mouse ↖ over ».

*Note: If you do not perform step **2**, the expanded menu will automatically appear after a few seconds.*

?

How can I make a command appear on the short version of a menu?

When you select a command from an expanded menu, PowerPoint automatically adds the command to the short version of the menu. The next time you display the short version of the menu, the command you selected will appear.

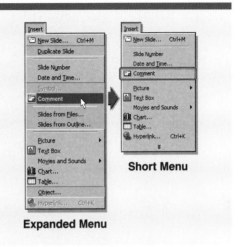

Short Menu

Expanded Menu

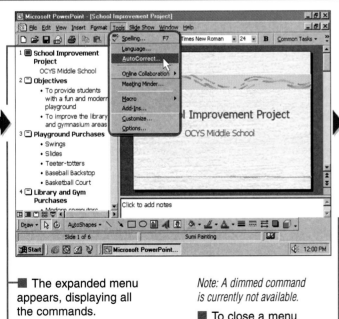

■ The expanded menu appears, displaying all the commands.

3 Click the command you want to use.

Note: A dimmed command is currently not available.

■ To close a menu without selecting a command, click outside the menu.

■ A dialog box appears if the command you selected displays three dots (...).

4 When you finish selecting options in the dialog box, click **OK** to confirm your changes.

■ To close the dialog box without making any changes, click **Cancel**.

CREATE A PRESENTATION USING THE AUTOCONTENT WIZARD

You can use the AutoContent Wizard to create a presentation. The wizard asks you a series of questions and then sets up a presentation based on your answers.

The wizard will organize the presentation and provide sample text to help you get started.

CREATE A PRESENTATION USING THE AUTOCONTENT WIZARD

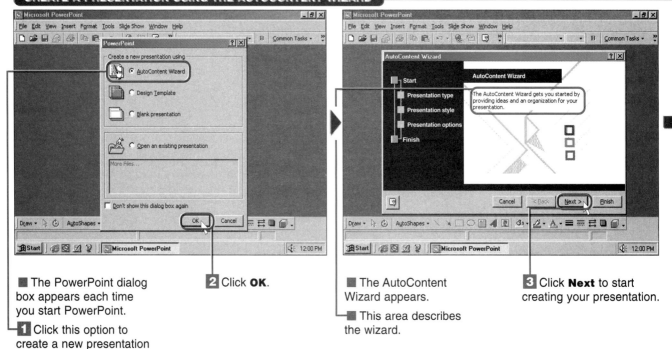

■ The PowerPoint dialog box appears each time you start PowerPoint.

1 Click this option to create a new presentation using the AutoContent Wizard (○ changes to ◉).

2 Click **OK**.

■ The AutoContent Wizard appears.

■ This area describes the wizard.

3 Click **Next** to start creating your presentation.

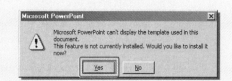

Why does a dialog box appear when I select a presentation in the AutoContent Wizard?

A dialog box appears if the presentation you selected is not installed on your computer. Insert the CD-ROM disc you used to install PowerPoint 2000 into your CD-ROM drive and then click **Yes** to install the presentation.

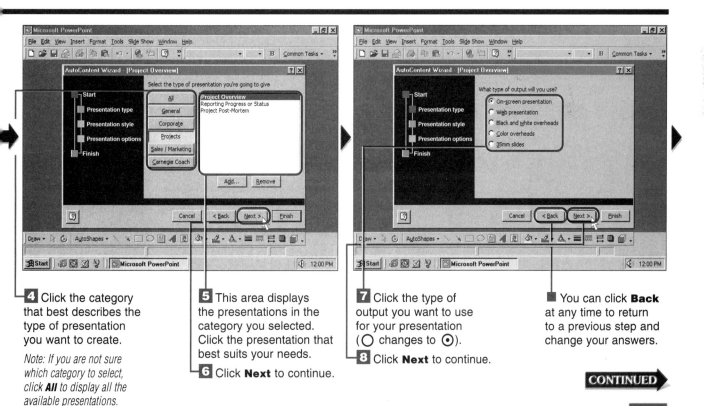

4 Click the category that best describes the type of presentation you want to create.

*Note: If you are not sure which category to select, click **All** to display all the available presentations.*

5 This area displays the presentations in the category you selected. Click the presentation that best suits your needs.

6 Click **Next** to continue.

7 Click the type of output you want to use for your presentation (○ changes to ⊙).

8 Click **Next** to continue.

■ You can click **Back** at any time to return to a previous step and change your answers.

CONTINUED

CREATE A PRESENTATION USING THE AUTOCONTENT WIZARD

The AutoContent Wizard allows you to specify a title for the first slide in your presentation. You can also specify information you want to appear on each slide.

Presentation title

Date last updated

Footer

Slide number

CREATE A PRESENTATION USING THE AUTOCONTENT WIZARD (CONTINUED)

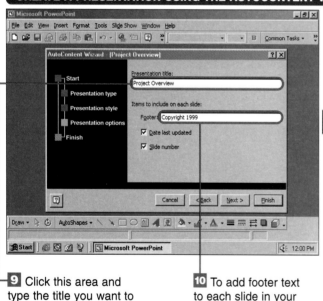

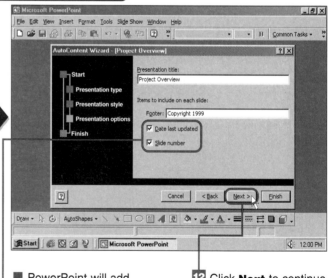

9 Click this area and type the title you want to appear on the first slide in your presentation.

10 To add footer text to each slide in your presentation, click this area and then type the text.

■ PowerPoint will add the current date and slide number to each slide in your presentation.

11 If you do not want to add the current date or slide number, click the option you do not want to add (☑ changes to ☐).

12 Click **Next** to continue.

Why does a slide in my presentation display a yellow light bulb (💡)?

A yellow light bulb indicates the Office Assistant has a suggestion for improving the slide. Click the light bulb to display the suggestion. For more information on the Office Assistant, see page 34.

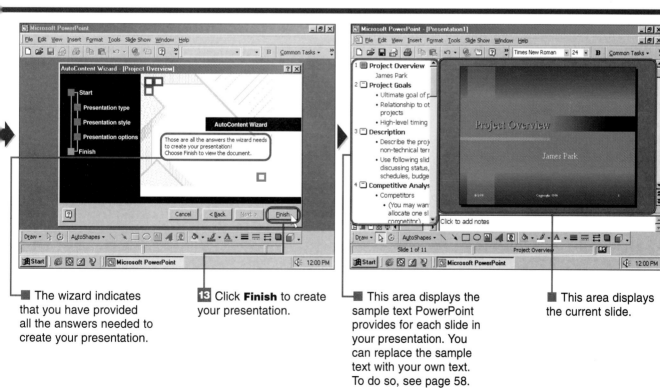

◼ The wizard indicates that you have provided all the answers needed to create your presentation.

🔢 Click **Finish** to create your presentation.

◼ This area displays the sample text PowerPoint provides for each slide in your presentation. You can replace the sample text with your own text. To do so, see page 58.

◼ This area displays the current slide.

CREATE A PRESENTATION USING A DESIGN TEMPLATE

You can use a design template to create a professional-looking presentation. Each design template uses fonts, backgrounds and colors to create a particular look.

When you create a presentation using a design template, PowerPoint creates only the first slide. You can add additional slides to your presentation as you need them.

CREATE A PRESENTATION USING A DESIGN TEMPLATE

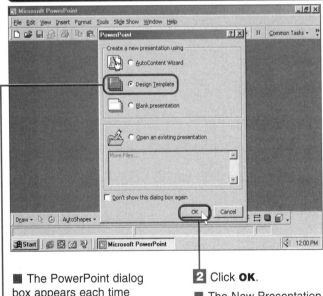

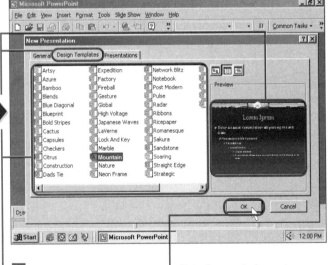

■ The PowerPoint dialog box appears each time you start PowerPoint.

1 Click this option to create a new presentation using a design template (○ changes to ⊙).

2 Click **OK**.

■ The New Presentation dialog box appears.

3 Click the **Design Templates** tab.

4 Click the design template you want to use.

■ This area displays a sample of the design template you selected.

Note: If a sample does not appear, you must install the design template on your computer. Insert the CD-ROM disc you used to install PowerPoint into your CD-ROM drive and then perform step 5.

5 Click **OK** to confirm your selection.

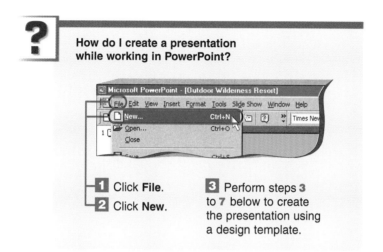

How do I create a presentation while working in PowerPoint?

1 Click **File**.

2 Click **New**.

3 Perform steps **3** to **7** below to create the presentation using a design template.

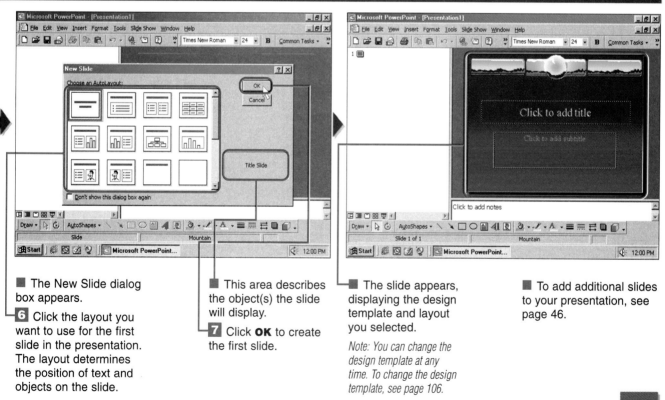

■ The New Slide dialog box appears.

6 Click the layout you want to use for the first slide in the presentation. The layout determines the position of text and objects on the slide.

■ This area describes the object(s) the slide will display.

7 Click **OK** to create the first slide.

■ The slide appears, displaying the design template and layout you selected.

Note: You can change the design template at any time. To change the design template, see page 106.

■ To add additional slides to your presentation, see page 46.

CREATE A BLANK PRESENTATION

You can use PowerPoint to create a blank presentation. Blank presentations are useful when you want to create your own design and content for the slides.

CREATE A BLANK PRESENTATION

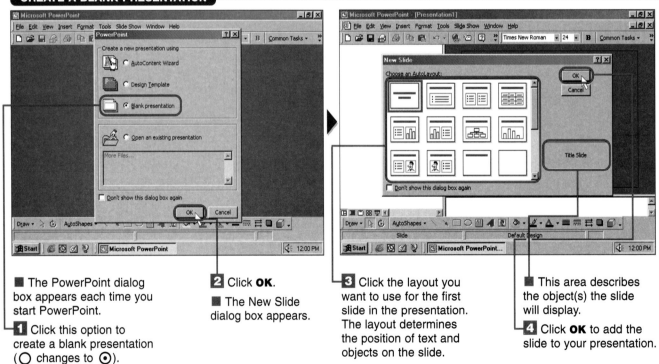

■ The PowerPoint dialog box appears each time you start PowerPoint.

1 Click this option to create a blank presentation (○ changes to ◉).

2 Click **OK**.

■ The New Slide dialog box appears.

3 Click the layout you want to use for the first slide in the presentation. The layout determines the position of text and objects on the slide.

■ This area describes the object(s) the slide will display.

4 Click **OK** to add the slide to your presentation.

?

PowerPoint created only one slide in my presentation. What is wrong?

When you create a blank presentation, PowerPoint creates only the first slide. You can add additional slides to your presentation as you need them. To add additional slides to your presentation, see page 46.

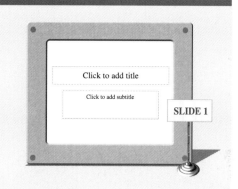

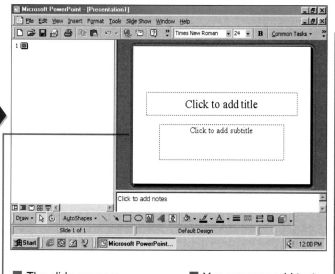

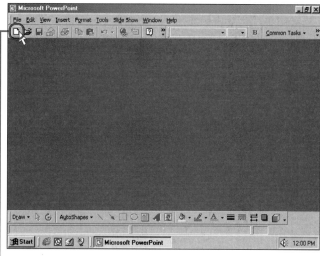

■ The slide appears, displaying the layout you selected. To change the layout at any time, see page 44.

■ You can now add text and objects and change the appearance of the slide to suit your needs.

While working in PowerPoint, you can create a blank presentation at any time.

1 Click 🗋 to display the New Slide dialog box. Then perform steps **3** and **4**.

Note: If 🗋 is not displayed, click 📄 on the Standard toolbar to display all the buttons.

SAVE A PRESENTATION

You can save your
presentation to
store it for future
use. This allows you
to later review and
make changes to
the presentation.

SAVE A PRESENTATION

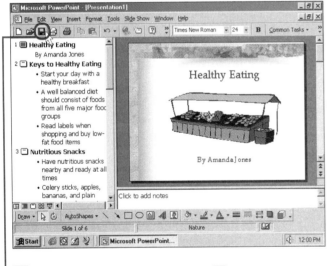

1 Click 🔲 to save
your presentation.

*Note: If 🔲 is not displayed,
click 》 on the Standard toolbar
to display all the buttons.*

■ The Save As dialog
box appears.

*Note: If you previously saved
your presentation, the Save As
dialog box will not appear since
you have already named the
presentation.*

2 Type a name for
the presentation.

24

? What are the commonly used folders I can access?

History

Provides access to folders and presentations you recently used.

My Documents

Provides a convenient place to store a presentation.

Desktop

Lets you store a presentation on the Windows desktop.

Favorites

Provides a place to store a presentation you will frequently access.

Web Folders

Can help you store a presentation on the Web.

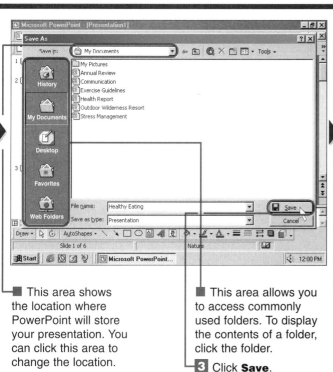

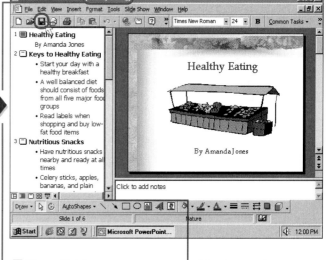

■ This area shows the location where PowerPoint will store your presentation. You can click this area to change the location.

■ This area allows you to access commonly used folders. To display the contents of a folder, click the folder.

3 Click **Save**.

■ PowerPoint saves your presentation and displays the name of the presentation at the top of your screen.

SAVE CHANGES

You should regularly save changes you make to a presentation to avoid losing your work.

1 Click 🖫 to save changes you make to your presentation.

CLOSE A PRESENTATION

When you finish working with a presentation, you can close the presentation to remove it from your screen.

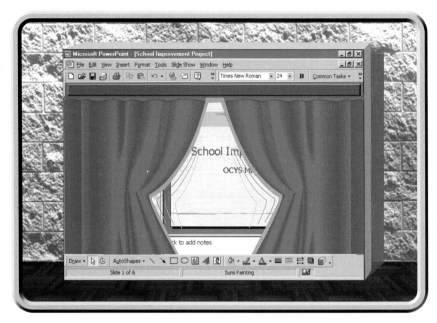

When you close a presentation, you do not exit the PowerPoint program. You can continue to work with other presentations.

CLOSE A PRESENTATION

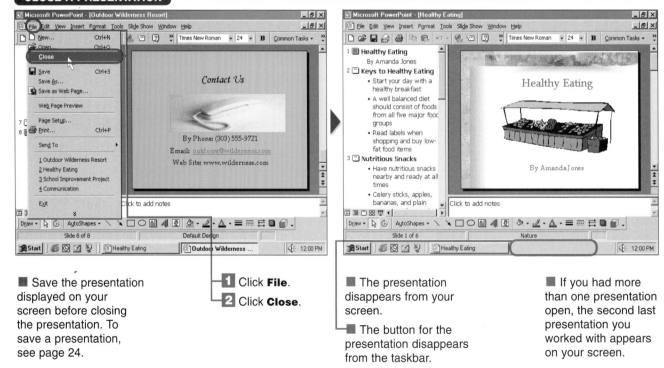

■ Save the presentation displayed on your screen before closing the presentation. To save a presentation, see page 24.

1 Click **File**.

2 Click **Close**.

■ The presentation disappears from your screen.

■ The button for the presentation disappears from the taskbar.

■ If you had more than one presentation open, the second last presentation you worked with appears on your screen.

EXIT POWERPOINT

When you finish
using PowerPoint,
you can exit the
program.

To prevent the loss of
data, you should always
exit all open programs
before turning off your
computer.

EXIT POWERPOINT

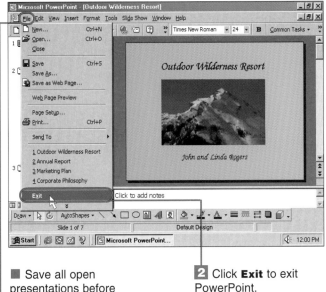

■ Save all open
presentations before
exiting PowerPoint. To
save a presentation,
see page 24.

1 Click **File**.

2 Click **Exit** to exit
PowerPoint.

■ The Microsoft
PowerPoint window
disappears from your
screen.

■ The button for the
program disappears
from the taskbar.

OPEN A PRESENTATION

You can open a presentation you previously created and display it on your screen. This lets you review and make changes to the presentation.

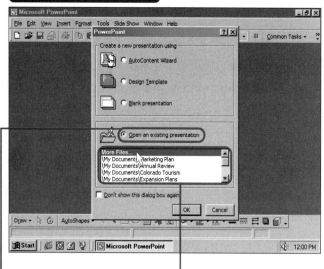

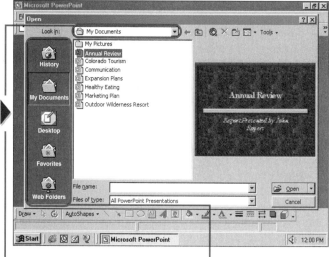

■ The PowerPoint dialog box appears each time you start PowerPoint.

1 Click this option to open an existing presentation (○ changes to ◉).

■ This area displays the names of the last presentations you worked with. To open one of these presentations, double-click the name of the presentation.

2 If the presentation you want to open is not listed, double-click **More Files**.

■ The Open dialog box appears.

■ This area shows the location of the displayed presentations. You can click this area to change the location.

■ This area allows you to access commonly used folders. To display the contents of a folder, click the folder.

Note: For information on the commonly used folders, see the top of page 25.

28

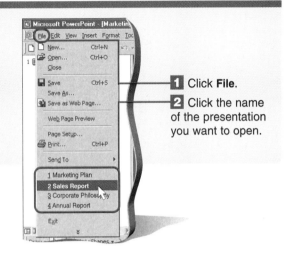

While working in PowerPoint, can I quickly open a presentation I recently worked with?

PowerPoint remembers the names of the last four presentations you worked with. You can quickly open one of these presentations.

1 Click **File**.

2 Click the name of the presentation you want to open.

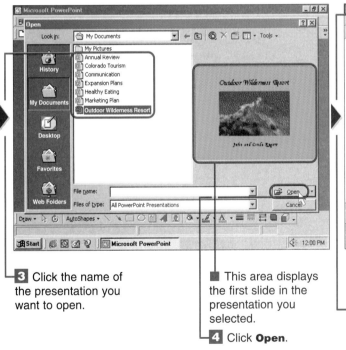

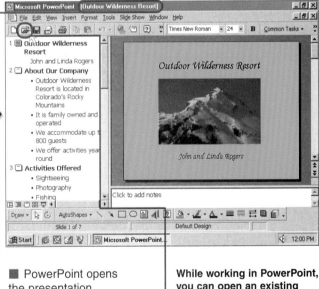

3 Click the name of the presentation you want to open.

■ This area displays the first slide in the presentation you selected.

4 Click **Open**.

■ PowerPoint opens the presentation.

■ The name of the presentation appears at the top of your screen.

While working in PowerPoint, you can open an existing presentation at any time.

1 Click 📄 to display the Open dialog box. Then perform steps **3** and **4**.

Note: If 📄 is not displayed, click 🔽 on the Standard toolbar to display all the buttons.

FIND A PRESENTATION

If you cannot remember
the name or location of
a presentation you want
to open, you can search
for the presentation.

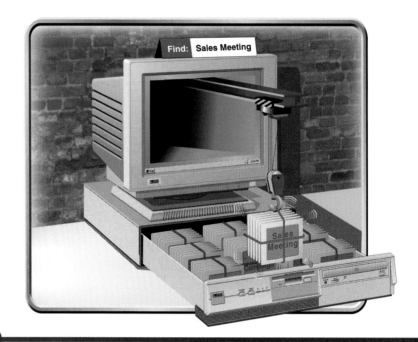

FIND A PRESENTATION

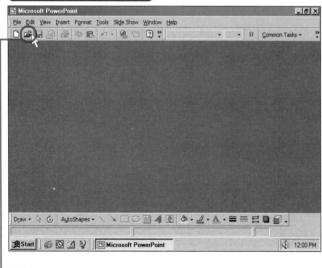

1 Click 📂 to display
the Open dialog box.

*Note: If 📂 is not displayed,
click 🔽 on the Standard
toolbar to display all the
buttons.*

■ The Open dialog
box appears.

2 Click **Tools**.

3 Click **Find**.

■ The Find dialog box
appears.

How can I search for a presentation?

When searching for a presentation, you must specify a property for the search. Common properties include the presentation contents, number of slides and file name. After you specify a property, you can specify a condition and value for the search.

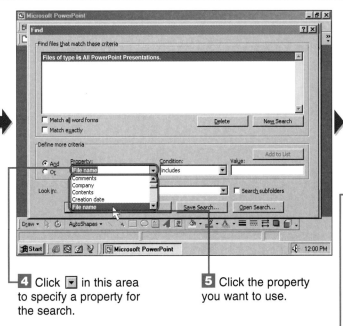

4 Click ▼ in this area to specify a property for the search.

5 Click the property you want to use.

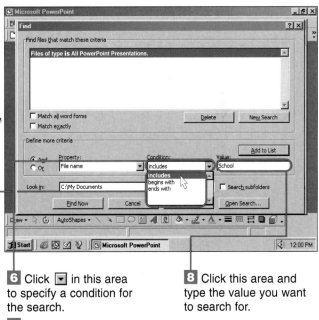

6 Click ▼ in this area to specify a condition for the search.

7 Click the condition you want to use.

Note: The available conditions depend on the property you selected in step 5.

8 Click this area and type the value you want to search for.

Note: If the value area is not available, you do not need to enter a value.

CONTINUED ▶

FIND A PRESENTATION

You can specify
the location where
you want to search
for a presentation.

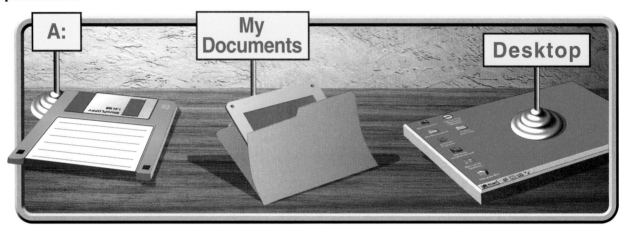

FIND A PRESENTATION (CONTINUED)

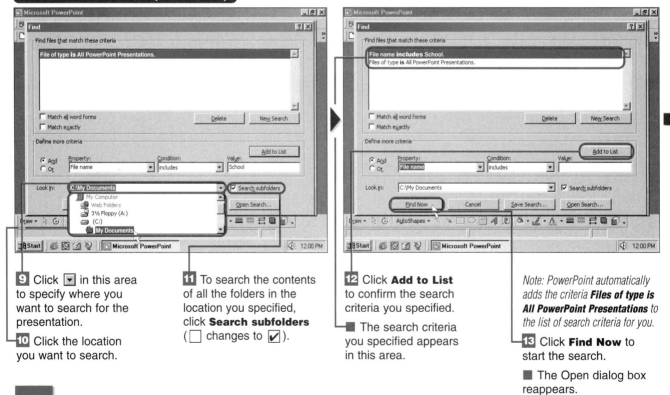

9 Click ▼ in this area
to specify where you
want to search for the
presentation.

10 Click the location
you want to search.

11 To search the contents
of all the folders in the
location you specified,
click **Search subfolders**
(☐ changes to ☑).

12 Click **Add to List**
to confirm the search
criteria you specified.

■ The search criteria
you specified appears
in this area.

*Note: PowerPoint automatically
adds the criteria **Files of type is
All PowerPoint Presentations** to
the list of search criteria for you.*

13 Click **Find Now** to
start the search.

■ The Open dialog box
reappears.

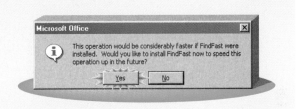

When I started the search, why did a dialog box appear, asking if I want to install FindFast?

FindFast is a feature that can help speed up your searches. To install FindFast, insert the CD-ROM disc you used to install PowerPoint into your CD-ROM drive. Then click **Yes** to install FindFast.

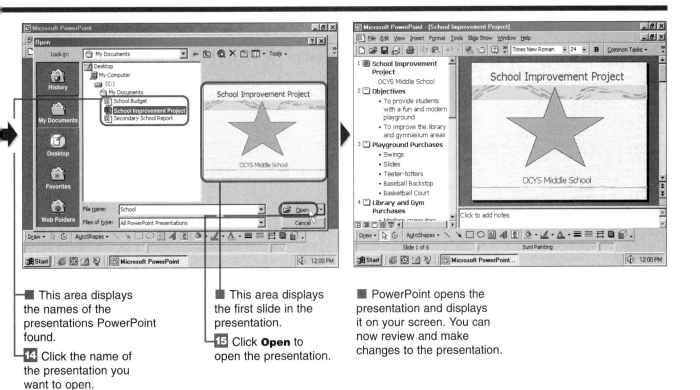

■ This area displays the names of the presentations PowerPoint found.

14 Click the name of the presentation you want to open.

■ This area displays the first slide in the presentation.

15 Click **Open** to open the presentation.

■ PowerPoint opens the presentation and displays it on your screen. You can now review and make changes to the presentation.

GETTING HELP

If you do not know how to perform a task, you can ask the Office Assistant for help.

USING THE OFFICE ASSISTANT

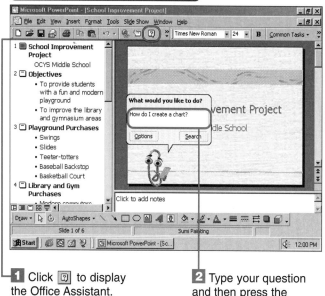

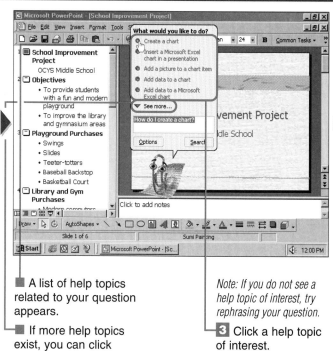

1 Click 🔲 to display the Office Assistant.

Note: If 🔲 is not displayed, click 🔋 on the Standard toolbar to display all the buttons.

2 Type your question and then press the **Enter** key.

Note: If the question area does not appear, click the Office Assistant.

■ A list of help topics related to your question appears.

■ If more help topics exist, you can click **See more** to view the additional topics.

Note: If you do not see a help topic of interest, try rephrasing your question.

3 Click a help topic of interest.

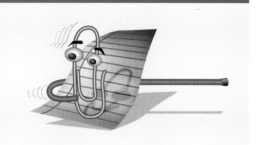

Can I move the Office Assistant?

If the Office Assistant covers information on your screen, you may need to move the Office Assistant. Position the mouse over the Office Assistant and then drag it to a new location.

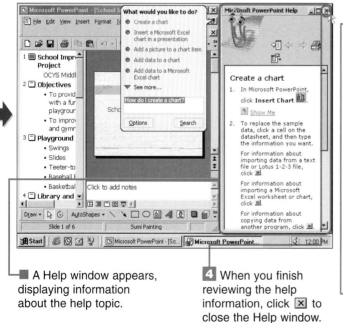

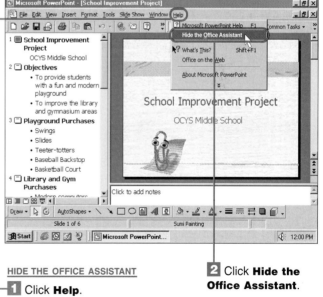

■ A Help window appears, displaying information about the help topic.

4 When you finish reviewing the help information, click ⊠ to close the Help window.

HIDE THE OFFICE ASSISTANT

1 Click **Help**.

2 Click **Hide the Office Assistant**.

GETTING HELP

You can use PowerPoint's help index to locate help topics of interest.

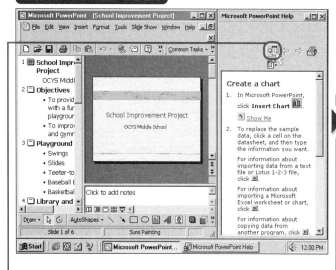

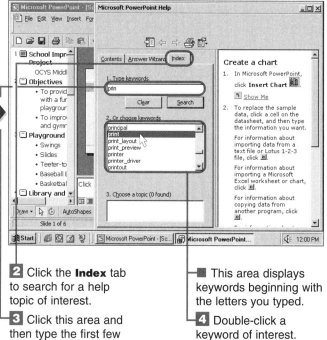

1 When viewing a help topic, click 🗗 to expand the Help window.

Note: To view a help topic, perform steps 1 to 3 on page 34.

■ The Help window expands.

2 Click the **Index** tab to search for a help topic of interest.

3 Click this area and then type the first few letters of a topic of interest.

■ This area displays keywords beginning with the letters you typed.

4 Double-click a keyword of interest.

Why do some words in the Help window appear in blue?

You can click a word or phrase that appears in blue without an underline to display a definition of the text. To hide the definition, click anywhere on your screen.

You can click a word or phrase that appears in blue with an underline to display a related help topic.

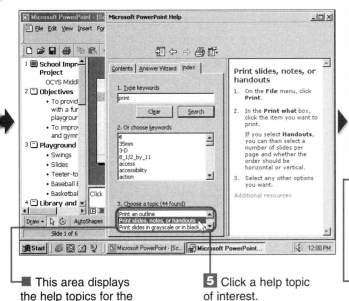

■ This area displays the help topics for the keyword you selected.

5 Click a help topic of interest.

■ This area displays information about the help topic.

Note: To display information for another help topic, repeat step 5.

6 When you finish reviewing the help information, click ⊠ to close the Help window.

CHAPTER 2

PowerPoint Basics

Are you ready to start working with your presentation? This chapter teaches you how.

CHANGE THE VIEW

PowerPoint offers several ways that you can view a presentation on your screen.

Each view displays the same presentation. If you make changes to your presentation in one view, the other views will also display the changes.

CHANGE THE VIEW

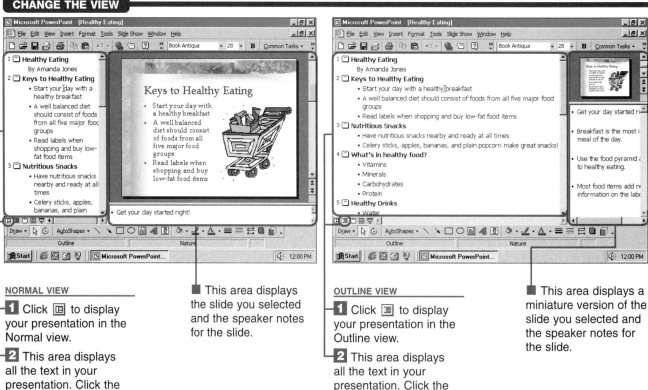

NORMAL VIEW

1 Click ⊞ to display your presentation in the Normal view.

2 This area displays all the text in your presentation. Click the text on a slide of interest.

■ This area displays the slide you selected and the speaker notes for the slide.

OUTLINE VIEW

1 Click ▤ to display your presentation in the Outline view.

2 This area displays all the text in your presentation. Click the text on a slide of interest.

■ This area displays a miniature version of the slide you selected and the speaker notes for the slide.

When would I use each view?

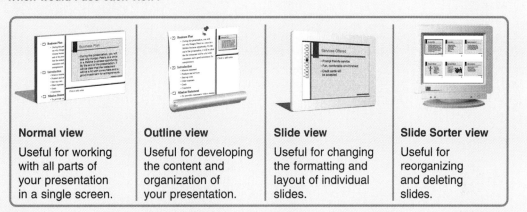

Normal view

Useful for working with all parts of your presentation in a single screen.

Outline view

Useful for developing the content and organization of your presentation.

Slide view

Useful for changing the formatting and layout of individual slides.

Slide Sorter view

Useful for reorganizing and deleting slides.

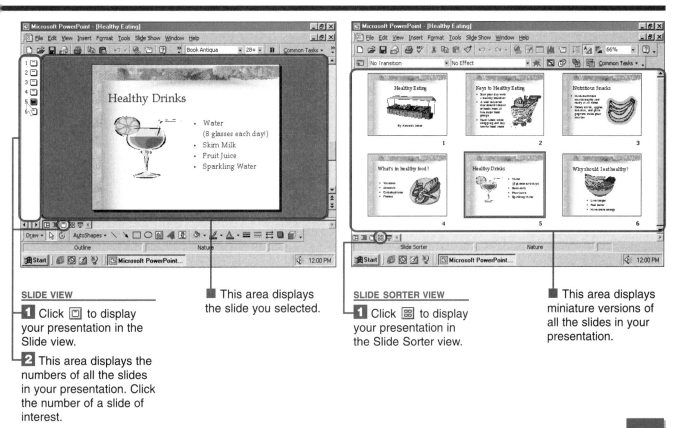

SLIDE VIEW

1 Click ▣ to display your presentation in the Slide view.

2 This area displays the numbers of all the slides in your presentation. Click the number of a slide of interest.

■ This area displays the slide you selected.

SLIDE SORTER VIEW

1 Click ▦ to display your presentation in the Slide Sorter view.

■ This area displays miniature versions of all the slides in your presentation.

BROWSE THROUGH A PRESENTATION

Your computer screen cannot display your entire presentation at once. You can browse through your presentation to view other areas of the presentation.

BROWSE THROUGH A PRESENTATION

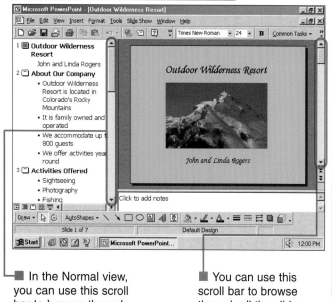

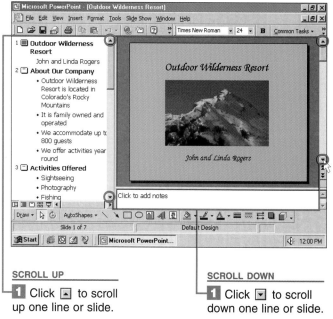

■ In the Normal view, you can use this scroll bar to browse through all the text in your presentation. To change the view, see page 40.

■ You can use this scroll bar to browse through all the slides in your presentation.

SCROLL UP

1 Click ▲ to scroll up one line or slide.

SCROLL DOWN

1 Click ▼ to scroll down one line or slide.

How do I use a wheeled mouse to browse through my presentation?

A wheeled mouse has a wheel between the left and right mouse buttons. You can move this wheel to browse through your presentation. The Microsoft IntelliMouse is a popular example of a wheeled mouse.

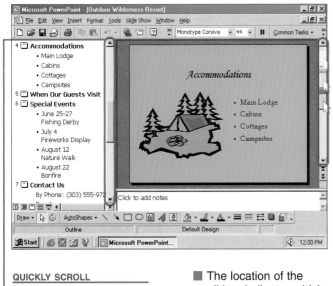

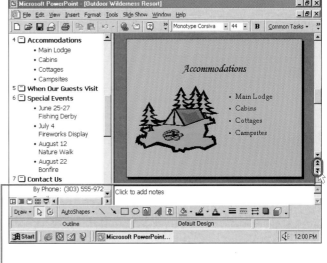

QUICKLY SCROLL

1 To quickly scroll through your presentation, drag the scroll box along the scroll bar.

■ The location of the scroll box indicates which part of your presentation you are viewing. To view the middle of your presentation, drag the scroll box halfway down the scroll bar.

DISPLAY PREVIOUS OR NEXT SLIDE

1 Click one of the following buttons.

⬢ Display previous slide

⬢ Display next slide

CHANGE THE SLIDE LAYOUT

You can change the layout of a slide in your presentation to accommodate text and objects you want to add.

Each slide layout displays a different arrangement of placeholders. Placeholders allow you to add objects you want to appear on a slide, such as a clip art image or chart.

CHANGE THE SLIDE LAYOUT

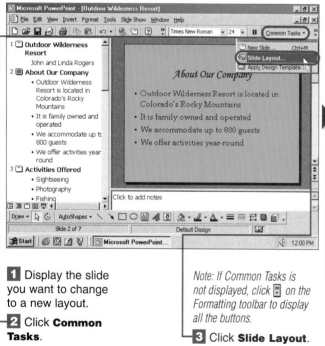

1 Display the slide you want to change to a new layout.

2 Click **Common Tasks**.

Note: If Common Tasks is not displayed, click ? on the Formatting toolbar to display all the buttons.

3 Click **Slide Layout**.

■ The Slide Layout dialog box appears.

■ This area displays the available layouts. You can use the scroll bar to browse through the layouts.

4 Click the layout you want to apply to the slide.

Can I change the slide layout at any time?

You should not change the slide layout after you have added an object to a slide. An object you have added will remain on the slide even after PowerPoint adds the placeholders for the new slide layout. This can cause the slide to become cluttered with overlapping objects and placeholders.

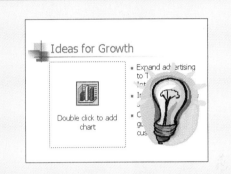

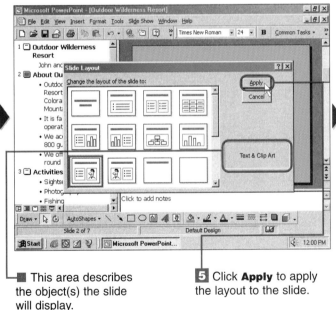

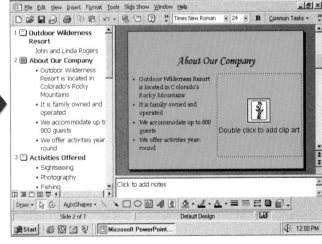

■ This area describes the object(s) the slide will display.

5 Click **Apply** to apply the layout to the slide.

■ The slide appears in the new layout.

ADD A NEW SLIDE

You can insert a
new slide into your
presentation to add
a new topic you
want to discuss.

ADD A NEW SLIDE

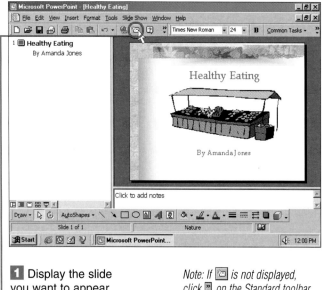

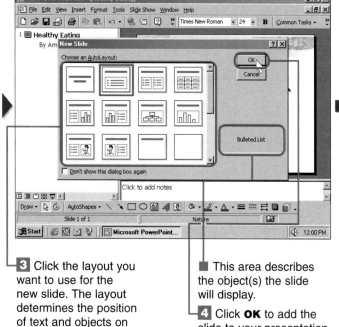

1 Display the slide
you want to appear
before the new slide.

2 Click 🖼 to add
a new slide.

*Note: If 🖼 is not displayed,
click 🔧 on the Standard toolbar
to display all the buttons.*

■ The New Slide dialog
box appears.

3 Click the layout you
want to use for the
new slide. The layout
determines the position
of text and objects on
the slide.

■ This area describes
the object(s) the slide
will display.

4 Click **OK** to add the
slide to your presentation.

How much text should I display on a slide?

You should be careful not to include too much text on a slide in your presentation. Too much text on a slide can make the slide difficult to read and minimize the impact of important ideas. If a slide contains too much text, you should add a new slide to accommodate some of the text.

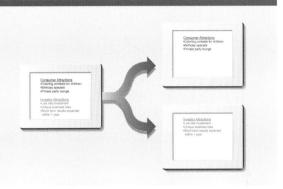

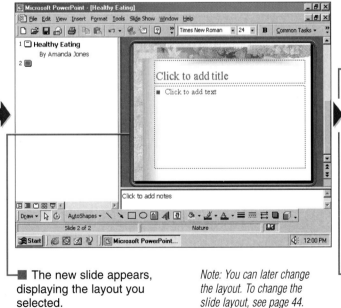

■ The new slide appears, displaying the layout you selected.

Note: You can later change the layout. To change the slide layout, see page 44.

5 If the slide layout provides an area for a title, click the area and then type the title.

6 If the slide layout provides an area for a list of points, click the area and then type a point. Press the `Enter` key each time you want to start a new point.

ZOOM IN OR OUT

PowerPoint allows you to enlarge or reduce the display of information on your screen.

Changing the zoom setting will not affect the way information appears when printed.

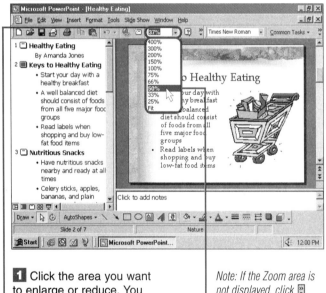

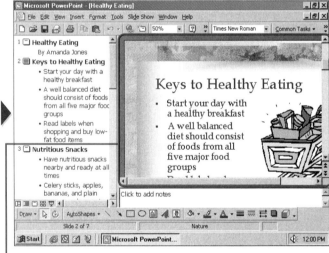

1 Click the area you want to enlarge or reduce. You can enlarge or reduce the area displaying the outline, current slide or speaker notes.

2 Click ⯆ in this area to display a list of zoom settings.

Note: If the Zoom area is not displayed, click ⯈ on the Standard toolbar to display all the buttons.

3 Click the zoom setting you want to use.

■ The area appears in the new zoom setting.

*Note: To return the current slide to its original zoom setting, repeat steps 1 to 3, except select **Fit** in step 3.*

PowerPoint lets you have several presentations open at once. You can easily switch from one open presentation to another.

SWITCH BETWEEN PRESENTATIONS

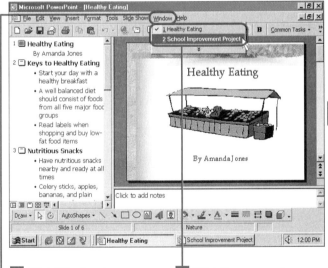

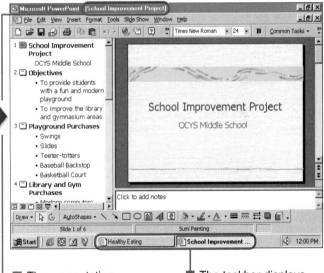

1 Click **Window** to display a list of all the presentations you have open.

2 Click the name of the presentation you want to switch to.

■ The presentation appears.

■ PowerPoint displays the name of the current presentation at the top of your screen.

■ The taskbar displays a button for each open presentation. You can also switch to a presentation by clicking its button on the taskbar.

DISPLAY OR HIDE A TOOLBAR

PowerPoint offers several toolbars that you can display or hide at any time. Each toolbar contains buttons that help you quickly perform common tasks.

You can choose which toolbars to display based on the tasks you perform most often.

DISPLAY OR HIDE A TOOLBAR

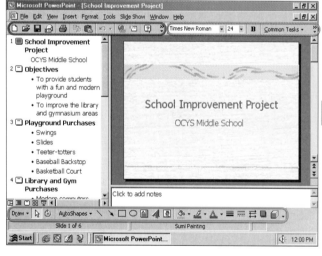

■ PowerPoint automatically displays three toolbars on your screen.

Standard toolbar

Formatting toolbar

Drawing toolbar

Note: PowerPoint displays different toolbars in the Slide Sorter view. For information on the views, see page 40.

■1 To display or hide a toolbar, click **View**.

2 Click **Toolbars**.

**Why would I want
to hide a toolbar?**

A screen displaying
fewer toolbars
provides a larger
and less cluttered
working area.

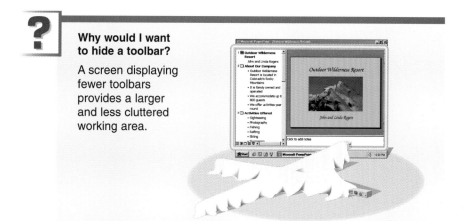

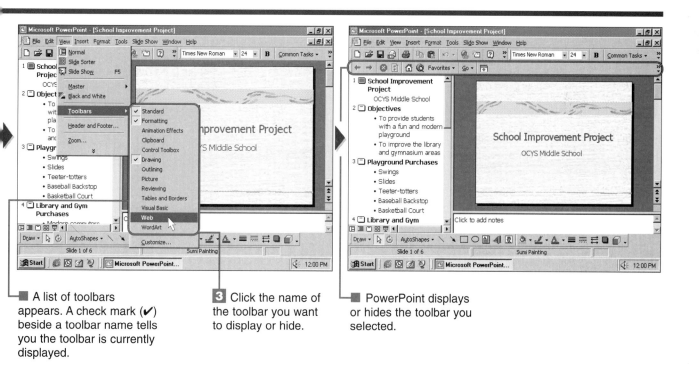

■ A list of toolbars
appears. A check mark (✔)
beside a toolbar name tells
you the toolbar is currently
displayed.

3 Click the name of
the toolbar you want
to display or hide.

■ PowerPoint displays
or hides the toolbar you
selected.

SIZE A TOOLBAR

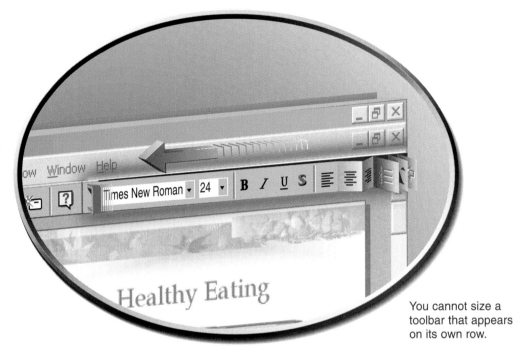

You can increase the size of a toolbar to display more buttons on the toolbar. This is useful when a toolbar appears on the same row as another toolbar and cannot display all of its buttons.

You cannot size a toolbar that appears on its own row.

SIZE A TOOLBAR

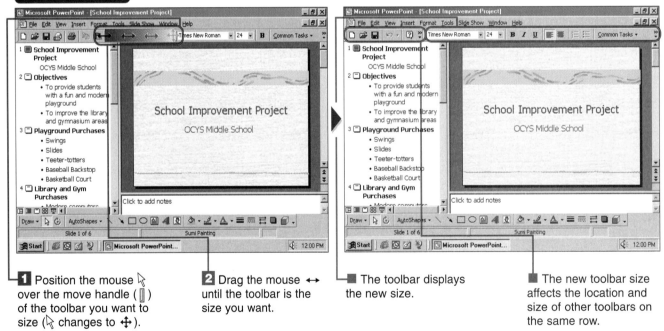

1 Position the mouse ⬚ over the move handle (⎸) of the toolbar you want to size (⬚ changes to ✛).

2 Drag the mouse ↔ until the toolbar is the size you want.

■ The toolbar displays the new size.

■ The new toolbar size affects the location and size of other toolbars on the same row.

You can move a toolbar to the top, bottom, right or left edge of your screen.

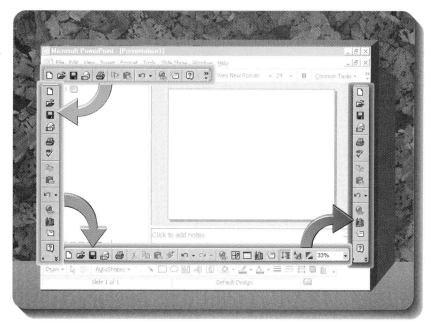

Moving a toolbar to its own row allows you to display more buttons on the toolbar.

MOVE A TOOLBAR

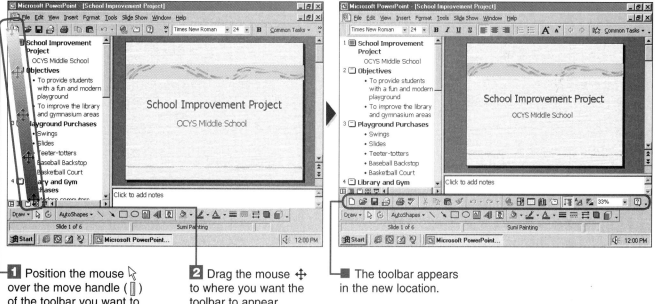

1 Position the mouse ⬚ over the move handle (▌) of the toolbar you want to move (⬚ changes to ✛).

2 Drag the mouse ✛ to where you want the toolbar to appear.

■ The toolbar appears in the new location.

Dictionary

MADDEN
BOOKS

1. ☐ **School Improvement Project**
   - OCVS Middle School

2. ☐ **Objectives**
   - To provide students with a fun and modern playground

   Playground Purchases

3. ☐ Library Book Depot Purchases
   - Modern Computers
   - New books and encyclopedias
   - Basketballs and volleyballs
   - Gymnastics equipment

5. ☐ **Benefits of Improvement**
   - Keeping up with latest technology
   - Students will have more interest in school
   - Better learning environment for students

CHAPTER 3

Edit Text

Do you want to edit the text in your presentation? In this chapter you will learn how to move and copy text, check for spelling errors, change the importance of text and more.

SELECT TEXT

Before changing text in your presentation, you will often need to select the text you want to work with. Selected text appears highlighted on your screen.

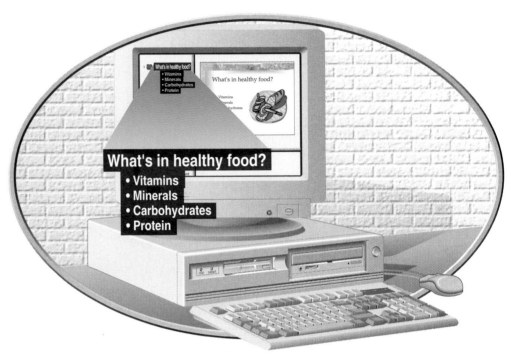

SELECT TEXT

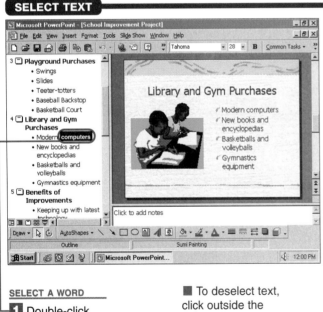

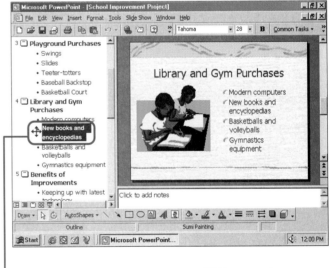

SELECT A WORD

1 Double-click the word you want to select.

■ To deselect text, click outside the selected area.

■ You can also use this method to select a word on a slide.

SELECT A POINT

1 Click the bullet (•) beside the point you want to select.

■ You can also use this method to select a point on a slide.

How do I select all the text in my presentation?

To quickly select all the text in your presentation, click the text in the Outline pane. Then press and hold down the `Ctrl` key as you press the `A` key.

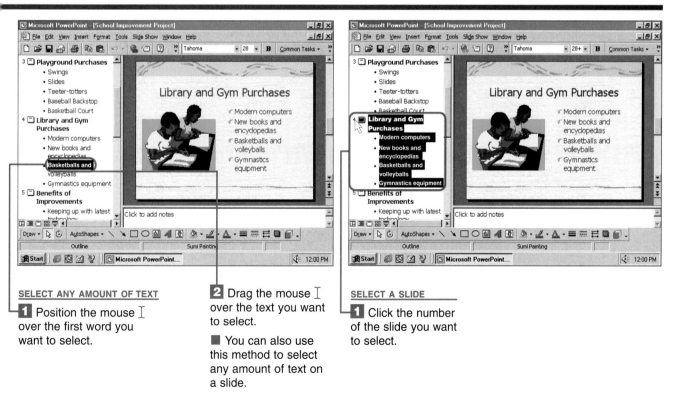

SELECT ANY AMOUNT OF TEXT

1 Position the mouse I over the first word you want to select.

2 Drag the mouse I over the text you want to select.

■ You can also use this method to select any amount of text on a slide.

SELECT A SLIDE

1 Click the number of the slide you want to select.

REPLACE SELECTED TEXT

You can replace text you have selected in your presentation with new text.

When you use the AutoContent Wizard to create a presentation, you need to replace the sample text provided by the wizard with your own text. For information on the AutoContent Wizard, see page 16.

REPLACE SELECTED TEXT

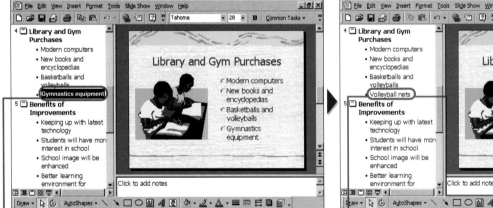

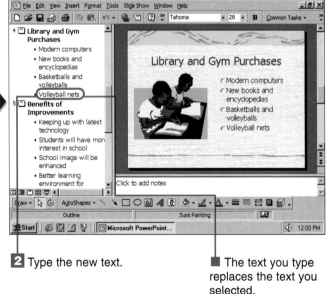

1 Select the text you want to replace with new text. To select text, see page 56.

2 Type the new text.

■ The text you type replaces the text you selected.

PowerPoint remembers the last changes you made to your presentation. If you regret these changes, you can cancel them by using the Undo feature.

The Undo feature can cancel your last editing and formatting changes.

UNDO CHANGES

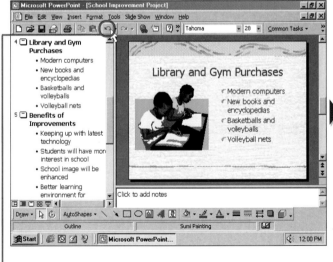

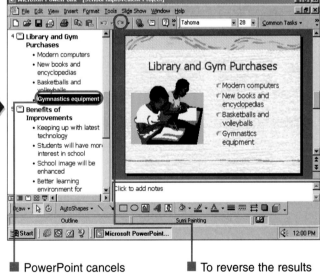

1 Click  to undo the last change you made to your presentation.

Note: If is not displayed, click on the Standard toolbar to display all the buttons.

■ PowerPoint cancels the last change you made to your presentation.

■ You can repeat step **1** to cancel previous changes you made.

■ To reverse the results of using the Undo feature, click .

Note: If is not displayed, click on the Standard toolbar to display all the buttons.

INSERT TEXT

You can add new text
to your presentation to
update the presentation.

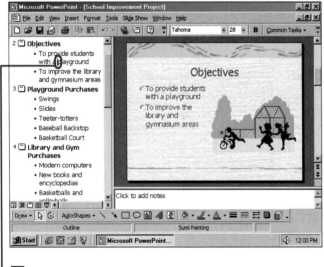

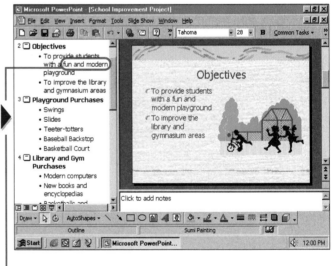

1 Click where you want
to insert the new text.

■ The text you type
will appear where the
insertion point flashes
on your screen.

Note: You can press the
← , ↓ , ↑ or → key
to move the insertion point.

2 Type the text
you want to insert.

■ To insert a blank space,
press the **Spacebar**.

60

Can I edit text directly on a slide?

The Normal view displays all the text for your presentation in the Outline pane and also displays the current slide. You can edit text in the Outline pane or directly on the current slide. Editing the text in one area will change the text in the other area.

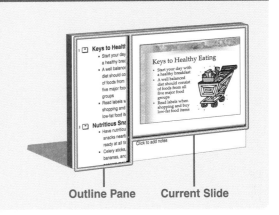

Outline Pane   Current Slide

INSERT A NEW POINT

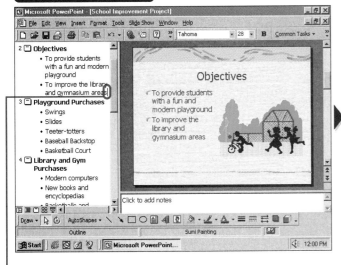

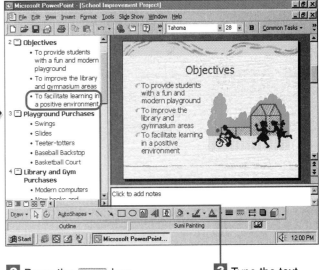

1 Click at the end of the point directly above where you want to insert a new point.

2 Press the Enter key to insert a blank line for the new point.

3 Type the text for the new point.

DELETE TEXT

You can remove text you no longer need from your presentation.

DELETE TEXT

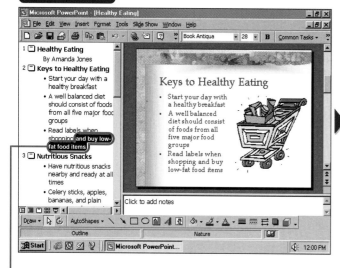

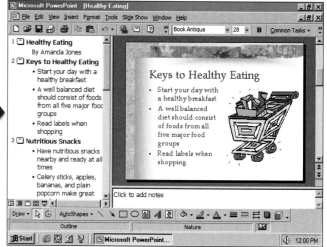

1 Select the text you want to delete. To select text, see page 56.

2 Press the Delete key to remove the text from your presentation.

■ The text disappears.

■ To delete one character at a time, click to the right of the first character you want to delete. Then press the ◆Backspace key once for each character you want to delete.

You can display only the titles for each slide in your presentation and hide the remaining text.

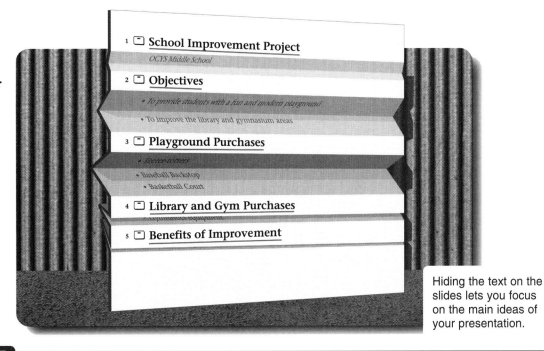

Hiding the text on the slides lets you focus on the main ideas of your presentation.

HIDE SLIDE TEXT

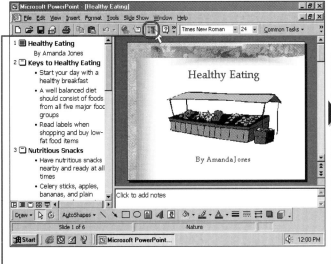

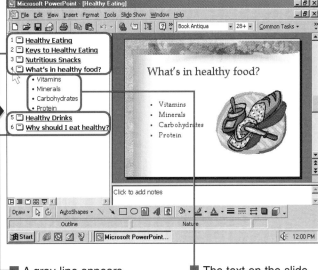

1 Click 🔲 to hide the text on all the slides in your presentation.

Note: If 🔲 is not displayed, click ⯈ on the Standard toolbar to display all the buttons.

■ A gray line appears below each slide title to indicate the text on the slide is hidden.

2 To display the text on a slide, double-click the number of the slide.

■ The text on the slide appears. You can repeat step **2** to once again hide the text.

■ To once again display the text on all the slides, repeat step **1**.

MOVE OR COPY TEXT

You can move or copy text
to a new location in your
presentation by dragging
and dropping the text.
This method is useful
when moving or copying
text short distances in
your presentation.

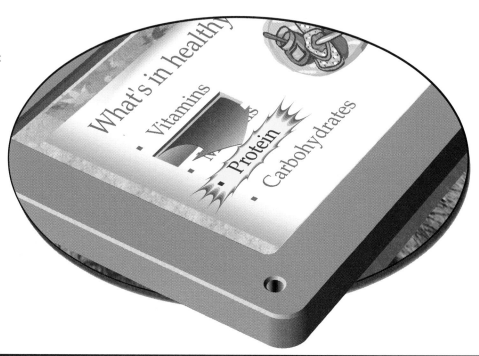

USING DRAG AND DROP

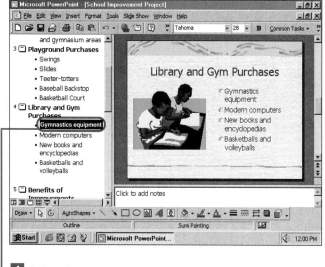

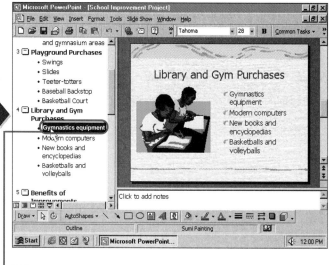

1 Select the text you
want to move or copy. To
select text, see page 56.

2 Position the mouse I
over the selected text
(I changes to ⌖).

What is the difference between moving and copying text?

Moving Text

Moving text allows you to rearrange information in your presentation. When you move text, the text disappears from its original location in your presentation.

Copying Text

Copying text allows you to repeat information in your presentation without having to retype the text. When you copy text, the text appears in both the original and new locations.

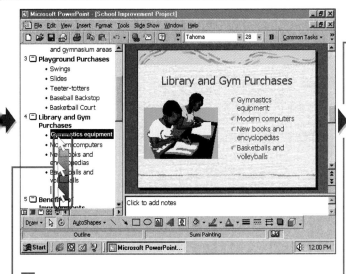

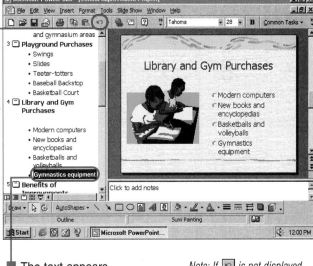

3 To move the text, drag the mouse to where you want to place the text.

■ To copy the text, press and hold down the `Ctrl` key as you drag the mouse to where you want to place the text.

■ The text will appear where you position the solid line or dotted insertion point on your screen.

■ The text appears in the new location.

■ To immediately cancel the move or copy, click ↶.

Note: If ↶ is not displayed, click ⏷ on the Standard toolbar to display all the buttons.

MOVE OR COPY TEXT

You can move or copy text to a new location in your presentation by using toolbar buttons. This method is useful when moving or copying text long distances in your presentation.

USING THE TOOLBAR BUTTONS

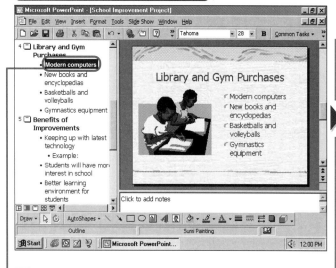

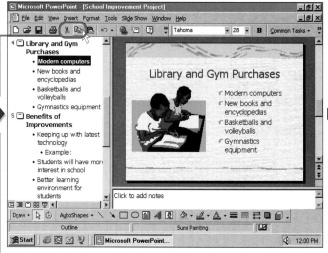

1 Select the text you want to move or copy. To select text, see page 56.

2 Click one of the following buttons.

✂ Move text

▣ Copy text

Note: If the button you want is not displayed, click [»] on the Standard toolbar to display all the buttons.

■ The Clipboard toolbar may appear. To hide the Clipboard toolbar, click [×] on the toolbar.

?

Why does the Clipboard toolbar appear when I move or copy text?

The Clipboard toolbar may appear when you move or copy text using the toolbar buttons. Each icon on the Clipboard toolbar represents text you have selected to move or copy.

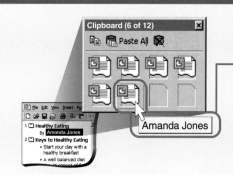

■ To see the text an icon represents, position the mouse ▷ over the icon. A yellow box appears, displaying the first few words. You can click the icon to place the text in your presentation.

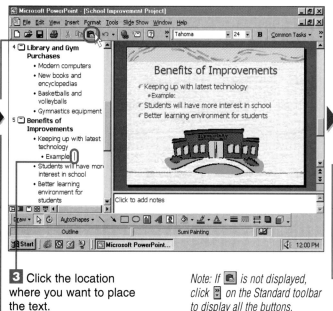

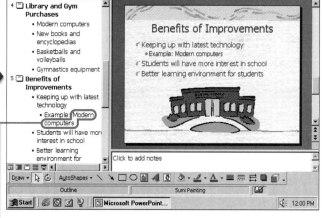

3 Click the location where you want to place the text.

4 Click 🔳 to place the text in the new location.

Note: If 🔳 is not displayed, click ▸ on the Standard toolbar to display all the buttons.

■ The text appears in the new location.

CHANGE IMPORTANCE OF TEXT

You can increase or decrease the importance of text in your presentation.

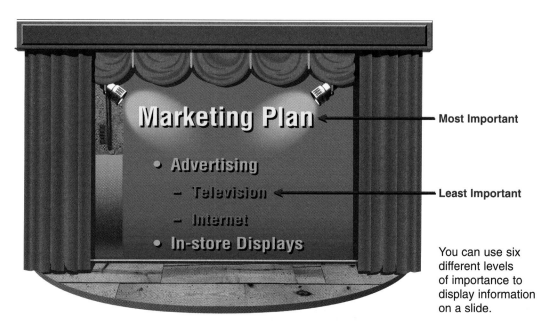

Most Important

Least Important

You can use six different levels of importance to display information on a slide.

CHANGE IMPORTANCE OF TEXT

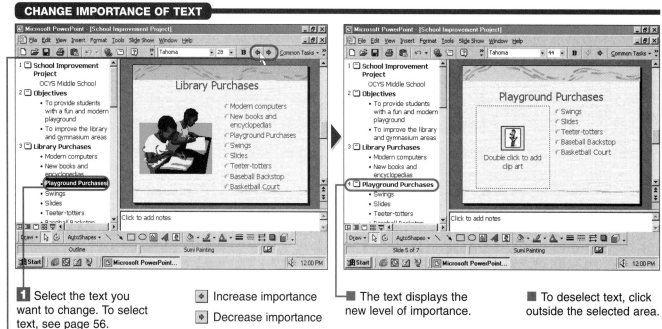

1 Select the text you want to change. To select text, see page 56.

2 Click one of these buttons.

⬅ Increase importance

➡ Decrease importance

Note: If the button you want is not displayed, click ⬄ on the Formatting toolbar to display all the buttons.

■ The text displays the new level of importance.

■ To deselect text, click outside the selected area.

You can duplicate
a slide in your
presentation. This
is useful if you want
to create a new slide
based on the content
and appearance of
an existing slide.

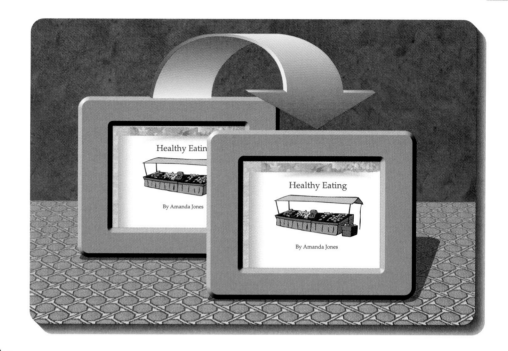

DUPLICATE A SLIDE

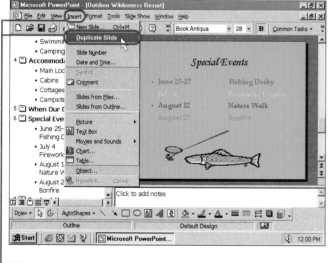

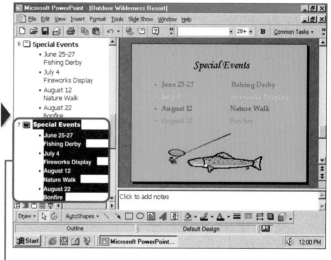

1 Click the slide you
want to duplicate.

2 Click **Insert**.

3 Click **Duplicate Slide**.

*Note: If Duplicate Slide does not
appear on the menu, position
the mouse ⤓ over the bottom
of the menu to display all the
menu commands.*

■ An exact copy of
the slide appears.

■ You can move
the duplicate slide to
another location in your
presentation. To move
a slide, see page 64.

INSERT SYMBOLS

You can add symbols
that do not appear
on your keyboard
to your slides.

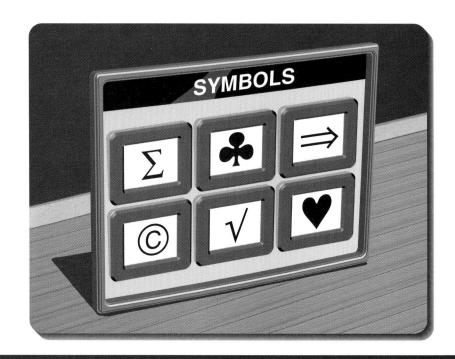

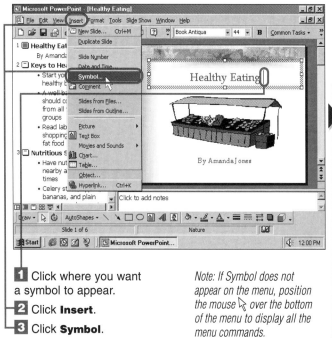

1 Click where you want
a symbol to appear.

2 Click **Insert**.

3 Click **Symbol**.

*Note: If Symbol does not
appear on the menu, position
the mouse ⬚ over the bottom
of the menu to display all the
menu commands.*

■ The Symbol dialog
box appears, displaying
the symbols for the
current font.

4 Click ▼ in this area
to display the symbols
for another font.

5 Click the font you
want to display.

■ The symbols for
the font you selected
appear.

? Which font should I select in the Symbol dialog box?

The Symbol and Wingdings fonts are two popular fonts available in the Symbol dialog box. The Symbol font contains a selection of symbols for mathematical equations. The Wingdings font contains a variety of bullet and arrow symbols.

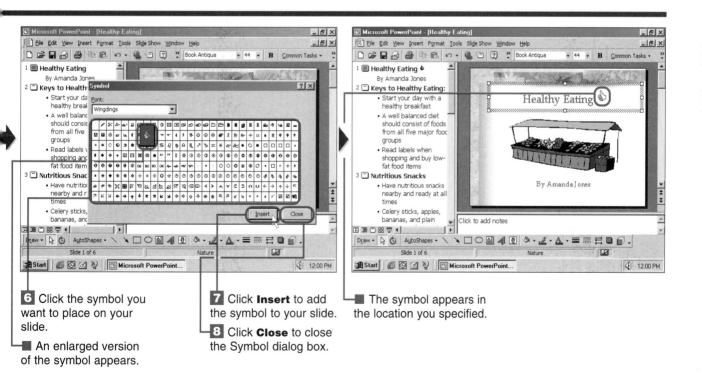

6 Click the symbol you want to place on your slide.

■ An enlarged version of the symbol appears.

7 Click **Insert** to add the symbol to your slide.

8 Click **Close** to close the Symbol dialog box.

■ The symbol appears in the location you specified.

FIND TEXT

You can use the Find feature to locate a word or phrase in your presentation.

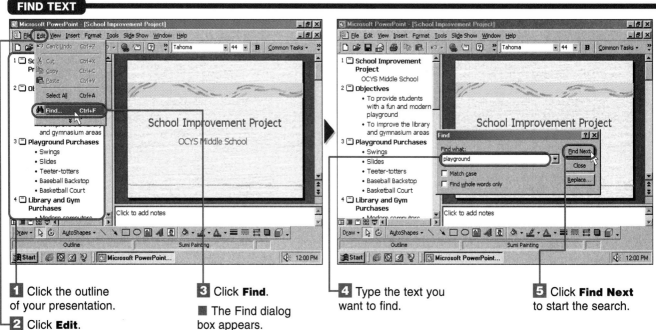

1 Click the outline of your presentation.

2 Click **Edit**.

3 Click **Find**.

■ The Find dialog box appears.

4 Type the text you want to find.

5 Click **Find Next** to start the search.

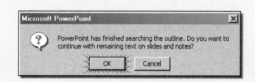

Why does this dialog box appear when I search for text in my presentation?

This dialog box appears if your presentation contains text that does not appear in the outline, such as speaker notes. Click **OK** to search the additional text your presentation.

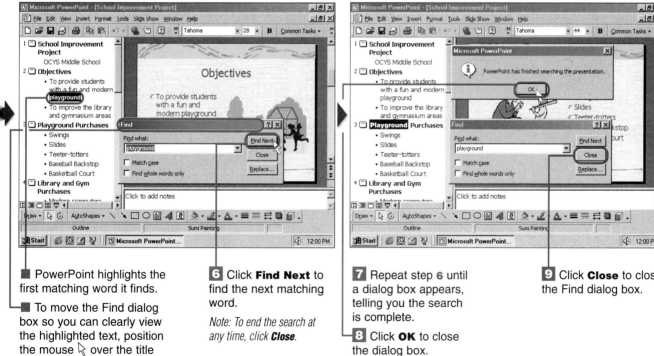

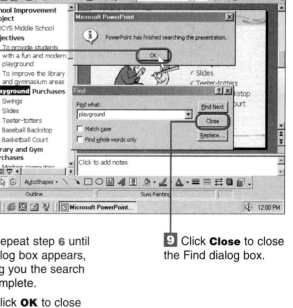

■ PowerPoint highlights the first matching word it finds.

■ To move the Find dialog box so you can clearly view the highlighted text, position the mouse ⬚ over the title bar and then drag the dialog box to a new location.

6 Click **Find Next** to find the next matching word.

*Note: To end the search at any time, click **Close**.*

7 Repeat step **6** until a dialog box appears, telling you the search is complete.

8 Click **OK** to close the dialog box.

9 Click **Close** to close the Find dialog box.

REPLACE TEXT

The Replace feature can locate and replace every occurrence of a word or phrase in your presentation. This is useful if you have frequently misspelled a name.

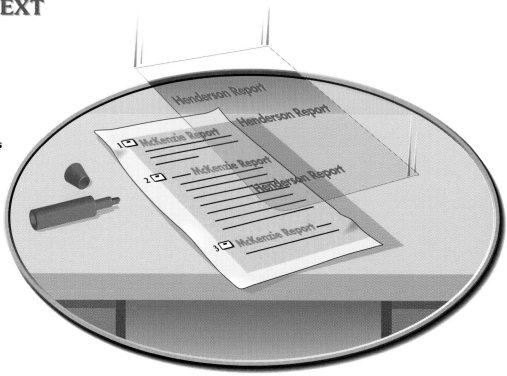

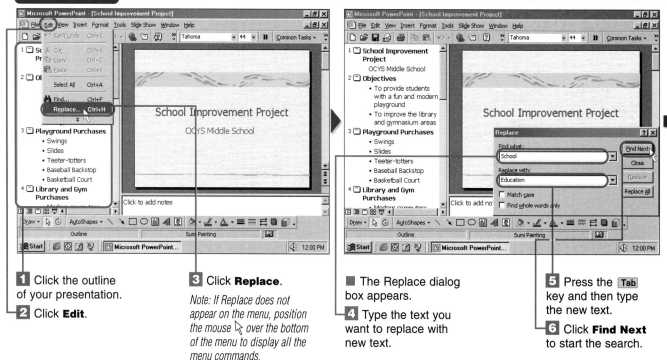

1 Click the outline of your presentation.

2 Click **Edit**.

3 Click **Replace**.

Note: If Replace does not appear on the menu, position the mouse over the bottom of the menu to display all the menu commands.

■ The Replace dialog box appears.

4 Type the text you want to replace with new text.

5 Press the Tab key and then type the new text.

6 Click **Find Next** to start the search.

Can I use the Replace feature to quickly enter text?

The Replace feature is useful when you have to type a long word or phrase, such as **University of Massachusetts**, many times in a presentation.

You can type a short form of the word or phrase, such as **UM**, throughout your presentation and then have PowerPoint replace the short form with the full word or phrase.

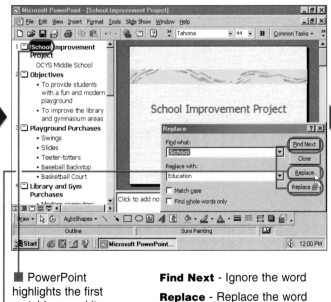

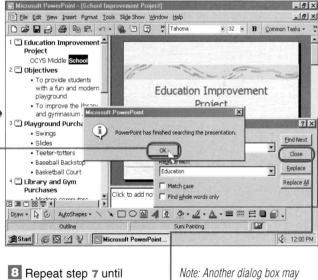

■ PowerPoint highlights the first matching word it finds.

7 Click one of these options.

Find Next - Ignore the word

Replace - Replace the word

Replace All - Replace the word and all other matching words in the presentation

Note: To end the search at any time, click ***Close***.

8 Repeat step **7** until a dialog box appears, telling you the search is complete.

9 Click **OK** to close the dialog box.

Note: Another dialog box may appear, asking if you want to search the remaining text on slides and notes. For more information, see the top of page 73.

10 Click **Close** to close the Replace dialog box.

CHECK SPELLING

PowerPoint automatically checks your presentation for spelling errors as you type. You can correct the errors that PowerPoint finds.

PowerPoint underlines spelling errors in red. The underlines will not appear when you view the slide show or print your presentation.

CORRECT AN ERROR

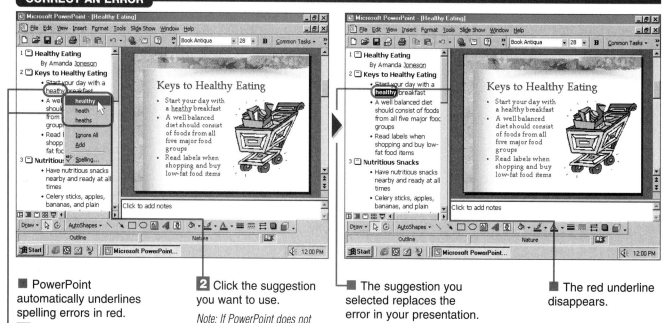

■ PowerPoint automatically underlines spelling errors in red.

1 Right-click an error in your presentation.

■ A menu appears with suggestions to correct the error.

2 Click the suggestion you want to use.

Note: If PowerPoint does not display a suggestion you want to use, click outside the menu to close the menu.

■ The suggestion you selected replaces the error in your presentation.

■ The red underline disappears.

Why did PowerPoint underline a correctly spelled word?

PowerPoint compares every word in your presentation to words in its dictionary. If a word in your presentation does not exist in PowerPoint's dictionary, the word is considered misspelled.

IGNORE AN ERROR

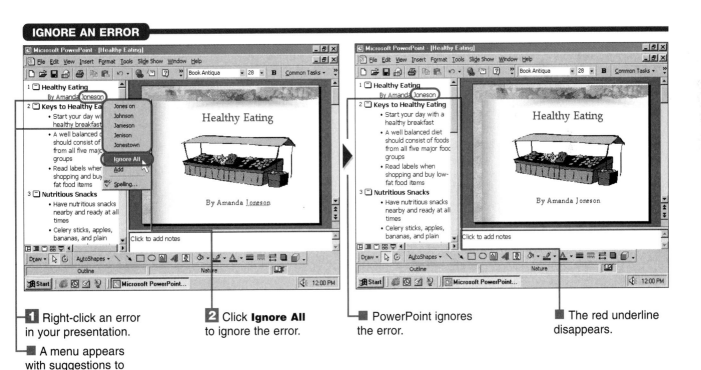

1 Right-click an error in your presentation.

■ A menu appears with suggestions to correct the error.

2 Click **Ignore All** to ignore the error.

■ PowerPoint ignores the error.

■ The red underline disappears.

CHECK SPELLING

You can find and correct all the spelling errors in your presentation at once.

CORRECT ENTIRE PRESENTATION

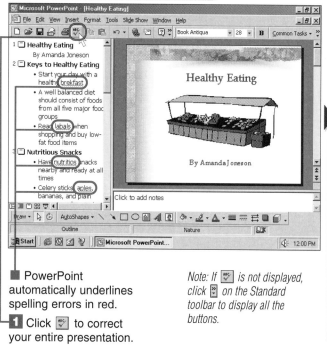

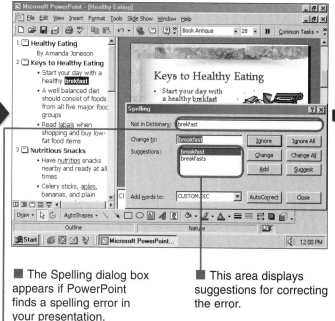

■ PowerPoint automatically underlines spelling errors in red.

1 Click 📝 to correct your entire presentation.

Note: If 📝 is not displayed, click 》 on the Standard toolbar to display all the buttons.

■ The Spelling dialog box appears if PowerPoint finds a spelling error in your presentation.

■ This area displays the spelling error.

■ This area displays suggestions for correcting the error.

Can PowerPoint automatically correct my typing mistakes?

PowerPoint's AutoCorrect feature automatically corrects common spelling errors as you type. For more information on the AutoCorrect feature, see page 80.

acheive	➡	achieve
claer	➡	clear
developement	➡	development
foriegn	➡	foreign
hte	➡	the
occassion	➡	occasion
recomend	➡	recommend
statment	➡	statement
wtih	➡	with

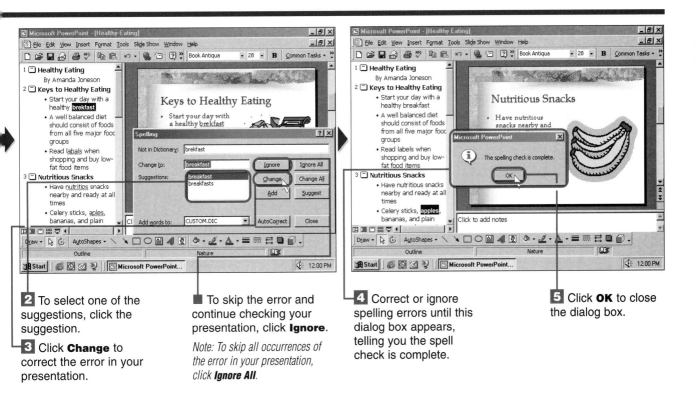

2 To select one of the suggestions, click the suggestion.

3 Click **Change** to correct the error in your presentation.

■ To skip the error and continue checking your presentation, click **Ignore**.

*Note: To skip all occurrences of the error in your presentation, click **Ignore All**.*

4 Correct or ignore spelling errors until this dialog box appears, telling you the spell check is complete.

5 Click **OK** to close the dialog box.

USING AUTOCORRECT

PowerPoint automatically corrects hundreds of typing, spelling and grammar errors as you type. You can create an AutoCorrect entry to add your own words and phrases to the list of errors that PowerPoint corrects.

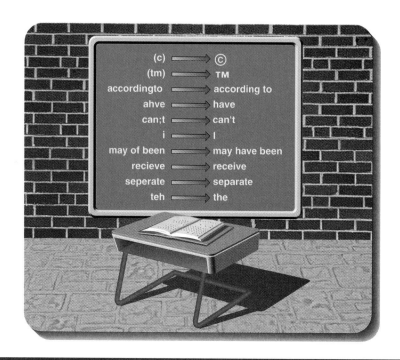

USING AUTOCORRECT

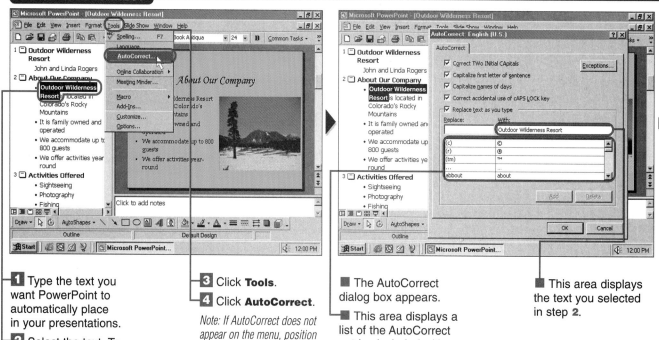

1 Type the text you want PowerPoint to automatically place in your presentations.

2 Select the text. To select text, see page 56.

3 Click **Tools**.

4 Click **AutoCorrect**.

Note: If AutoCorrect does not appear on the menu, position the mouse ⌇ over the bottom of the menu to display all the menu commands.

■ The AutoCorrect dialog box appears.

■ This area displays a list of the AutoCorrect entries included with PowerPoint.

■ This area displays the text you selected in step **2**.

What types of AutoCorrect entries can I create?

You can create AutoCorrect entries for typing, spelling and grammar errors you often make. You can also create AutoCorrect entries to quickly enter words and phrases you frequently use, such as your name.

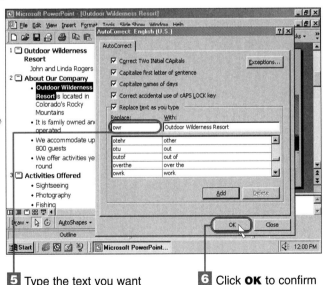

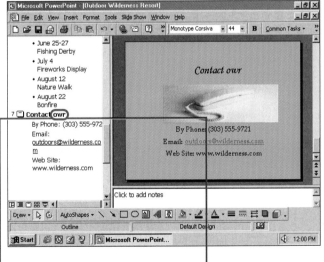

5 Type the text you want PowerPoint to replace automatically with the text you selected in step **2**. The text should not contain spaces and should not be a real word.

6 Click **OK** to confirm your changes.

INSERT AN AUTOCORRECT ENTRY

■ After you create an AutoCorrect entry, PowerPoint will automatically insert the entry each time you type the corresponding text.

1 Click where you want the AutoCorrect entry to appear in your presentation.

2 Type the text PowerPoint will automatically replace.

3 Press the **Spacebar** and the AutoCorrect entry replaces the text you typed.

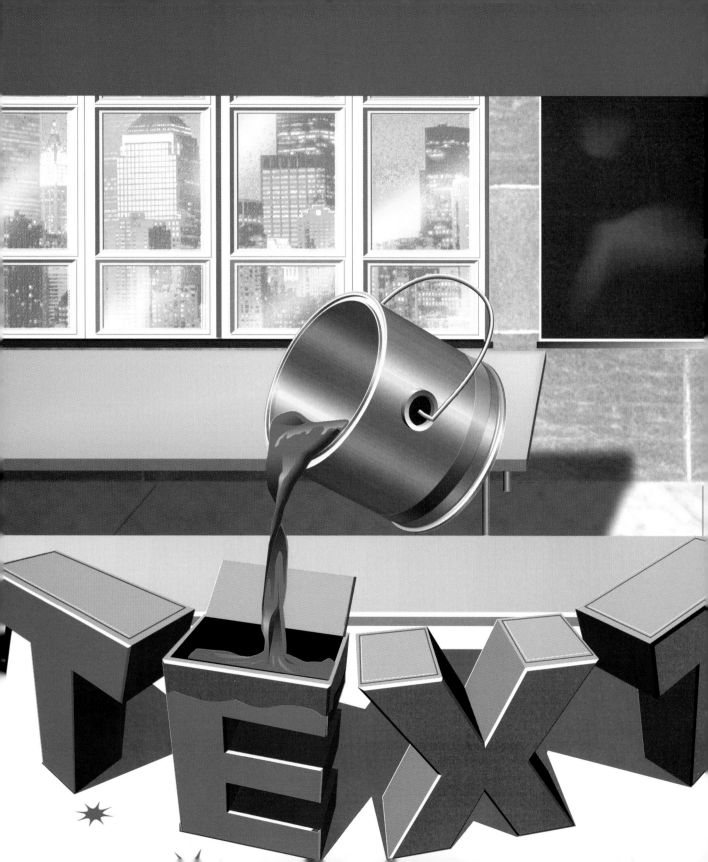

CHAPTER 4

Format Text

Would you like to improve the appearance of your text? This chapter shows you how to change the style and color of text, work with bullets and numbers and more.

CHANGE STYLE OF TEXT

You can use the Bold, Italic, Underline and Shadow features to change the style of text on a slide.

CHANGE STYLE OF TEXT

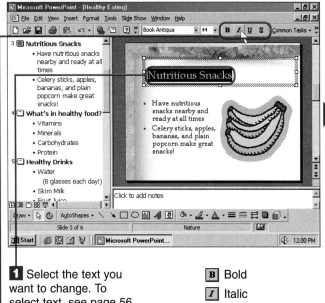

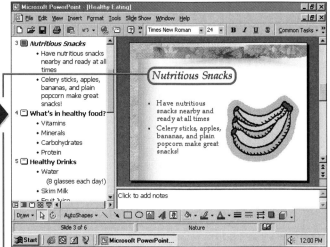

1 Select the text you want to change. To select text, see page 56.

2 Click one of these buttons.

B	Bold
I	Italic
U	Underline
S	Shadow

Note: If the button you want is not displayed, click ⟩⟩ *on the Formatting toolbar to display all the buttons.*

■ The text you selected appears in the new style.

■ To deselect text, click outside the selected area.

■ To remove a style, repeat steps **1** and **2**.

You can enhance
the appearance of
a slide by changing
the design, or font,
of text.

CHANGE FONT OF TEXT

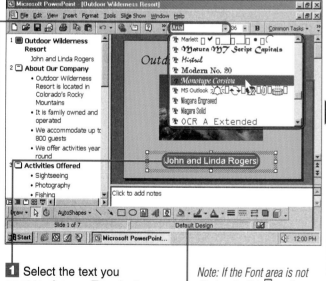

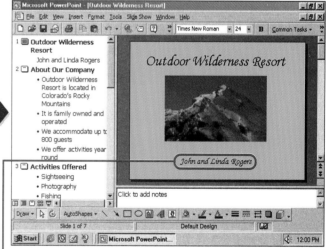

1 Select the text you
want to change. To select
text, see page 56.

2 Click 🔽 in this area
to display a list of the
available fonts.

*Note: If the Font area is not
displayed, click ≫ on the
Formatting toolbar to display
all the buttons.*

3 Click the font you
want to use.

■ The text you selected
changes to the new font.

■ To deselect text,
click outside the
selected area.

CHANGE SIZE OF TEXT

You can increase or decrease the size of text on a slide.

PowerPoint measures the size of text in points. There are 72 points in an inch.

CHANGE SIZE OF TEXT

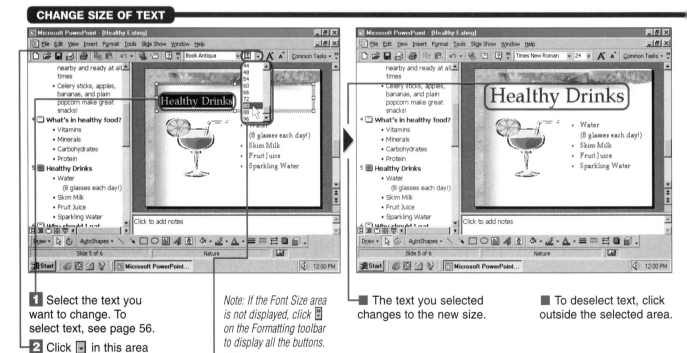

1 Select the text you want to change. To select text, see page 56.

2 Click ▾ in this area to display a list of the available sizes.

Note: If the Font Size area is not displayed, click ▸ on the Formatting toolbar to display all the buttons.

3 Click the size you want to use.

■ The text you selected changes to the new size.

■ To deselect text, click outside the selected area.

Why would I change the size of text on a slide?

You may want to increase the size of text on a slide to help emphasize important information. You can decrease the size of text to fit more information on a slide. When changing the size of text on a slide, make sure the audience will be able to read the text from several feet away.

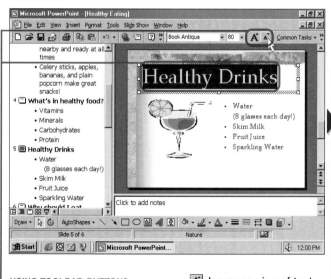

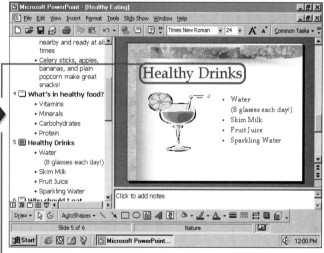

USING TOOLBAR BUTTONS

1 Select the text you want to change. To select text, see page 56.

2 Click one of these buttons to change the size of the text.

A̅ Increase size of text

A̤ Decrease size of text

Note: If the button you want is not displayed, click ⁝ on the Formatting toolbar to display all the buttons.

■ The size of the text increases or decreases.

3 Repeat step 2 until the text is the size you want.

■ To deselect text, click outside the selected area.

CHANGE ALIGNMENT OF TEXT

You can enhance the
appearance of a slide
by aligning text in
different ways.

CHANGE ALIGNMENT OF TEXT

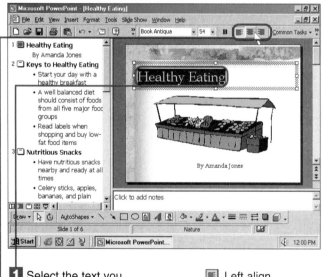

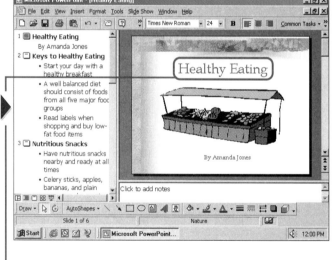

1 Select the text you
want to align differently.
To select text, see
page 56.

2 Click one of these
buttons.

▤ Left align

▤ Center

▤ Right align

*Note: If the button you want
is not displayed, click ⊠
on the Formatting toolbar
to display all the buttons.*

■ The text you selected
displays the new alignment.

■ To deselect text,
click outside the
selected area.

88

You can change the color of text on a slide to enhance the appearance of the slide and draw attention to important information.

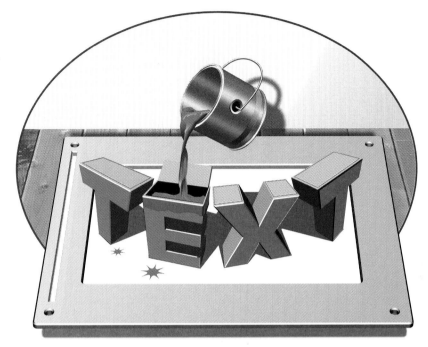

CHANGE COLOR OF TEXT

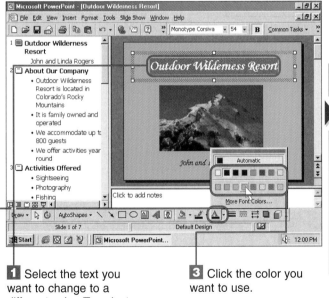

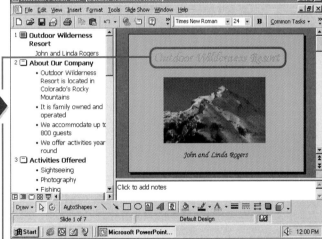

1 Select the text you want to change to a different color. To select text, see page 56.

2 Click ⬚ in this area to select a color.

3 Click the color you want to use.

Note: The available colors depend on the color scheme of the slide. For information on color schemes, see page 108.

■ The text you selected appears in the new color.

■ To deselect text, click outside the selected area.

■ To once again display the text in the default color, repeat steps **1** to **3**, except select **Automatic** in step **3**.

CHANGE APPEARANCE OF TEXT

You can make text in your presentation look more attractive by using various fonts, styles, sizes, special effects and colors.

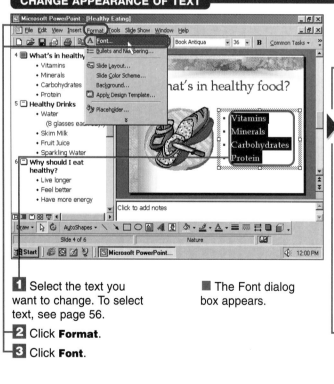

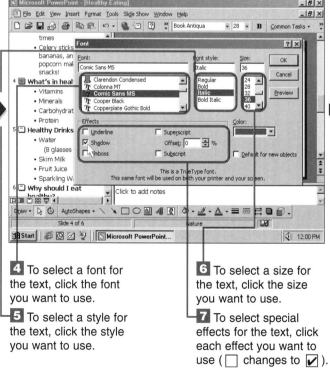

1 Select the text you want to change. To select text, see page 56.

2 Click **Format**.

3 Click **Font**.

■ The Font dialog box appears.

4 To select a font for the text, click the font you want to use.

5 To select a style for the text, click the style you want to use.

6 To select a size for the text, click the size you want to use.

7 To select special effects for the text, click each effect you want to use (☐ changes to ☑).

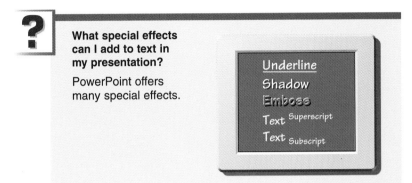

What special effects can I add to text in my presentation?

PowerPoint offers many special effects.

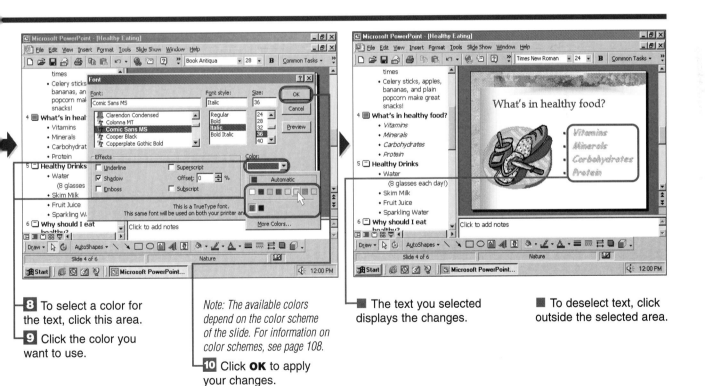

8 To select a color for the text, click this area.

9 Click the color you want to use.

Note: The available colors depend on the color scheme of the slide. For information on color schemes, see page 108.

10 Click **OK** to apply your changes.

■ The text you selected displays the changes.

■ To deselect text, click outside the selected area.

CHANGE CASE OF TEXT

You can change the case of text in your presentation without retyping the text. PowerPoint offers five case styles you can choose from.

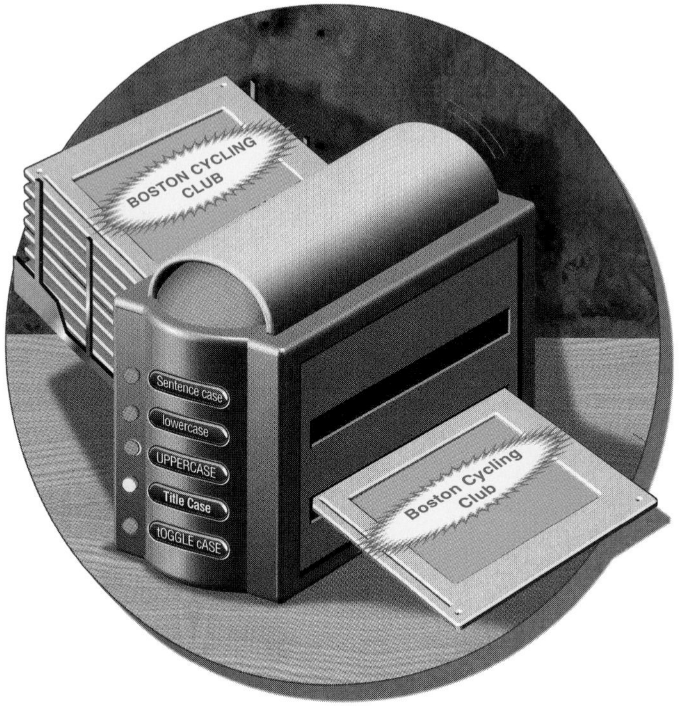

CHANGE CASE OF TEXT

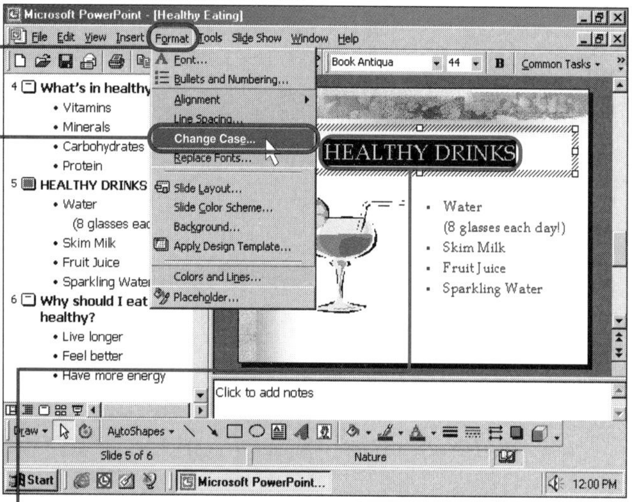

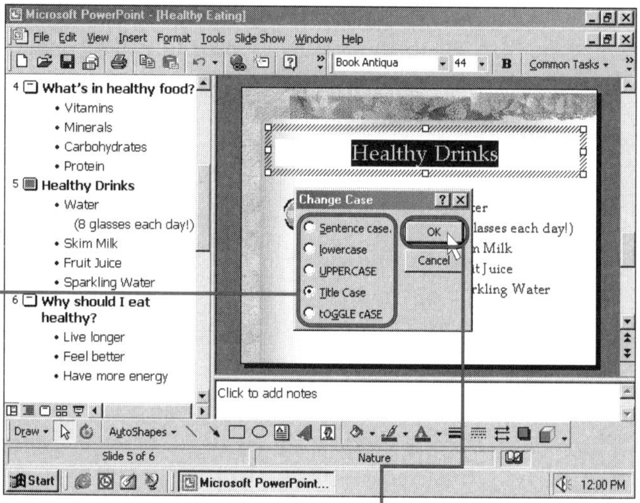

1 Select the text you want to change. To select text, see page 56.

2 Click **Format**.

3 Click **Change Case**.

Note: If Change Case does not appear on the menu, position the mouse over the bottom of the menu to display all the menu commands.

■ The Change Case dialog box appears.

4 Click the case style you want to use (○ changes to ⊙).

5 Click **OK** to confirm your selection.

■ The text you selected changes to the new case style.

■ To deselect text, click outside the selected area.

You can display the formatting of all the text in your presentation. Displaying the formatting of text allows you to see how the text in your speaker notes or outline will appear when printed.

DISPLAY TEXT FORMATTING

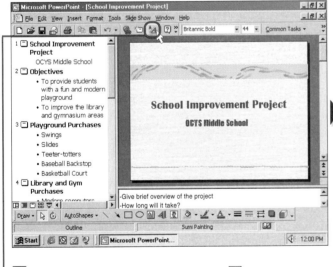

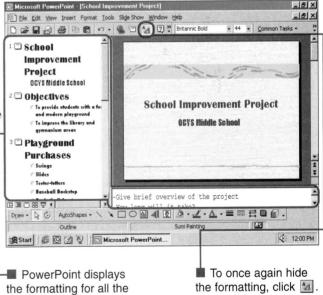

1 Click 🔲 to display the formatting of all the text in your presentation.

Note: If 🔲 is not displayed, click 🔲 on the Standard toolbar to display all the buttons.

■ PowerPoint displays the formatting for all the text in your presentation.

■ To once again hide the formatting, click 🔲.

COPY FORMATTING

You can make one area of text in your presentation look exactly like another.

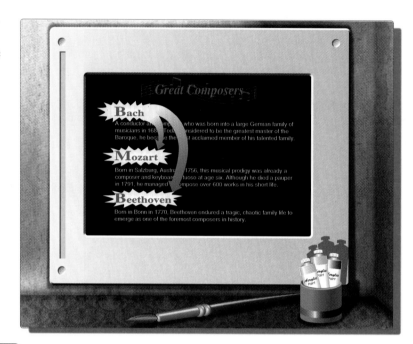

You may want to copy the formatting of text to make all the headings or important words in your presentation look the same. This will give your slides a consistent appearance.

COPY FORMATTING

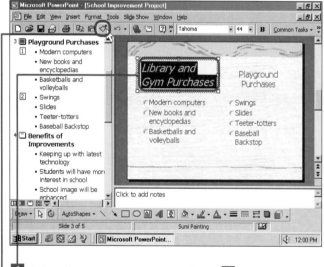

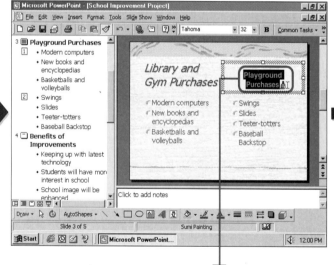

1 Select the text that displays the formatting you want to copy. To select text, see page 56.

2 Click to copy the formatting.

Note: If is not displayed, click on the Standard toolbar to display all the buttons.

■ The mouse changes to when over the slide.

3 Select the text you want to display the same formatting.

94

? **How do I copy formatting between slides in my presentation?**

To copy formatting between slides, perform steps **1** and **2** on page 94. Then display the slide containing the text you want to display the same formatting and select the text.

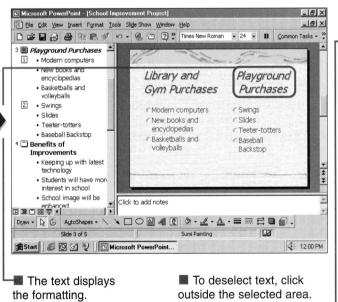

■ The text displays the formatting.

■ To deselect text, click outside the selected area.

COPY FORMATTING TO SEVERAL AREAS

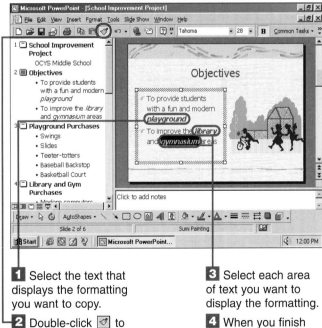

1 Select the text that displays the formatting you want to copy.

2 Double-click 🖋 to copy the formatting.

Note: If 🖋 is not displayed, click ⥥ on the Standard toolbar to display all the buttons.

3 Select each area of text you want to display the formatting.

4 When you finish copying the formatting, press the Esc key.

REPLACE A FONT

If you do not like a font used throughout your presentation, you can replace all occurrences of the font with a font you prefer.

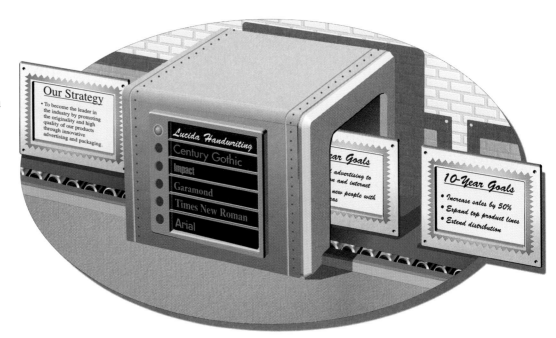

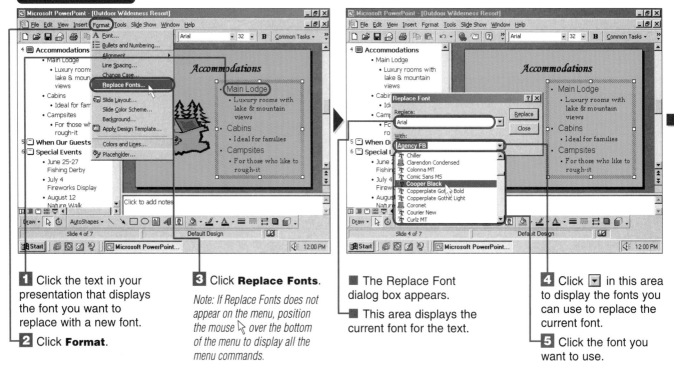

1 Click the text in your presentation that displays the font you want to replace with a new font.

2 Click **Format**.

3 Click **Replace Fonts**.

Note: If Replace Fonts does not appear on the menu, position the mouse ⌖ over the bottom of the menu to display all the menu commands.

■ The Replace Font dialog box appears.

■ This area displays the current font for the text.

4 Click ▼ in this area to display the fonts you can use to replace the current font.

5 Click the font you want to use.

96

What determines which fonts are available on my computer?

The fonts available on your computer may be different from the fonts on other computers. The available fonts depend on your printer and the setup of your computer.

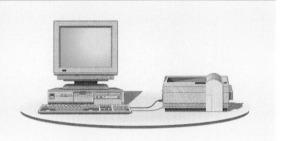

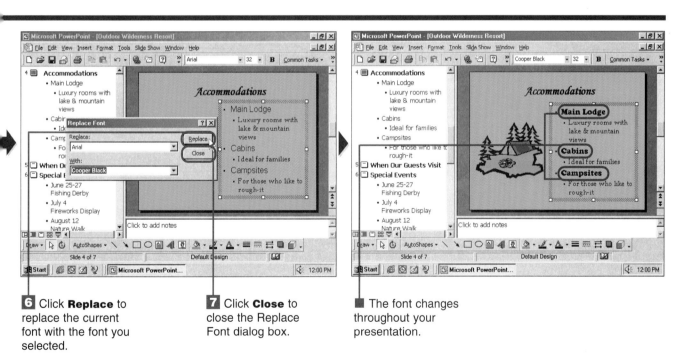

6 Click **Replace** to replace the current font with the font you selected.

7 Click **Close** to close the Replace Font dialog box.

■ The font changes throughout your presentation.

WORK WITH BULLETS AND NUMBERS

You can change
the appearance of
bullets or numbers
on a slide.

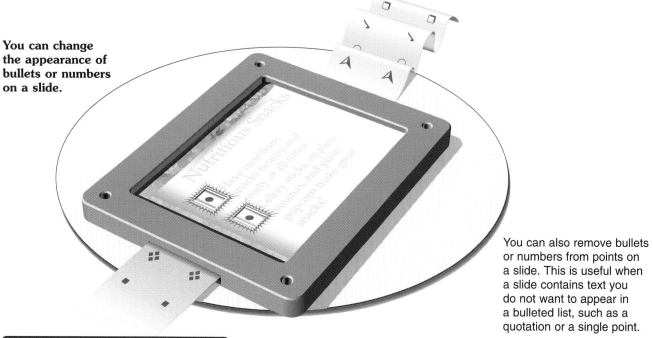

You can also remove bullets
or numbers from points on
a slide. This is useful when
a slide contains text you
do not want to appear in
a bulleted list, such as a
quotation or a single point.

WORK WITH BULLETS AND NUMBERS

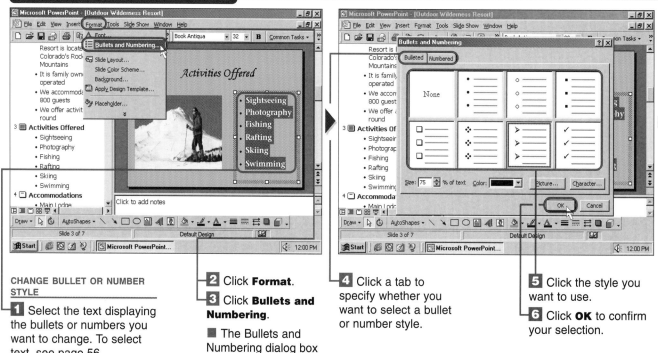

CHANGE BULLET OR NUMBER STYLE

1 Select the text displaying
the bullets or numbers you
want to change. To select
text, see page 56.

2 Click **Format**.

3 Click **Bullets and Numbering**.

■ The Bullets and
Numbering dialog box
appears.

4 Click a tab to
specify whether you
want to select a bullet
or number style.

5 Click the style you
want to use.

6 Click **OK** to confirm
your selection.

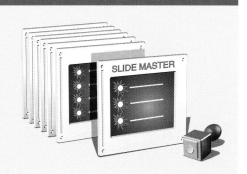

Can I make changes to the bullets on all my slides at once?

You can perform the steps below to make changes to the bullets on the Slide Master. Changing the bullets on the Slide Master will change the bullets on all the slides in your presentation. For information on the Slide Master, see page 118.

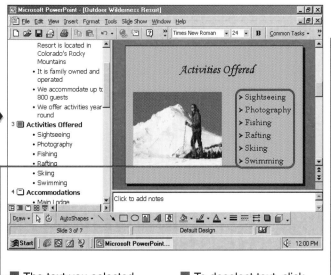

■ The text you selected displays the new bullets or numbers.

■ To deselect text, click outside the selected area.

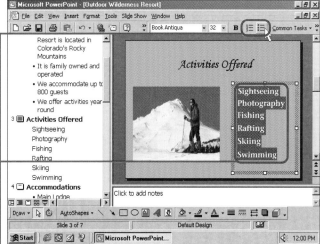

QUICKLY ADD OR REMOVE BULLETS OR NUMBERS

1 Select the text where you want to add or remove bullets or numbers. To select text, see page 56.

2 Click one of these buttons.

▤ Bullets

▤ Numbers

Note: If the button you want is not displayed, click ▸▸ on the Standard toolbar to display all the buttons.

CHANGE INDENTATION OF TEXT

You can change the indentation of text to emphasize the start of a new paragraph.

Indent first line

Indent all but first line

CHANGE INDENTATION OF TEXT

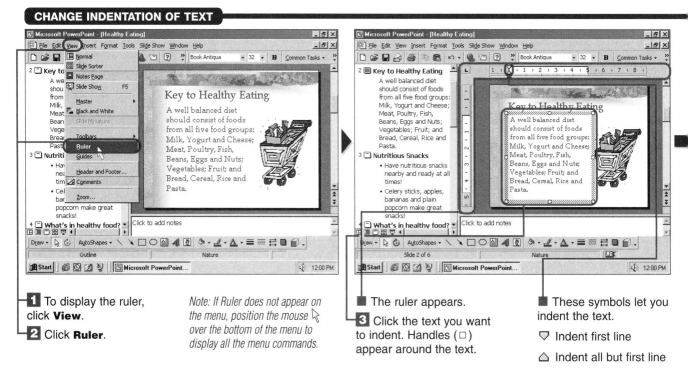

1 To display the ruler, click **View**.

2 Click **Ruler**.

Note: If Ruler does not appear on the menu, position the mouse over the bottom of the menu to display all the menu commands.

■ The ruler appears.

3 Click the text you want to indent. Handles (□) appear around the text.

■ These symbols let you indent the text.

▽ Indent first line

△ Indent all but first line

I tried to indent all but the first line of text, but it did not work properly. What is wrong?

If the text you are indenting displays bullets, all the text will indent to the same location. To indent all but the first line of text, you must first remove the bullets. For information on removing bullets, see page 99.

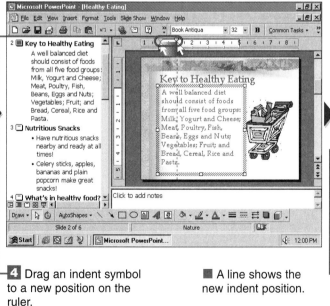

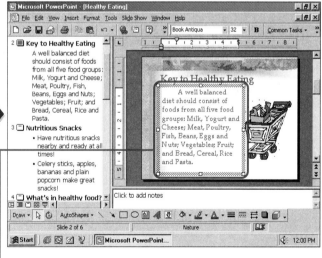

4 Drag an indent symbol to a new position on the ruler.

■ A line shows the new indent position.

■ PowerPoint indents the text.

■ To hide the ruler, repeat steps **1** and **2**.

ADD TABS

You can use tabs to line up columns of text on a slide. PowerPoint offers four types of tabs that you can choose from.

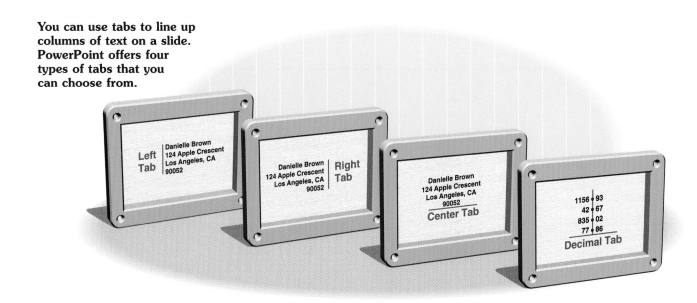

ADD TABS

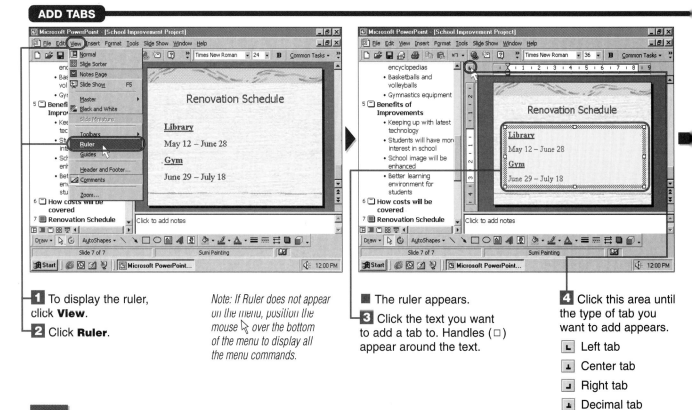

1 To display the ruler, click **View**.

2 Click **Ruler**.

Note: If Ruler does not appear on the menu, position the mouse ⟍ over the bottom of the menu to display all the menu commands.

■ The ruler appears.

3 Click the text you want to add a tab to. Handles (□) appear around the text.

4 Click this area until the type of tab you want to add appears.

◻ Left tab

◻ Center tab

◻ Right tab

◻ Decimal tab

How do I remove a tab I added to a slide?

When you no longer need a tab, you can remove the tab from the ruler.

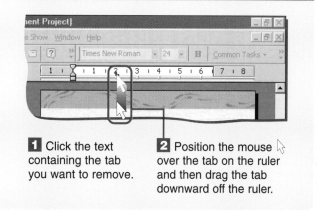

1 Click the text containing the tab you want to remove.

2 Position the mouse over the tab on the ruler and then drag the tab downward off the ruler.

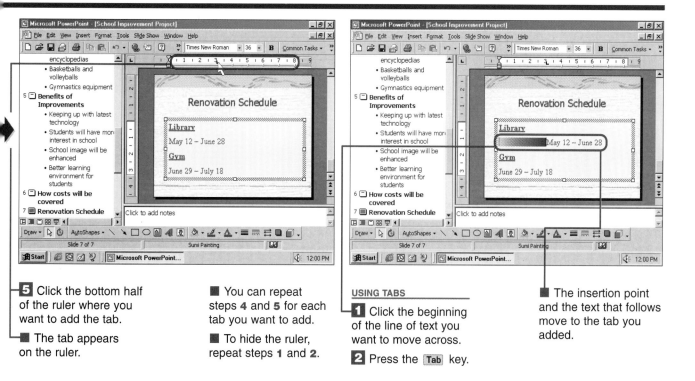

5 Click the bottom half of the ruler where you want to add the tab.

■ The tab appears on the ruler.

■ You can repeat steps **4** and **5** for each tab you want to add.

■ To hide the ruler, repeat steps **1** and **2**.

USING TABS

1 Click the beginning of the line of text you want to move across.

2 Press the Tab key.

■ The insertion point and the text that follows move to the tab you added.

CHAPTER 5

Change Appearance of Slides

Are you wondering how to change the overall look of the slides in your presentation? In this chapter you will learn how to change the design template, color scheme and background of your slides.

CHANGE DESIGN TEMPLATE

PowerPoint offers many design templates that you can choose from to give the slides in your presentation a new appearance.

CHANGE DESIGN TEMPLATE

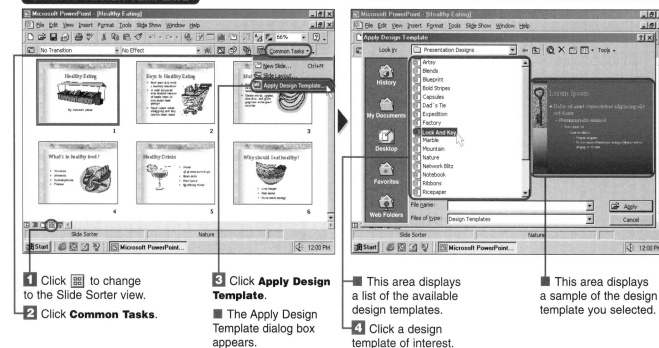

1 Click ⊞ to change to the Slide Sorter view.

2 Click **Common Tasks**.

3 Click **Apply Design Template**.

■ The Apply Design Template dialog box appears.

■ This area displays a list of the available design templates.

4 Click a design template of interest.

■ This area displays a sample of the design template you selected.

106

When I changed the design template for my presentation, why did some parts of my slides not change?

The new design template may not affect parts of a slide you have previously changed. For example, if you changed the color of text before changing the design template, the new design template will not affect the text you changed.

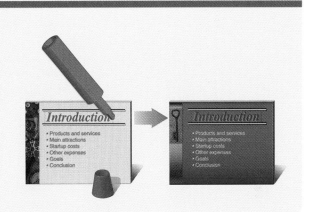

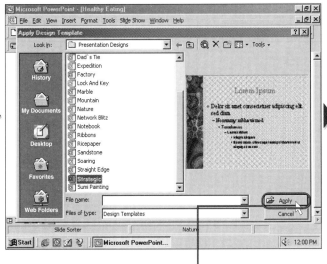

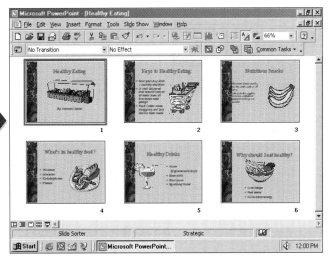

5 Repeat step **4** until the design template you want to use appears.

6 Click **Apply** to apply the design template to every slide in your presentation.

■ The slides in your presentation display the new design template.

CHANGE COLOR SCHEME

You can change
the color scheme
of your entire
presentation.

If you will be using
overheads, you should
choose a color scheme
with a light background.
If you will be using 35mm
slides or delivering your
presentation on a computer
screen, you should choose
a color scheme with a dark
background.

CHANGE COLOR SCHEME

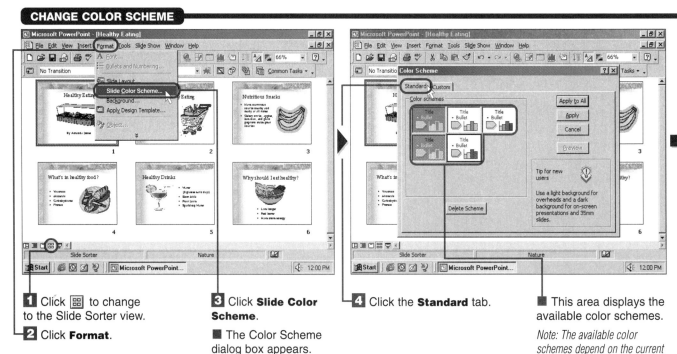

1 Click ⊞ to change
to the Slide Sorter view.

2 Click **Format**.

3 Click **Slide Color
Scheme**.

■ The Color Scheme
dialog box appears.

4 Click the **Standard** tab.

■ This area displays the
available color schemes.

*Note: The available color
schemes depend on the current
design template. To change the
design template, see page 106.*

Can I use a color scheme to emphasize one slide in my presentation?

You can change the color scheme for one slide to make the slide stand out from the rest of your presentation. To change the color scheme for a single slide, click the slide you want to change. Then perform steps **2** to **6** below, except select **Apply** in step **6**.

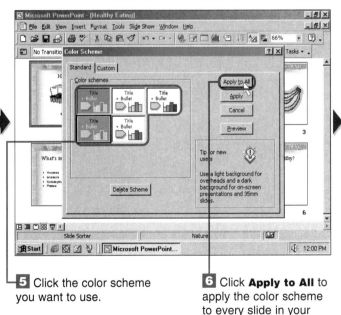

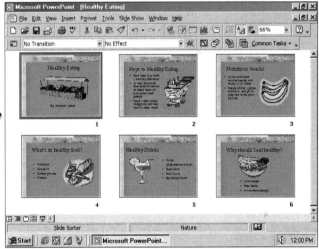

5 Click the color scheme you want to use.

6 Click **Apply to All** to apply the color scheme to every slide in your presentation.

■ All the slides in your presentation display the new color scheme.

CHANGE SLIDE BACKGROUND

You can change the
background color of
your slides to make
your presentation
more attractive.

CHANGE BACKGROUND COLOR

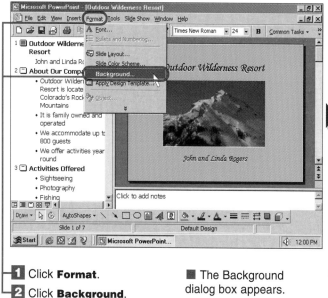

1 Click **Format**.

2 Click **Background**.

■ The Background
dialog box appears.

3 Click this area
to display the colors
you can use for the
background.

4 Click the color you
want to use for the
background of the slide.

Note: The available colors
depend on the color scheme
of the slide. For information on
color schemes, see page 108.

Why didn't the entire background change?

Some text or objects on the Slide Master may not be affected by the new background. You can hide text and objects on the Slide Master to change the entire background of your slides. Perform steps **1** and **2** below. Click **Omit background graphics from master** (☐ changes to ☑) and then perform step **5**. For more information on the Slide Master, see page 118.

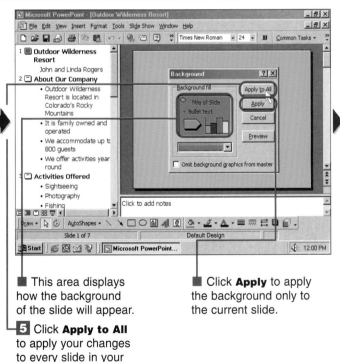

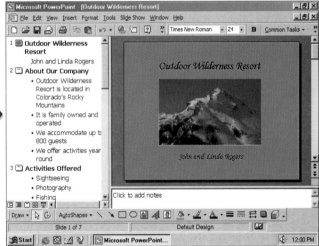

■ This area displays how the background of the slide will appear.

5 Click **Apply to All** to apply your changes to every slide in your presentation.

■ Click **Apply** to apply the background only to the current slide.

■ The slides in your presentation display the new background color.

Note: The new background color may not affect parts of a slide you have previously changed. For example, if you previously changed the background color of a text box on a slide, the text box will not be affected by the new background color.

CHANGE SLIDE BACKGROUND

You can apply a
gradient, pattern
or texture to the
background of
your slides.

APPLY A GRADIENT, PATTERN OR TEXTURE

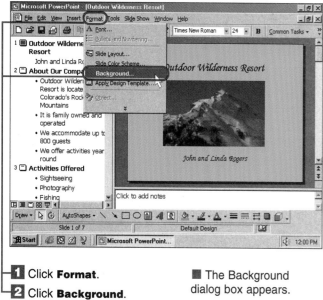

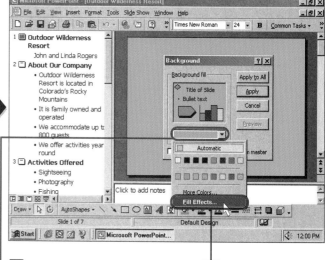

1 Click **Format**.

2 Click **Background**.

■ The Background
dialog box appears.

3 Click this area
to apply a gradient,
pattern or texture to
the background of
your slides.

4 Click **Fill Effects**.

■ The Fill Effects
dialog box appears.

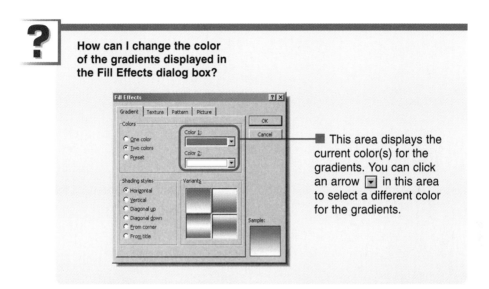

? How can I change the color
of the gradients displayed in
the Fill Effects dialog box?

■ This area displays the
current color(s) for the
gradients. You can click
an arrow ▼ in this area
to select a different color
for the gradients.

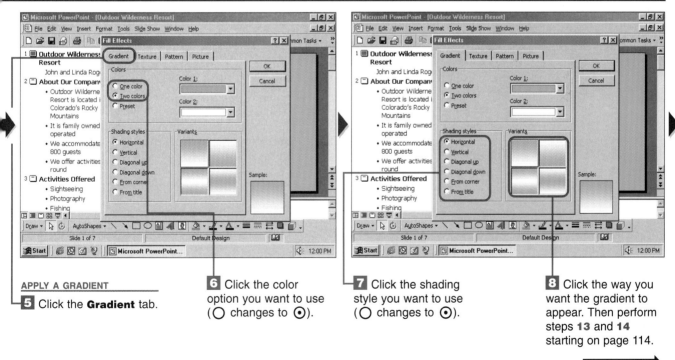

APPLY A GRADIENT

5 Click the **Gradient** tab.

6 Click the color
option you want to use
(○ changes to ◉).

7 Click the shading
style you want to use
(○ changes to ◉).

8 Click the way you
want the gradient to
appear. Then perform
steps **13** and **14**
starting on page 114.

CONTINUED

CHANGE SLIDE BACKGROUND

You can choose to display a background you selected on every slide in your presentation or only on one slide.

Displaying a different background on one slide can help emphasize a slide or introduce a new part of your presentation.

APPLY A GRADIENT, PATTERN OR TEXTURE (CONTINUED)

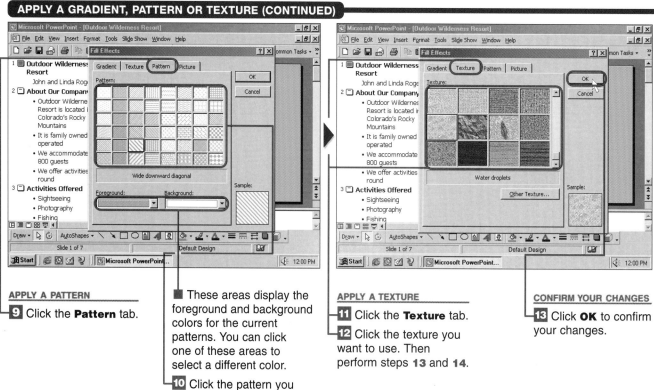

APPLY A PATTERN

9 Click the **Pattern** tab.

■ These areas display the foreground and background colors for the current patterns. You can click one of these areas to select a different color.

10 Click the pattern you want to use. Then perform steps **13** and **14**.

APPLY A TEXTURE

11 Click the **Texture** tab.

12 Click the texture you want to use. Then perform steps **13** and **14**.

CONFIRM YOUR CHANGES

13 Click **OK** to confirm your changes.

What slide background should I choose?

When selecting a slide background, make sure the gradient, pattern or texture you choose does not make the text on the slides difficult to read. You may need to change the color of the text on the slides to make the text easier to read. To change the color of text, see page 89.

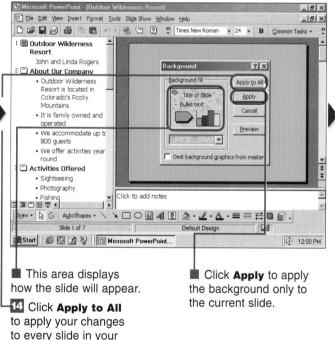

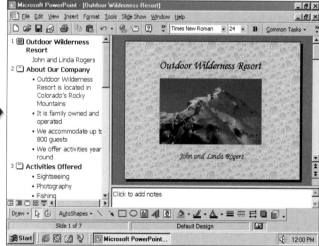

■ This area displays how the slide will appear.

14 Click **Apply to All** to apply your changes to every slide in your presentation.

■ Click **Apply** to apply the background only to the current slide.

■ The slides in your presentation display the new background.

Note: If the entire slide background does not change, see the top of page 111.

CHANGE A HEADER OR FOOTER

You can display specific information on every slide in your presentation. For example, you may want to display your company name on each slide.

You can display the date and time, slide number and footer text on each slide.

When you use the AutoContent Wizard to create a presentation, PowerPoint may automatically add header or footer information to your slides for you. For information on the AutoContent Wizard, see page 16.

CHANGE A HEADER OR FOOTER

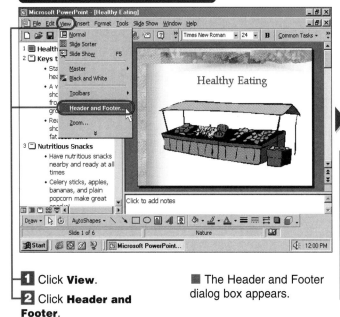

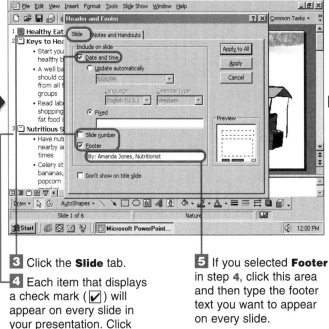

1 Click **View**.

2 Click **Header and Footer**.

■ The Header and Footer dialog box appears.

3 Click the **Slide** tab.

4 Each item that displays a check mark (✔) will appear on every slide in your presentation. Click an item to add (✔) or remove (☐) a check mark.

5 If you selected **Footer** in step **4**, click this area and then type the footer text you want to appear on every slide.

Can I change the header and footer displayed on my speaker notes and handouts?

Yes. Perform steps **1** to **7** below, except click the **Notes and Handouts** tab in step **3**. Then perform step **9** to apply the changes to all your speaker notes and handouts.

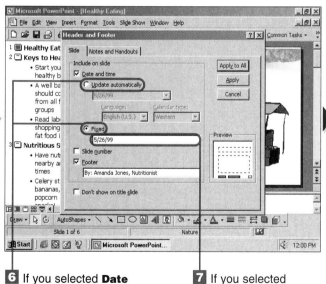

6 If you selected **Date and time** in step **4**, click one of the following options (○ changes to ⊙).

Update automatically
Display current date

Fixed
Display date you specify

7 If you selected **Fixed** in step **6**, type the date you want to display on your slides.

8 If you do not want the information you specified to appear on the title slide, click this option (☐ changes to ☑).

9 Click **Apply to All** to apply your changes to every slide in your presentation.

■ To apply your changes to only the current slide, click **Apply**.

USING THE SLIDE MASTER

You can use the Slide Master to change the appearance of all the slides in your presentation at once.

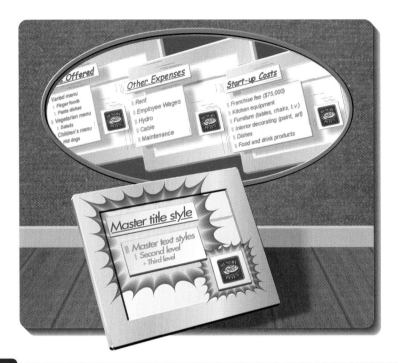

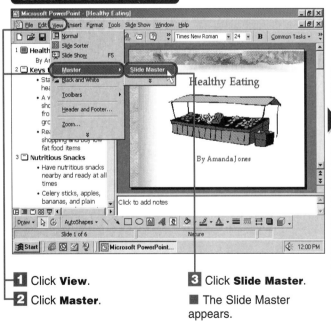

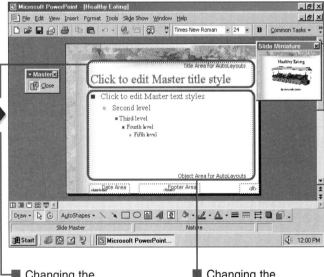

1 Click **View**.

2 Click **Master**.

3 Click **Slide Master**.

■ The Slide Master appears.

■ Changing the appearance of this text will change the appearance of the title on each slide.

■ Changing the appearance of this text will change the appearance of the points on each slide.

Note: To change the appearance of text, see pages 84 to 91.

Can I use the Slide Master to add my company logo to every slide in my presentation?

Yes. You can add an object, such as a picture, clip art image or AutoShape, to the Slide Master as you would add an object to any slide in your presentation. To add an object to a slide, see pages 124 to 133.

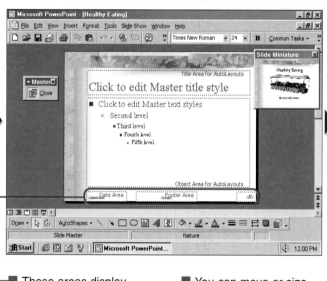

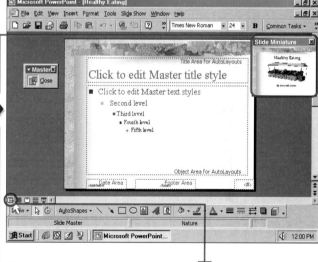

■ These areas display the date, footer text and slide number on each slide.

Note: To change this information, see page 116.

■ You can move or size a placeholder on the Slide Master as you would move or size any object on a slide. To move or size an object, see page 170.

■ This area displays a miniature version of a slide in your presentation. This allows you to preview any changes you make.

4 When you finish making changes to the Slide Master, click 🔲 to close the Slide Master and return to the Normal view.

CREATE A TEMPLATE

You can create a template that stores the formatting, color schemes and text you use most often. You can then use the template to quickly create a new presentation at any time.

CREATE A TEMPLATE

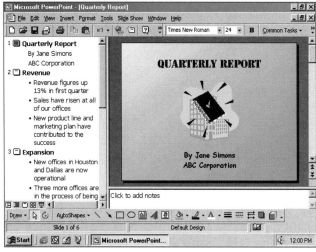

1 Open the presentation you want to use as the basis for the template. To open a presentation, see page 28.

2 Click **File**.

3 Click **Save As**.

■ The Save As dialog box appears.

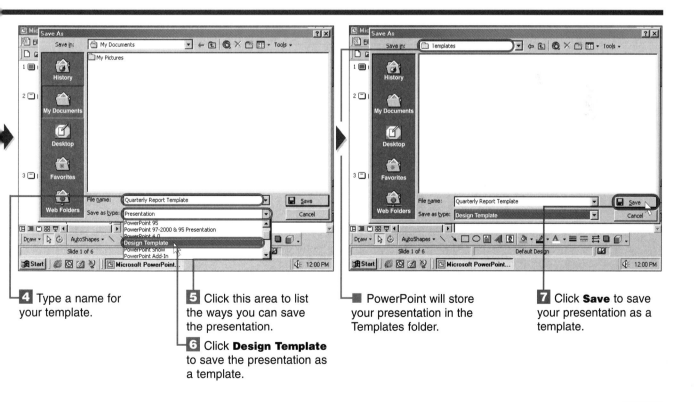

How do I use a template I created?

To create a presentation using a template you created, perform steps **1** to **5** on page 20, except select the **General** tab in step **3**.

4 Type a name for your template.

5 Click this area to list the ways you can save the presentation.

6 Click **Design Template** to save the presentation as a template.

■ PowerPoint will store your presentation in the Templates folder.

7 Click **Save** to save your presentation as a template.

CHAPTER 6

Add Simple Objects

Would you like to learn how to add simple objects to your slides? This chapter shows you how to add objects such as text effects, clip art images and pictures.

Product Availability

• Department stores
• Catalogues*

*Not available Texas and Arizona

ADD AN AUTOSHAPE

You can add
simple shapes,
called AutoShapes,
to the slides in
your presentation.

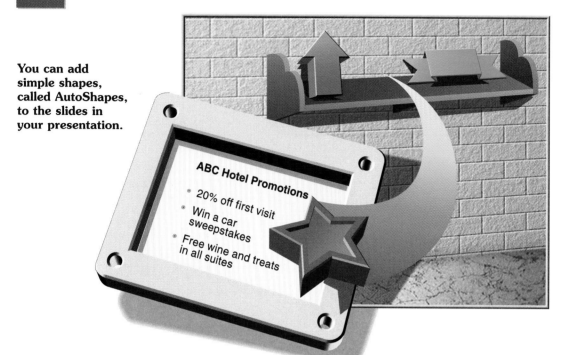

You can add
AutoShapes such
as rectangles,
arrows, stars
and banners.

ADD AN AUTOSHAPE

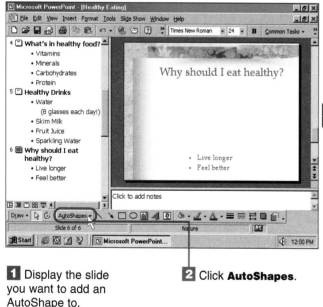

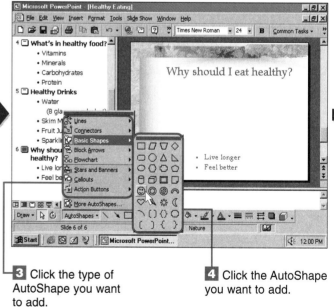

1 Display the slide
you want to add an
AutoShape to.

2 Click **AutoShapes**.

3 Click the type of
AutoShape you want
to add.

*Note: If the type of AutoShape
you want does not appear on
the menu, position the mouse*
*over the bottom of the menu to
display all the menu commands.*

4 Click the AutoShape
you want to add.

?

Can I add text to an AutoShape?

You can add text to most AutoShapes. This is particularly useful for AutoShapes such as banners. To add text to an AutoShape, click the AutoShape and then type the text you want the AutoShape to display.

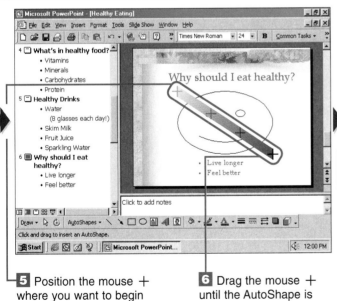

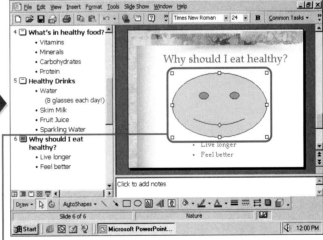

5 Position the mouse + where you want to begin drawing the AutoShape.

6 Drag the mouse + until the AutoShape is the size you want.

■ The AutoShape appears on the slide. The handles (□) around the AutoShape let you change the size of the AutoShape.

7 To hide the handles, click outside the AutoShape.

Note: To move, size or delete an AutoShape, see pages 170 to 172.

ADD A TEXT BOX

You can add a text box to a slide to include additional information in your presentation.

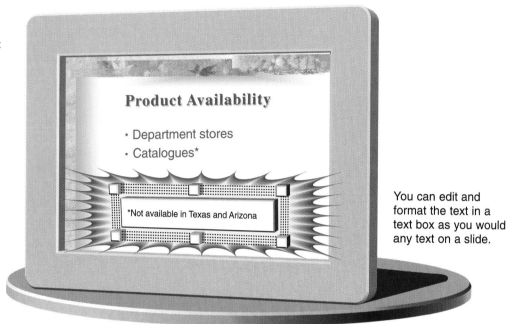

You can edit and format the text in a text box as you would any text on a slide.

ADD A TEXT BOX

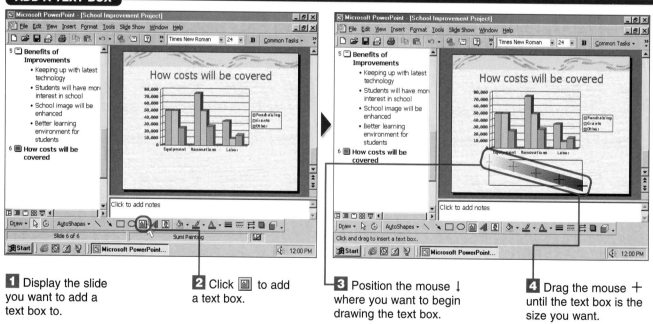

1 Display the slide you want to add a text box to.

2 Click 📝 to add a text box.

3 Position the mouse ↓ where you want to begin drawing the text box.

4 Drag the mouse ┼ until the text box is the size you want.

Why doesn't the text in the text box I added appear in the outline of my presentation?

The text in a text box you added will not appear in the outline of your presentation. To have the text appear in the outline, you must enter the text in a text placeholder. To change the layout of a slide to one that includes a text placeholder, see page 44.

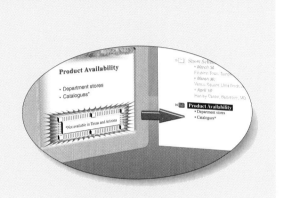

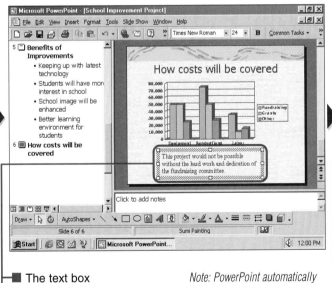

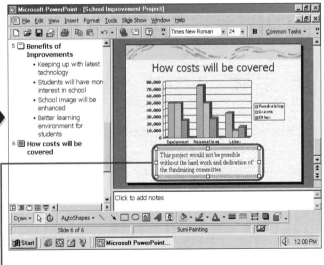

■ The text box appears on the slide.

5 Type the text you want the text box to display.

Note: PowerPoint automatically adjusts the height of the text box to accommodate the text you type.

■ The handles (□) around the text box let you change the size of the text box.

6 To hide the handles, click outside the text box.

Note: To move, size or delete a text box, see pages 170 to 173.

ADD A TEXT EFFECT

You can add a text effect to a slide in your presentation. Text effects can enhance the appearance of a title or draw attention to an important point.

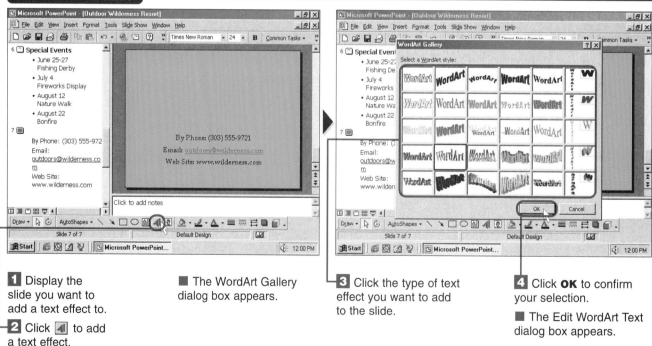

1 Display the slide you want to add a text effect to.

2 Click ◀ to add a text effect.

■ The WordArt Gallery dialog box appears.

3 Click the type of text effect you want to add to the slide.

4 Click **OK** to confirm your selection.

■ The Edit WordArt Text dialog box appears.

128

?

How do I edit a text effect?

Double-click the text effect to display the Edit WordArt Text dialog box. Then edit the text in the dialog box. When you finish editing the text effect, click **OK** to display the changes on the slide.

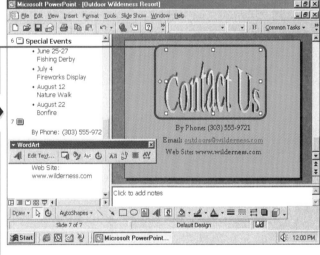

5 Type the text you want the text effect to display.

6 Click **OK** to add the text effect to the slide.

■ The text effect appears on the slide. The handles (□) around the text effect let you change the size of the text effect.

7 To hide the handles, click outside the text effect.

Note: To move, size or delete a text effect, see pages 170 to 172.

ADD CLIP ART

You can add a
clip art image to
a slide to make
your presentation
more interesting
and entertaining.

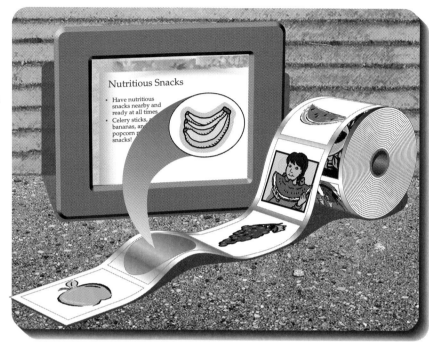

PowerPoint provides
thousands of clip art
images that you can
choose from.

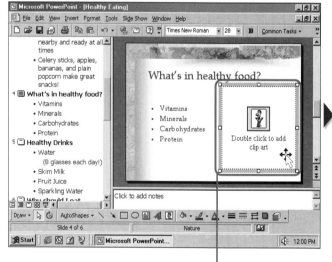

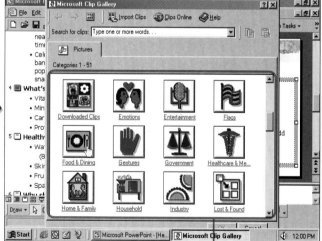

1 Display the slide you want
to add a clip art image to.

2 Change the layout of the
slide to one that includes
a placeholder for a clip art
image. To change the slide
layout, see page 44.

3 Double-click this
area to add a clip art
image to the slide.

■ The Microsoft Clip
Gallery dialog box appears.

4 Click the category
of clip art images you
want to display.

130

?

Where can I find more clip art images?

If you are connected to the Internet, you can visit Microsoft's Clip Gallery Live Web site to find additional clip art images. In the Microsoft Clip Gallery dialog box, click **Clips Online**. In the dialog box that appears, click **OK** to connect to the Web site.

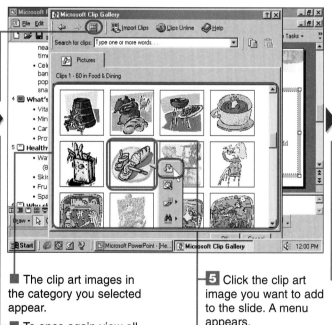

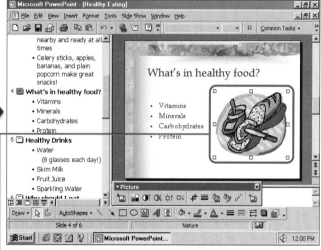

■ The clip art images in the category you selected appear.

■ To once again view all the categories, click 🔳.

5 Click the clip art image you want to add to the slide. A menu appears.

6 Click 🖾 to add the clip art image to the slide.

■ The clip art image appears on the slide. The handles (□) around the image let you change the size of the image.

7 To hide the handles, click outside the clip art image.

Note: To move, size or delete a clip art image, see pages 170 to 172.

ADD A PICTURE

You can add a
picture stored
on your computer
to a slide in your
presentation.

Adding a picture
is useful if you
want to display
your company logo
or a picture of your
products on a slide.

ADD A PICTURE

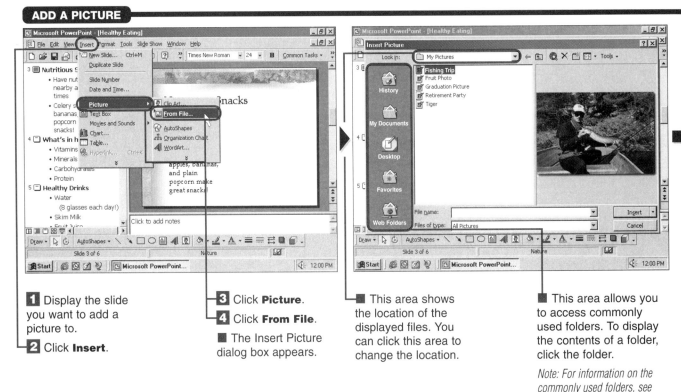

1 Display the slide
you want to add a
picture to.

2 Click **Insert**.

3 Click **Picture**.

4 Click **From File**.

■ The Insert Picture
dialog box appears.

■ This area shows
the location of the
displayed files. You
can click this area to
change the location.

■ This area allows you
to access commonly
used folders. To display
the contents of a folder,
click the folder.

*Note: For information on the
commonly used folders, see
the top of page 25.*

How can I have the same picture appear on every slide in my presentation?

You can perform the steps below to add a picture to the Slide Master. Adding a picture to the Slide Master will add the picture to every slide in your presentation. For information on the Slide Master, see page 118.

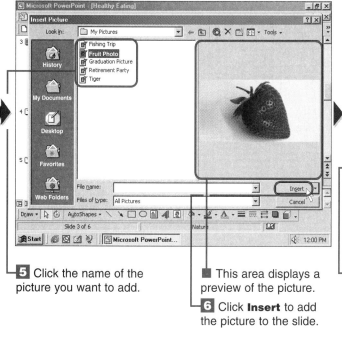

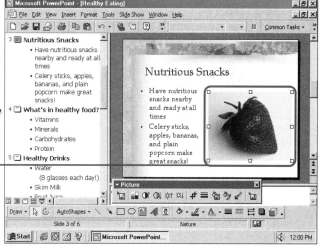

5 Click the name of the picture you want to add.

■ This area displays a preview of the picture.

6 Click **Insert** to add the picture to the slide.

■ The picture appears on the slide. The handles (□) around the picture let you change the size of the picture.

7 To hide the handles, click outside the picture.

Note: To move, size or delete a picture, see pages 170 to 172.

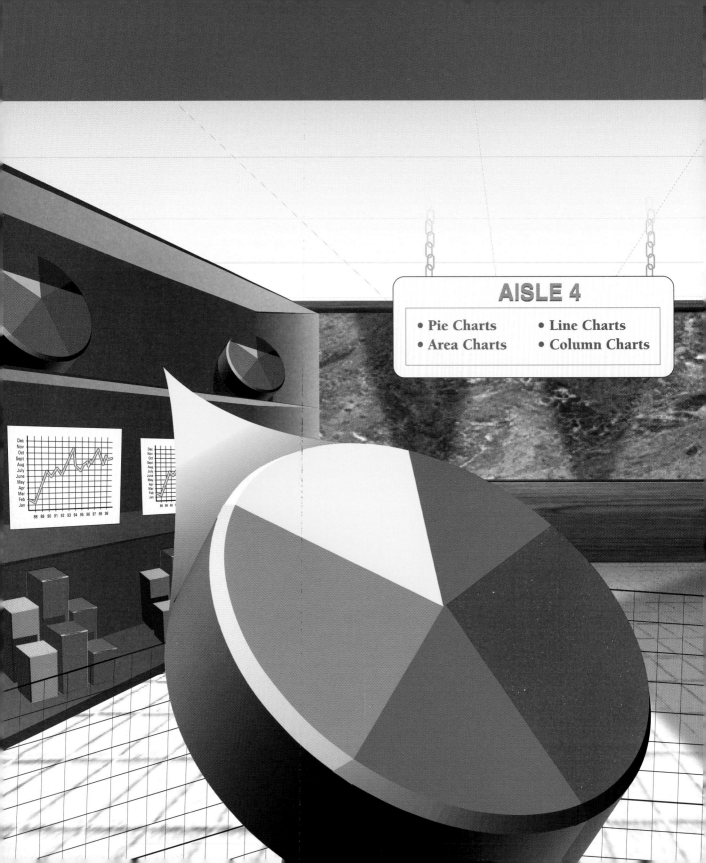

CHAPTER 7

Add Charts

Do you want to use a chart to visually display information on a slide? This chapter shows you how to create and work with charts in your presentation.

ADD A CHART

You can add a
chart to a slide to
show trends and
compare data.

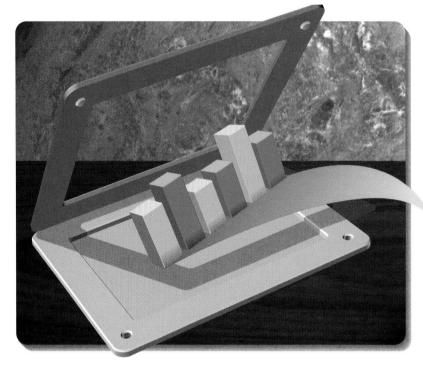

A chart is more
appealing and
often easier to
understand than
a list of numbers.

ADD A CHART

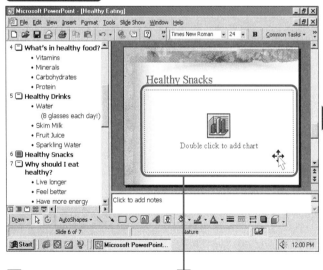

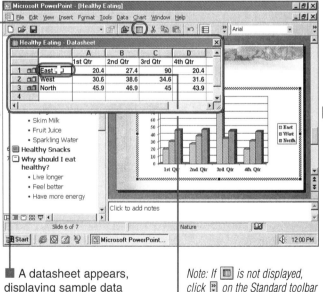

1 Display the slide you
want to add a chart to.

2 Change the layout
of the slide to one that
includes a placeholder
for a chart. To change the
slide layout, see page 44.

3 Double-click this area
to add a chart to the slide.

■ A datasheet appears,
displaying sample data
to show you where to
enter information.

■ If the datasheet does
not appear, click 🔲 to
display the datasheet.

*Note: If 🔲 is not displayed,
click ⯈ on the Standard toolbar
to display all the buttons.*

4 To replace the data
in a cell, click the cell.
A thick border appears
around the cell.

How do I change the data displayed in my chart?

Double-click the chart to activate the chart and display the datasheet. You can then perform steps **4** to **7** below to change the data displayed in the chart.

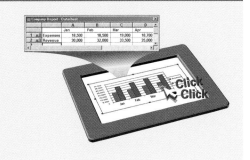

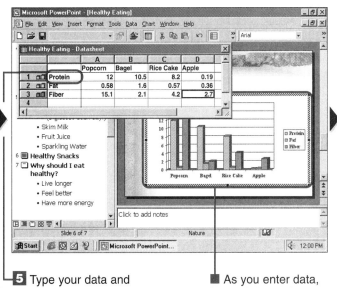

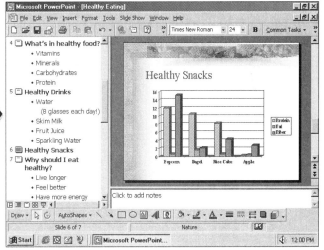

5 Type your data and then press the `Enter` key.

Note: To remove data from a cell and leave the cell empty, click the cell and then press the `Delete` *key.*

6 Repeat steps **4** and **5** until you finish entering all your data.

■ As you enter data, PowerPoint updates the chart on the slide.

7 When you finish entering data for the chart, click a blank area on your screen.

■ The datasheet disappears and you can clearly view the chart on the slide.

Note: To move, size or delete a chart, see pages 170 to 172.

CHANGE THE CHART TYPE

You can change the chart type to better suit your data.

The type of chart you should use depends on your data. For example, area, column and line charts are ideal for showing changes to values over time. Pie charts are ideal for showing percentages.

CHANGE THE CHART TYPE

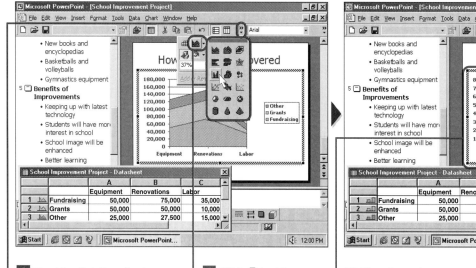

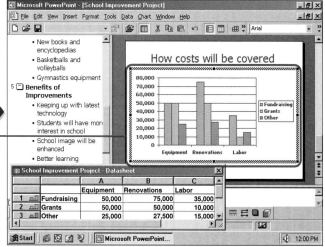

1 Double-click the chart you want to change.

2 Click 📊 on the Standard toolbar to display all the toolbar buttons.

3 Click ▼ in this area to select the type of chart you want to use.

4 Click the type of chart you want to use.

■ The chart changes to the new chart type.

5 Click a blank area on your screen to hide the datasheet and return to the slide.

138

You can change the way data is plotted in your chart. This allows you to emphasize different information in the chart.

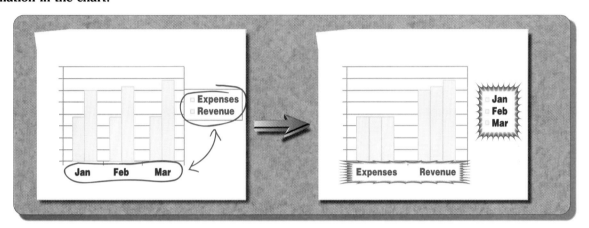

CHANGE THE WAY DATA IS PLOTTED

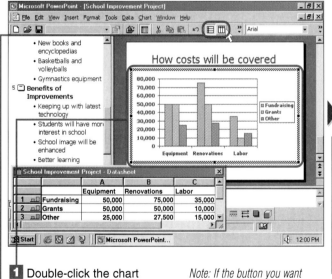

1 Double-click the chart you want to change.

2 Click one of the following buttons.

▤ Plot data by row

▥ Plot data by column

Note: If the button you want is not displayed, click ⟩⟩ on the Standard toolbar to display all the buttons.

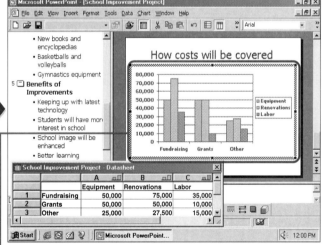

■ The chart displays the change.

3 Click a blank area on your screen to hide the datasheet and return to the slide.

ADD A DATA TABLE

The datasheet is not displayed during a slide show or when you print your presentation. If you want to display or print the information from the datasheet, you must add a data table to your chart.

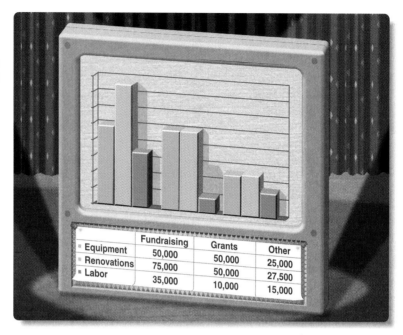

You cannot add a data table to some types of charts.

ADD A DATA TABLE

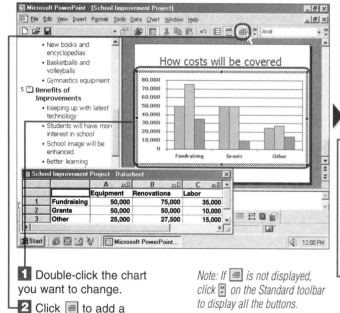

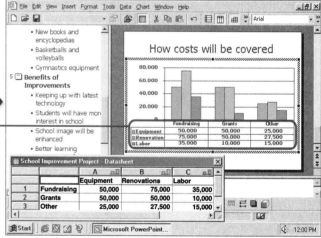

1 Double-click the chart you want to change.

2 Click ▦ to add a data table to the chart.

Note: If ▦ is not displayed, click ▸ on the Standard toolbar to display all the buttons.

■ The data table appears in the chart.

3 Click a blank area on your screen to hide the datasheet and return to the slide.

■ To remove a data table from a chart, repeat steps **1** to **3**.

140

ROTATE TEXT

You can rotate text on a chart axis to improve the appearance of the chart.

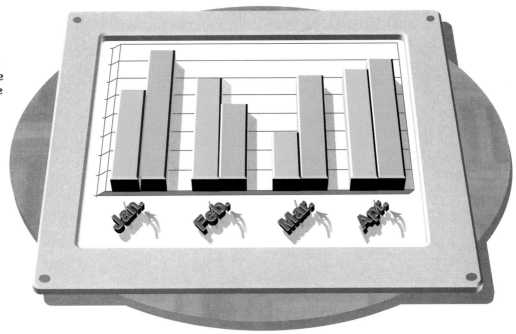

ROTATE TEXT

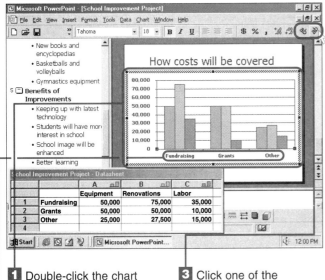

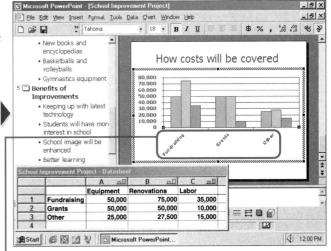

1 Double-click the chart you want to change.

2 Click the text you want to rotate.

3 Click one of the following buttons.

⬢ Rotate text downward

⬢ Rotate text upward

Note: If the button you want is not displayed, click ⬚ on the Formatting toolbar to display all the buttons.

■ The text is rotated.

4 Click a blank area on your screen to hide the datasheet and return to the slide.

■ To return the text to its original position, repeat steps **1** to **4**.

FORMAT NUMBERS

You can change the appearance of numbers in a chart without retyping the numbers.

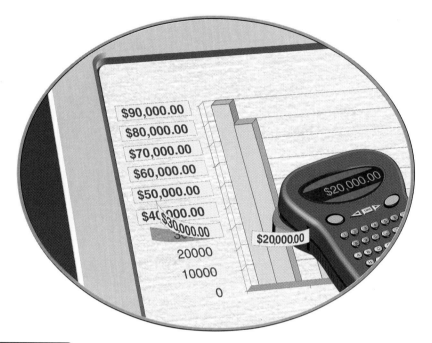

CHANGE THE NUMBER STYLE

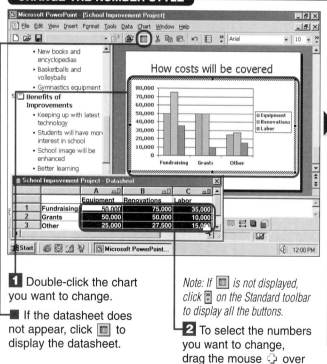

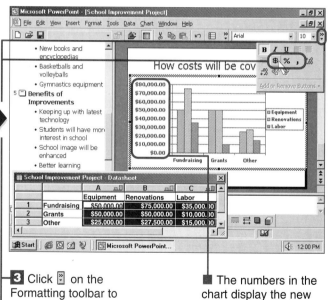

1 Double-click the chart you want to change.

■ If the datasheet does not appear, click 🔳 to display the datasheet.

Note: If 🔳 is not displayed, click 🔋 on the Standard toolbar to display all the buttons.

2 To select the numbers you want to change, drag the mouse ⊕ over the cells containing the numbers.

3 Click 🔋 on the Formatting toolbar to display all the toolbar buttons.

4 Click one of the following buttons.

⑤ Currency

％ Percent

，Comma

■ The numbers in the chart display the new style.

5 Click a blank area on your screen to hide the datasheet and return to the slide.

Why do number signs (#) appear in the datasheet?

Number signs (#) appear in the datasheet when a number is too long to fit in a cell.

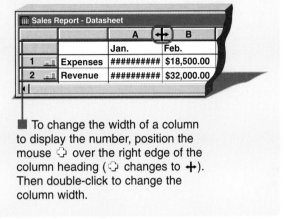

■ To change the width of a column to display the number, position the mouse ⇦ over the right edge of the column heading (⇦ changes to ✛). Then double-click to change the column width.

ADD OR REMOVE A DECIMAL PLACE

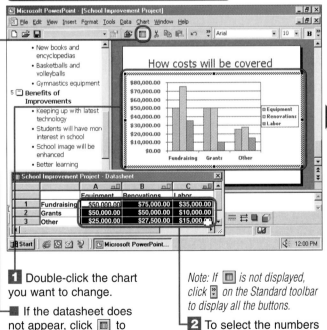

1 Double-click the chart you want to change.

■ If the datasheet does not appear, click 🔲 to display the datasheet.

Note: If 🔲 is not displayed, click 🔋 on the Standard toolbar to display all the buttons.

2 To select the numbers you want to change, drag the mouse ⇦ over the cells containing the numbers.

3 Click 🔋 on the Formatting toolbar to display all the toolbar buttons.

4 Click one of the following buttons.

🔢 Add decimal place

🔢 Remove decimal place

■ The number of decimal places displayed in the chart increases or decreases.

5 Click a blank area on your screen to hide the datasheet and return to the slide.

143

ADD A PATTERN TO A DATA SERIES

You can add a pattern to a data series in a chart. A pattern can make it easier to identify the data series when the slide is displayed in black and white.

ADD A PATTERN TO A DATA SERIES

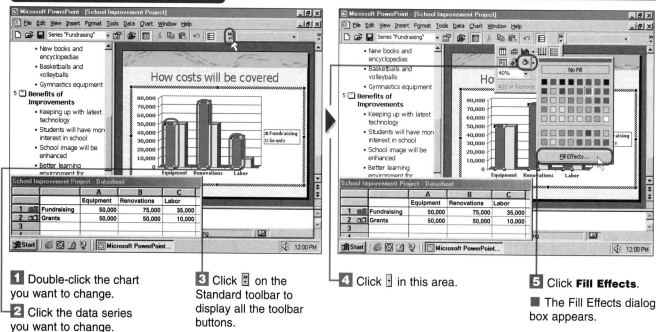

1 Double-click the chart you want to change.

2 Click the data series you want to change. Handles (■) appear on the data series.

3 Click 🔧 on the Standard toolbar to display all the toolbar buttons.

4 Click 🔽 in this area.

5 Click **Fill Effects**.

■ The Fill Effects dialog box appears.

144

Can I change the color of a data series?

Yes. Perform steps **1** to **4** below and then click the color you want to use for the data series.

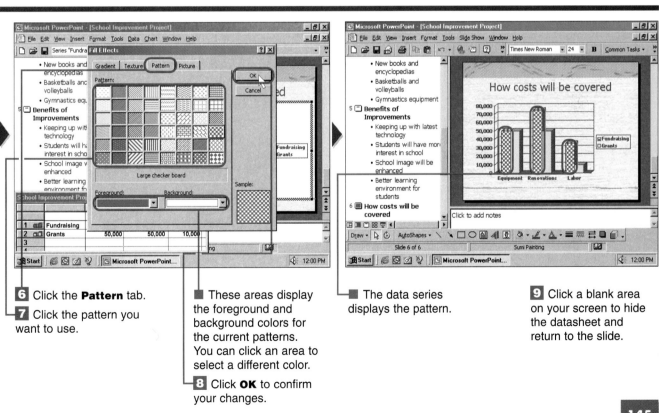

■6 Click the **Pattern** tab.

■7 Click the pattern you want to use.

■ These areas display the foreground and background colors for the current patterns. You can click an area to select a different color.

■8 Click **OK** to confirm your changes.

■ The data series displays the pattern.

■9 Click a blank area on your screen to hide the datasheet and return to the slide.

ADD AN ORGANIZATION CHART

You can add an
organization chart to a
slide in your presentation.
Organization charts are
useful for showing
information such
as the structure
of a company.

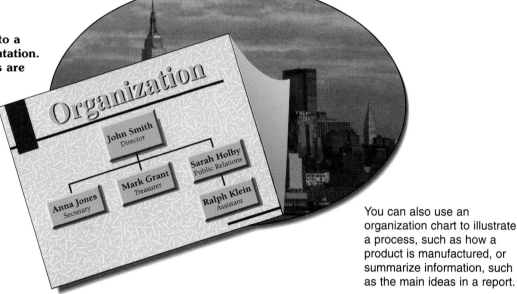

You can also use an
organization chart to illustrate
a process, such as how a
product is manufactured, or
summarize information, such
as the main ideas in a report.

ADD AN ORGANIZATION CHART

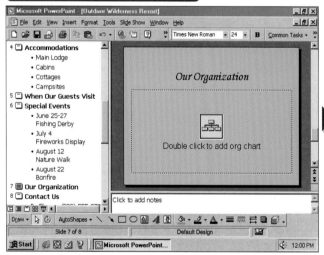

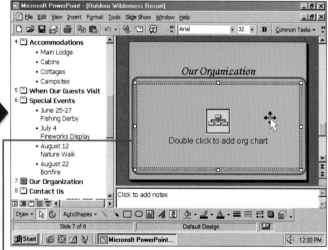

1 Display the slide
you want to add an
organization chart to.

2 Change the layout
of the slide to one that
includes a placeholder
for an organization chart.
To change the slide
layout, see page 44.

3 Double-click this area
to add an organization
chart.

Why does this dialog box appear when I try to add an organization chart?

This dialog box appears if the Microsoft Organization Chart feature is not installed on your computer. Insert the CD-ROM disc you used to install PowerPoint into your CD-ROM drive and then click **Yes** to install the feature.

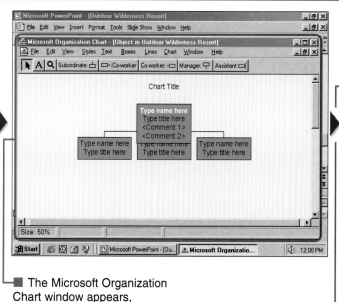

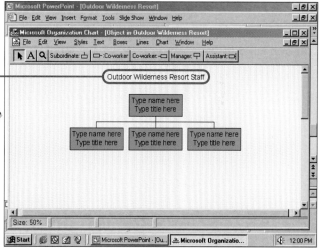

■ The Microsoft Organization Chart window appears, displaying a simple organization chart that you can customize.

CHANGE THE TITLE

4 To change the title of the organization chart, drag the mouse I over the existing title and then type a new title.

■ If you do not want the organization chart to display a title, drag the mouse I over the existing title and then press the Delete key.

CONTINUED

ADD AN ORGANIZATION CHART

You can enter text into each box in an organization chart. You can also add a new box to include an additional person, such as a co-worker or manager.

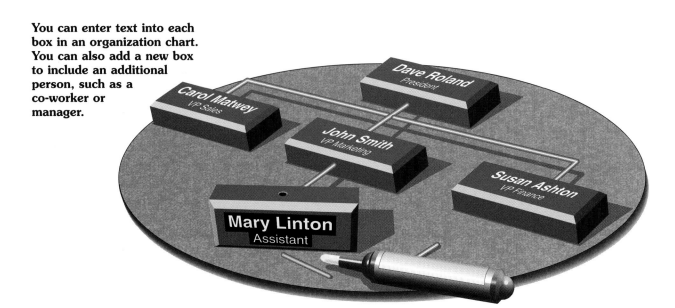

ADD AN ORGANIZATION CHART (CONTINUED)

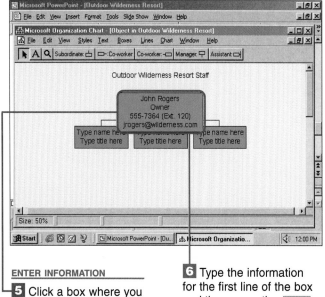

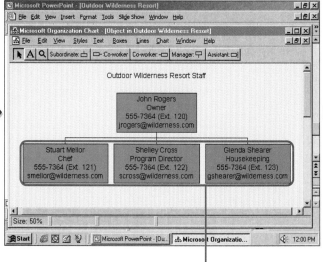

ENTER INFORMATION

5 Click a box where you want to enter information.

6 Type the information for the first line of the box and then press the `Enter` key. Repeat this step until you have typed all the information for the box.

Note: You can enter up to four lines of information in each box.

7 When you finish entering the information for the box, click outside the box.

8 Repeat steps **5** to **7** for each box you want to display information.

?

What type of information can I enter into a box?

Although each box prompts you to enter a name, title and comments, you can enter any information you want into a box. The information you enter will depend on the purpose of the organization chart and the information you want to display.

Type name here
Type title here
<Comment 1>
<Comment 2>

Step 5
Glue pieces together
Use only a small
amount of glue

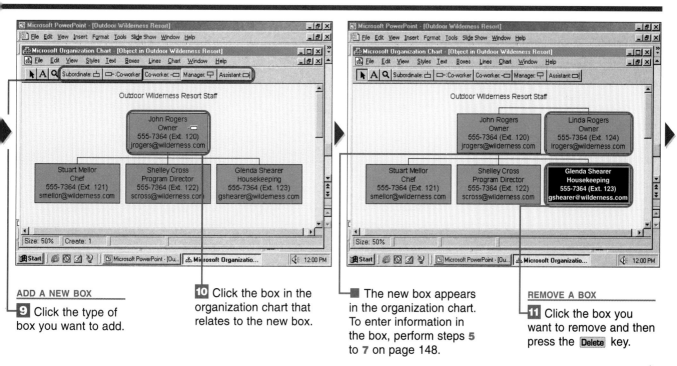

ADD A NEW BOX

9 Click the type of box you want to add.

10 Click the box in the organization chart that relates to the new box.

■ The new box appears in the organization chart. To enter information in the box, perform steps **5** to **7** on page 148.

REMOVE A BOX

11 Click the box you want to remove and then press the `Delete` key.

CONTINUED ▶

ADD AN ORGANIZATION CHART

You can move boxes in an organization chart to reflect changes in the structure of your company.

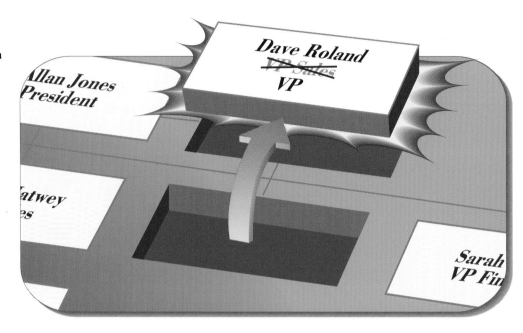

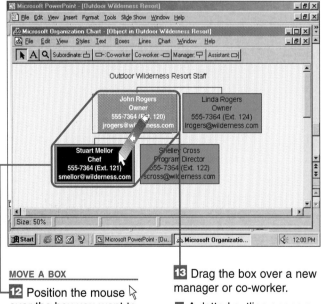

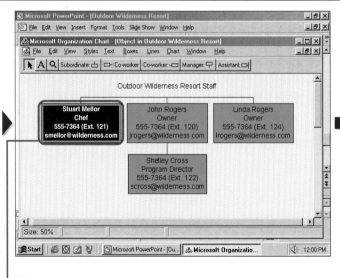

MOVE A BOX

12 Position the mouse ⅄ over the box you want to move.

13 Drag the box over a new manager or co-worker.

■ A dotted outline appears when you drag the box. An arrow (◁ or ▷) or icon (🗗) displays where the box will appear in relation to the manager or co-worker.

■ The box moves to the new location.

Can I make changes to an organization chart after adding the chart to a slide?

Yes. Double-click the organization chart on the slide to display the chart in the Microsoft Organization Chart window. You can then make changes to the organization chart.

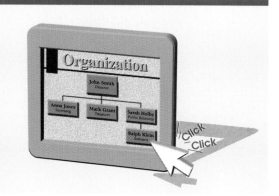

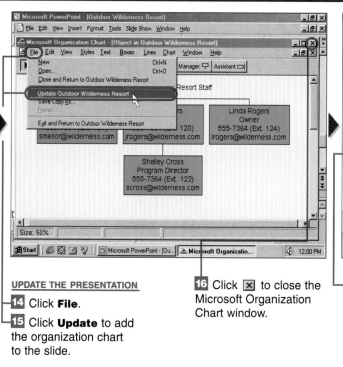

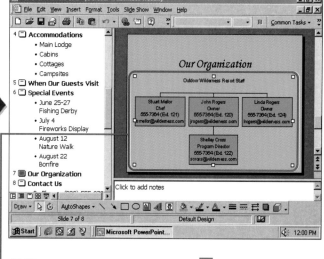

UPDATE THE PRESENTATION

■14 Click **File**.

■15 Click **Update** to add the organization chart to the slide.

■16 Click ☒ to close the Microsoft Organization Chart window.

■ The organization chart appears on the slide. The handles (□) around the chart let you change the size of the chart.

■17 To hide the handles, click outside the organization chart.

Note: To move, size or delete an organization chart, see pages 170 to 172.

CHAPTER 8

Add Tables

Are you interested in using a table to organize information on a slide? In this chapter you will learn how to create and work with tables.

ADD A TABLE

You can add a table to
neatly display information
on a slide. Tables can
help you organize lists
of information, such as
a schedule of events or
a price list.

ADD A TABLE

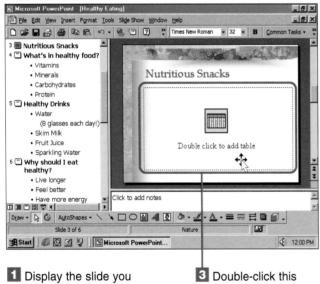

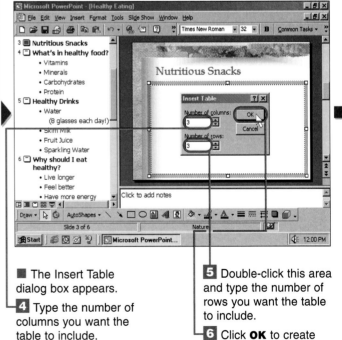

1 Display the slide you
want to add a table to.

2 Change the layout
of the slide to one that
includes a placeholder
for a table. To change the
slide layout, see page 44.

3 Double-click this
area to add a table
to the slide.

■ The Insert Table
dialog box appears.

4 Type the number of
columns you want the
table to include.

5 Double-click this area
and type the number of
rows you want the table
to include.

6 Click **OK** to create
the table.

What are cells, columns and rows in a table?

A **cell** is the area where a row and column intersect.

A **column** is a vertical line of cells.

A **row** is a horizontal line of cells.

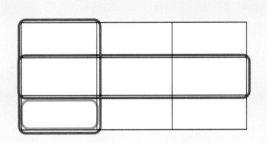

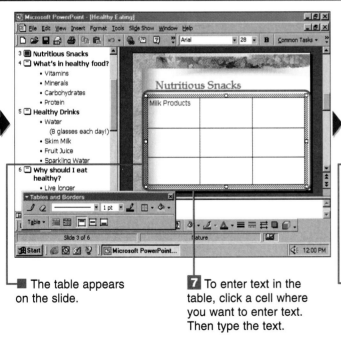

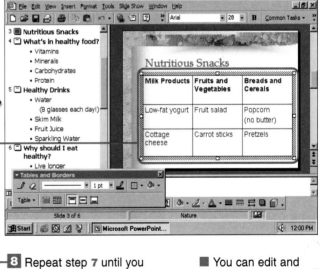

■ The table appears on the slide.

7 To enter text in the table, click a cell where you want to enter text. Then type the text.

8 Repeat step **7** until you have typed all the text.

9 When you finish entering text in the table, click outside the table.

■ You can edit and format the text in a table as you would any text on a slide.

Note: To move, size or delete a table, see pages 170 to 173.

CHANGE COLUMN WIDTH

You can improve
the appearance
of your table by
changing the width
of the columns.

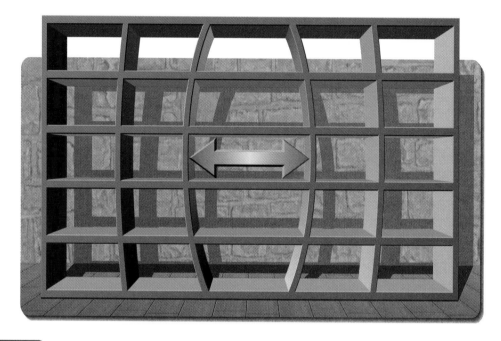

CHANGE COLUMN WIDTH

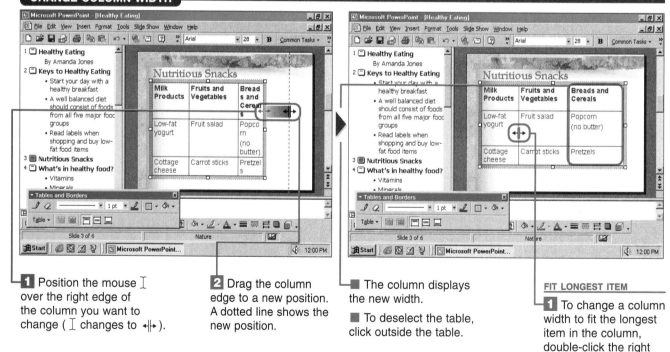

1 Position the mouse I
over the right edge of
the column you want to
change (I changes to ↔).

2 Drag the column
edge to a new position.
A dotted line shows the
new position.

■ The column displays
the new width.

■ To deselect the table,
click outside the table.

FIT LONGEST ITEM

1 To change a column
width to fit the longest
item in the column,
double-click the right
edge of the column.

You can change the
height of rows to change
the amount of space
between the rows of
information in your table.

CHANGE ROW HEIGHT

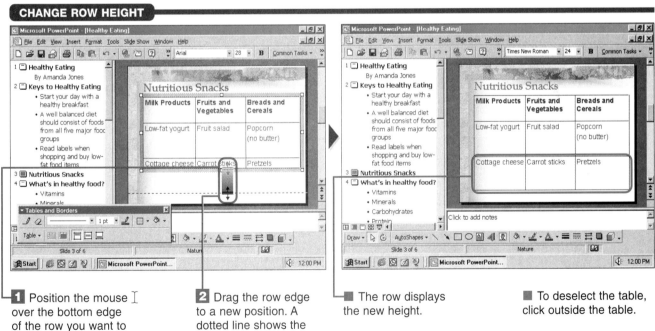

1 Position the mouse I
over the bottom edge
of the row you want to
change (I changes to ↨).

2 Drag the row edge
to a new position. A
dotted line shows the
new position.

■ The row displays
the new height.

■ To deselect the table,
click outside the table.

ADD A ROW OR COLUMN

You can add a row or column to your table when you want to insert additional information.

ADD A ROW

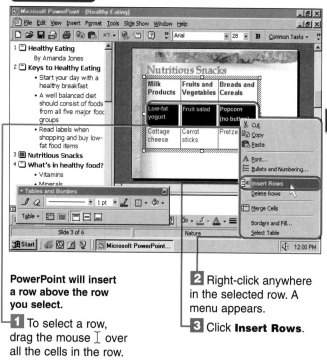

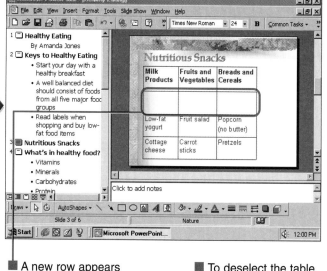

PowerPoint will insert a row above the row you select.

1 To select a row, drag the mouse I over all the cells in the row.

2 Right-click anywhere in the selected row. A menu appears.

3 Click **Insert Rows**.

■ A new row appears and all the rows that follow shift downward.

■ You may need to move or size the table to fit the table on the slide. To move or size the table, see page 170.

■ To deselect the table, click outside the table.

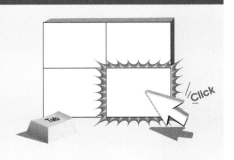

Can I add a row to the bottom of my table?

Yes. To add a row to the bottom of your table, click the bottom right cell in the table and then press the `Tab` key.

ADD A COLUMN

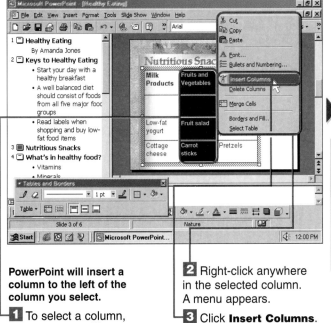

PowerPoint will insert a column to the left of the column you select.

1 To select a column, drag the mouse I over all the cells in the column.

2 Right-click anywhere in the selected column. A menu appears.

3 Click **Insert Columns**.

■ A new column appears and all the columns that follow shift to the right.

■ You may need to move or size the table to fit the table on the slide. To move or size the table, see page 170.

■ To deselect the table, click outside the table.

DELETE A ROW OR COLUMN

You can delete a
row or column that
you no longer need
from your table.

When you delete a row
or column, the Clipboard
toolbar may appear.
To hide the Clipboard
toolbar, see page 50.

DELETE A ROW

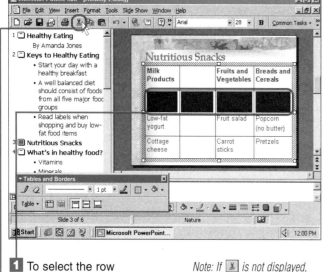

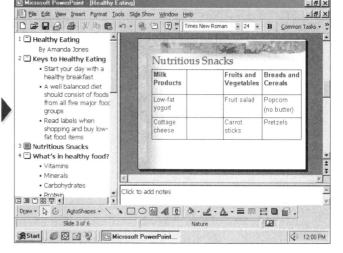

1 To select the row
you want to delete,
drag the mouse I over
all the cells in the row.

2 Click ✂ to delete
the row.

*Note: If ✂ is not displayed,
click ？ on the Standard toolbar
to display all the buttons.*

■ The row disappears
and all the rows that
follow shift upward.

■ To deselect the table,
click outside the table.

?

Can I delete the information in a row or column without removing the row or column from my table?

Yes. To select the cells displaying the information you want to delete, drag the mouse I over the cells. Then press the `Delete` key to delete the information.

DELETE A COLUMN

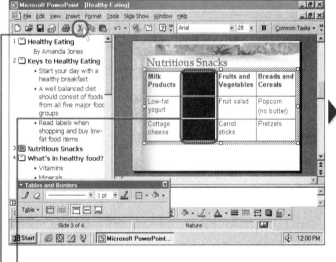

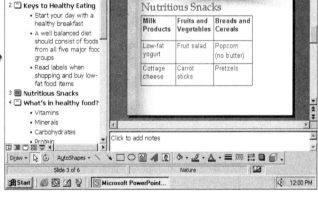

1 To select the column you want to delete, drag the mouse I over all the cells in the column.

2 Click 🔏 to delete the column.

Note: If 🔏 is not displayed, click 🔧 on the Standard toolbar to display all the buttons.

■ The column disappears and all the columns that follow shift to the left.

■ To deselect the table, click outside the table.

MERGE CELLS

You can combine two or more cells in your table to create one large cell. This is useful when you want to display a title in a cell at the top of your table.

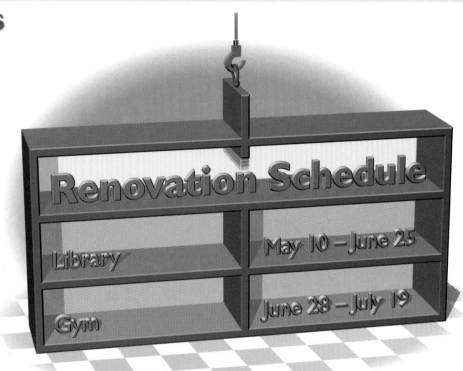

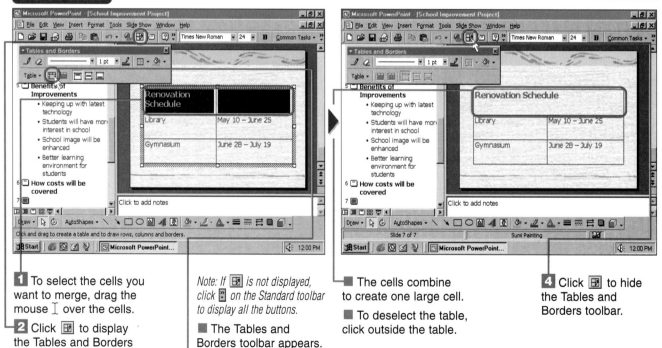

1 To select the cells you want to merge, drag the mouse I over the cells.

2 Click 🖼 to display the Tables and Borders toolbar.

Note: If 🖼 is not displayed, click 🔅 on the Standard toolbar to display all the buttons.

■ The Tables and Borders toolbar appears.

3 Click 🖼 to merge the cells.

■ The cells combine to create one large cell.

■ To deselect the table, click outside the table.

4 Click 🖼 to hide the Tables and Borders toolbar.

162

You can split one
cell in your table
into two smaller
cells.

SPLIT CELLS

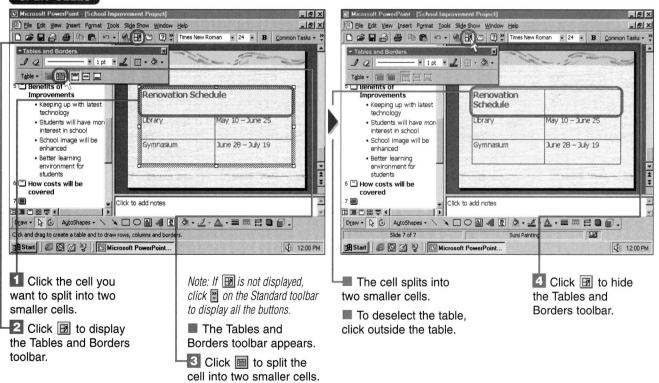

1 Click the cell you
want to split into two
smaller cells.

2 Click 🔢 to display
the Tables and Borders
toolbar.

*Note: If 🔢 is not displayed,
click 🔽 on the Standard toolbar
to display all the buttons.*

■ The Tables and
Borders toolbar appears.

3 Click 🔲 to split the
cell into two smaller cells.

■ The cell splits into
two smaller cells.

■ To deselect the table,
click outside the table.

4 Click 🔢 to hide
the Tables and
Borders toolbar.

ADD COLOR TO CELLS

You can make a table in your presentation more attractive by adding color to cells.

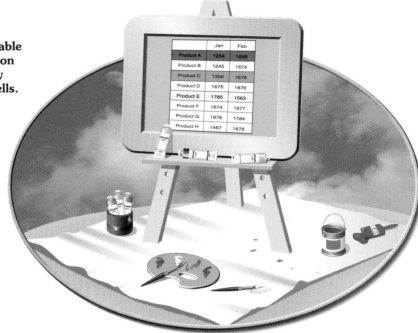

Changing the color for specific cells in your table can help you emphasize important information in the table.

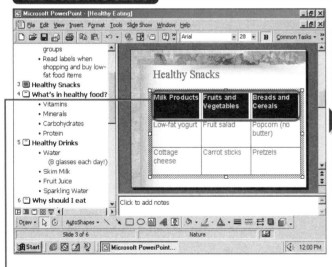

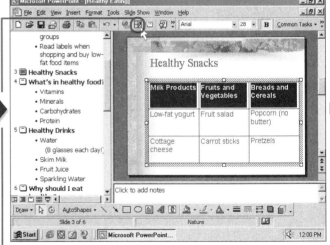

1 To select the cells you want to display color, drag the mouse I over the cells.

2 Click ⊞ to display the Tables and Borders toolbar.

Note: If ⊞ is not displayed, click ⁝ on the Standard toolbar to display all the buttons.

■ The Tables and Borders toolbar appears.

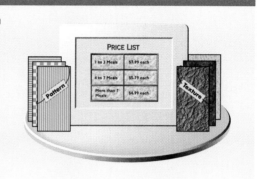

Can I add a texture or pattern to the cells in my table?

Yes. Perform steps **1** to **3** below. Then perform steps **3** to **8** starting on page 178 to add a texture or pattern to cells in your table.

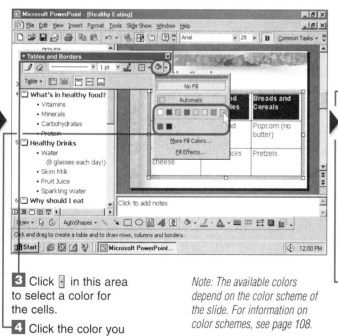

3 Click ⬝ in this area to select a color for the cells.

4 Click the color you want to use.

Note: The available colors depend on the color scheme of the slide. For information on color schemes, see page 108.

■ The cells you selected display the color.

■ To deselect the table, click outside the table.

5 Click 🔲 to hide the Tables and Borders toolbar.

■ To remove color from cells, repeat steps **1** to **5**, except select **No Fill** in step **4**.

CHANGE TABLE BORDERS

You can change the borders in a table to enhance the appearance of a slide in your presentation.

CHANGE TABLE BORDERS

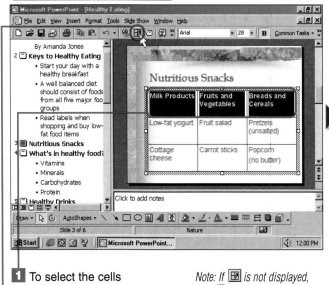

1 To select the cells you want to display a different border, drag the mouse I over the cells.

2 Click 🖽 to display the Tables and Borders toolbar.

Note: If 🖽 is not displayed, click 🗒 on the Standard toolbar to display all the buttons.

■ The Tables and Borders toolbar appears.

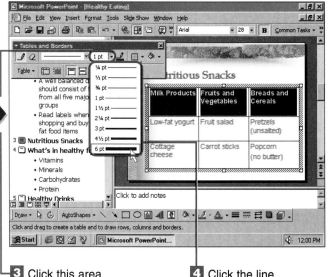

3 Click this area to display a list of the available line thicknesses for the border.

4 Click the line thickness you want to use.

166

Can I change the color of a table border?

Yes. Perform steps **1** to **4** below. Click 🖊 and select the border color you want to use. Then perform steps **5** to **7** below.

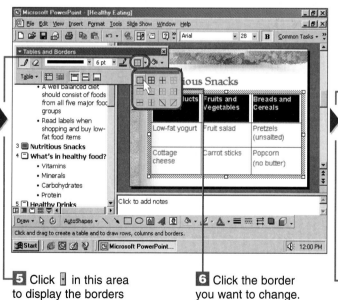

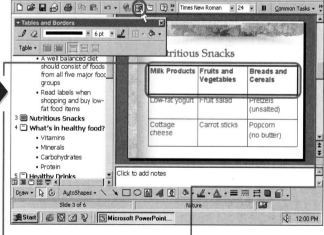

5 Click ⬝ in this area to display the borders you can change.

6 Click the border you want to change.

■ The cells you selected display the new border.

■ To deselect the table, click outside the table.

7 Click 🔳 to hide the Tables and Borders toolbar.

■ To remove a border from your table, perform steps **1** and **2**. Then perform steps **5** to **7**, except select 🔳 in step **6**.

CHAPTER 9

Work With Objects

Do you want to customize the objects on your slides? Read this chapter to learn how to change the size or color of an object and how to make an object 3-D.

MOVE OR SIZE AN OBJECT

You can change
the location or
size of an object
on a slide.

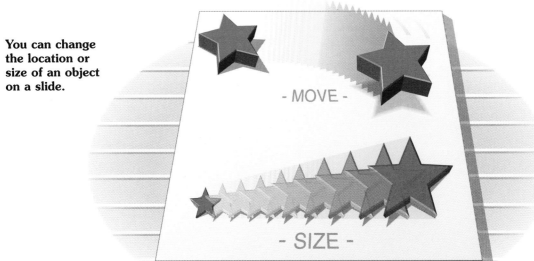

An object can include an
AutoShape, chart, clip
art image, picture, table,
text box or text effect.

MOVE AN OBJECT

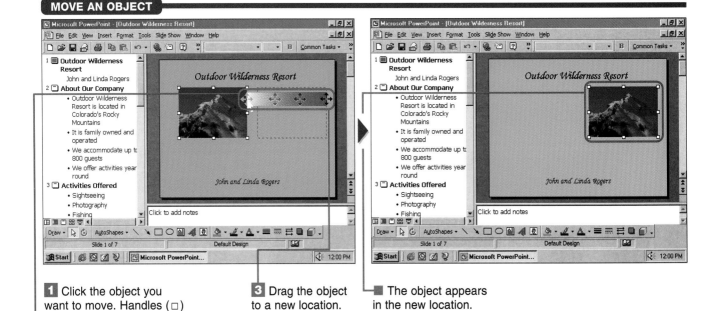

1 Click the object you
want to move. Handles (□)
appear around the object.

2 Position the mouse ⍐
over an edge of the object
(⍐ changes to ✛).

3 Drag the object
to a new location.

■ The object appears
in the new location.

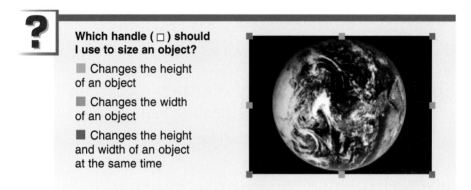

Which handle (□) should I use to size an object?

■ Changes the height of an object

■ Changes the width of an object

■ Changes the height and width of an object at the same time

SIZE AN OBJECT

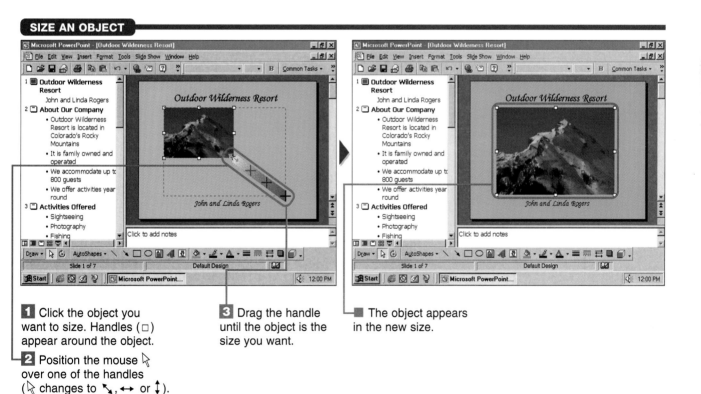

1 Click the object you want to size. Handles (□) appear around the object.

2 Position the mouse ⌖ over one of the handles (⌖ changes to ↘, ↔ or ↕).

3 Drag the handle until the object is the size you want.

■ The object appears in the new size.

DELETE AN OBJECT

You can delete
an object you
no longer want
to appear on a
slide.

You can delete
an object such as
a clip art image,
picture or text box.

DELETE AN OBJECT

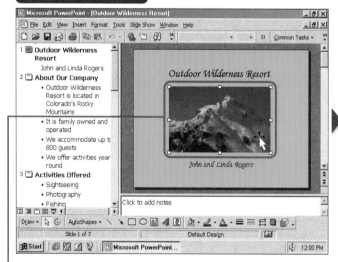

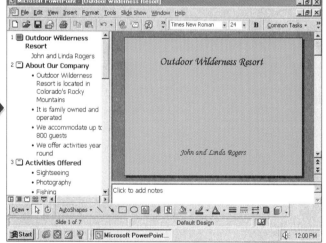

1 Click the object
you want to delete.
Handles (□) appear
around the object.

2 Press the Delete key
to delete the object.

■ You may need to
press the Delete key
again to completely
remove the object from
the slide.

■ The object disappears
from the slide.

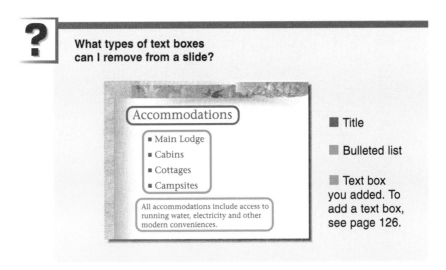

What types of text boxes can I remove from a slide?

Accommodations

- Main Lodge
- Cabins
- Cottages
- Campsites

All accommodations include access to running water, electricity and other modern conveniences.

■ Title

■ Bulleted list

■ Text box you added. To add a text box, see page 126.

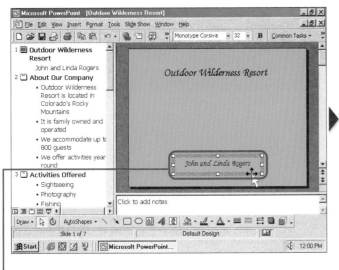

DELETE A TEXT BOX OR TABLE

1 Click the text box or table you want to delete. Handles (□) appear around the object.

2 Click an edge of the text box or table.

3 Press the Delete key to delete the text box or table.

■ You may need to press the Delete key again to completely remove the object from the slide.

■ The text box or table disappears from the slide.

CHANGE OBJECT COLOR

You can change the
color of an object on
a slide to enhance
the appearance of
the slide.

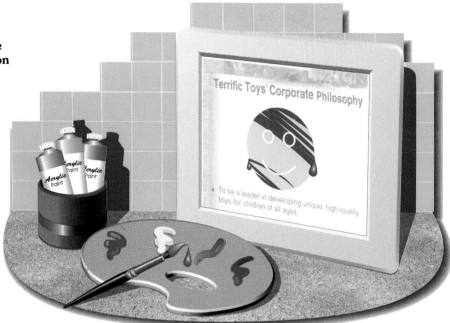

CHANGE OBJECT COLOR

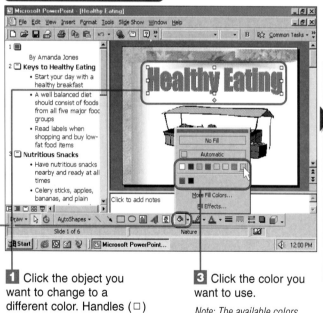

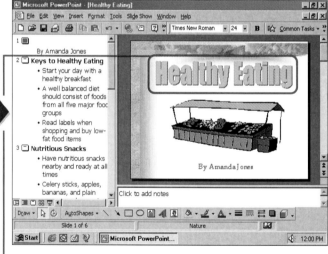

1 Click the object you
want to change to a
different color. Handles (□)
appear around the object.

2 Click ⊟ in this area
to select a color.

3 Click the color you
want to use.

*Note: The available colors
depend on the color scheme
of the slide. For information on
color schemes, see page 108.*

■ The object appears
in the new color.

■ To deselect the object,
click outside the object.

You can change
the color of the
line surrounding
an object on a
slide.

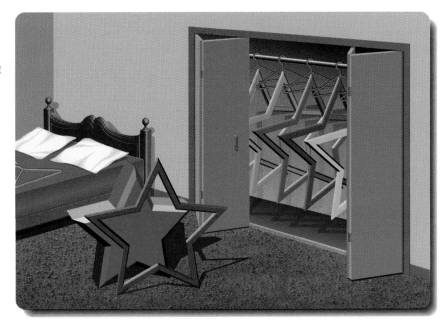

You can change the
line color for objects
such as text boxes,
pictures, charts and
AutoShapes.

CHANGE LINE COLOR

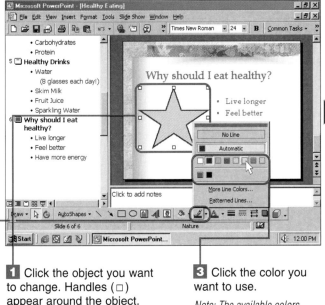

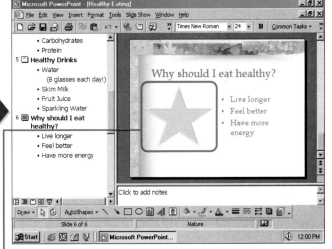

1 Click the object you want
to change. Handles (□)
appear around the object.

2 Click ▼ in this area to
display the available line
colors.

3 Click the color you
want to use.

*Note: The available colors
depend on the color scheme
of the slide. For information on
color schemes, see page 108.*

■ The line surrounding
the object displays the
new color.

■ To deselect the object,
click outside the object.

■ To remove the line
surrounding an object,
repeat steps **1** to **3**,
except select **No Line**
in step **3**.

CHANGE LINE THICKNESS

You can emphasize
an object by
changing the
thickness of the
line surrounding
the object.

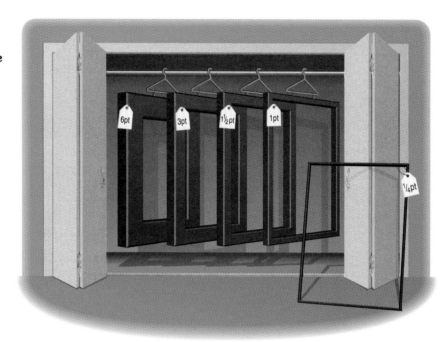

You can change
the line thickness
for objects such
as text boxes,
pictures, charts
and AutoShapes.

CHANGE LINE THICKNESS

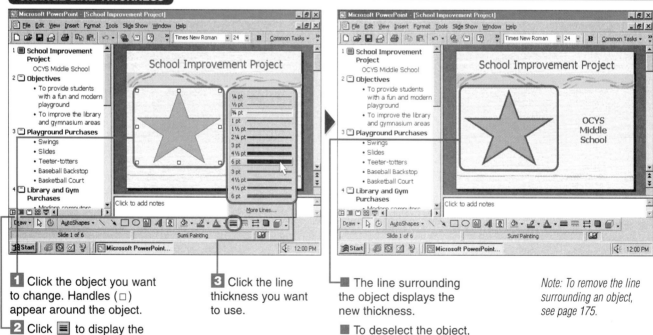

1 Click the object you want
to change. Handles (□)
appear around the object.

2 Click ≡ to display the
available line thicknesses.

3 Click the line
thickness you want
to use.

■ The line surrounding
the object displays the
new thickness.

■ To deselect the object,
click outside the object.

*Note: To remove the line
surrounding an object,
see page 175.*

You can change the
line surrounding an
object to a dashed
or dotted line.

CHANGE DASH STYLE

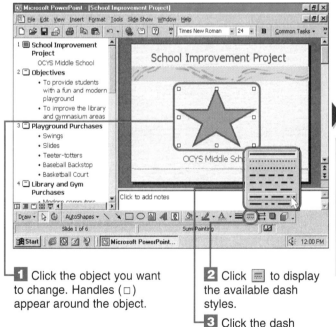

1 Click the object you want to change. Handles (□) appear around the object.

2 Click ▤ to display the available dash styles.

3 Click the dash style you want to use.

■ The line surrounding the object displays the dash style.

■ To deselect the object, click outside the object.

Note: To remove the line surrounding an object, see page 175.

ADD A TEXTURE OR PATTERN

You can enhance the appearance of an object on a slide by adding a texture or pattern to the object.

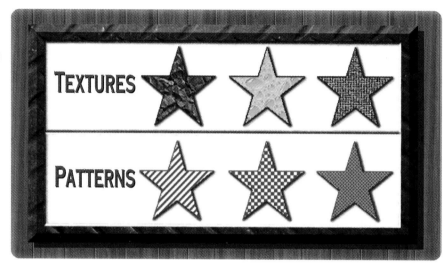

You can add a texture or pattern to several types of objects, including AutoShapes, text effects and text boxes.

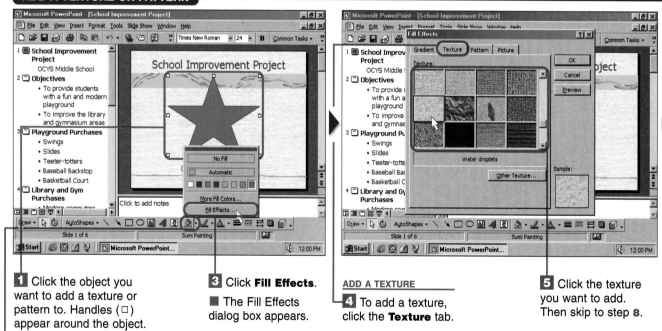

1 Click the object you want to add a texture or pattern to. Handles (□) appear around the object.

2 Click ▪ in this area.

3 Click **Fill Effects**.

■ The Fill Effects dialog box appears.

ADD A TEXTURE

4 To add a texture, click the **Texture** tab.

5 Click the texture you want to add. Then skip to step **8**.

178

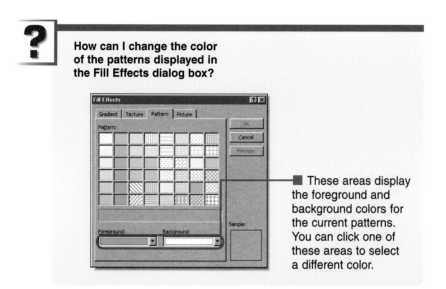

How can I change the color of the patterns displayed in the Fill Effects dialog box?

■ These areas display the foreground and background colors for the current patterns. You can click one of these areas to select a different color.

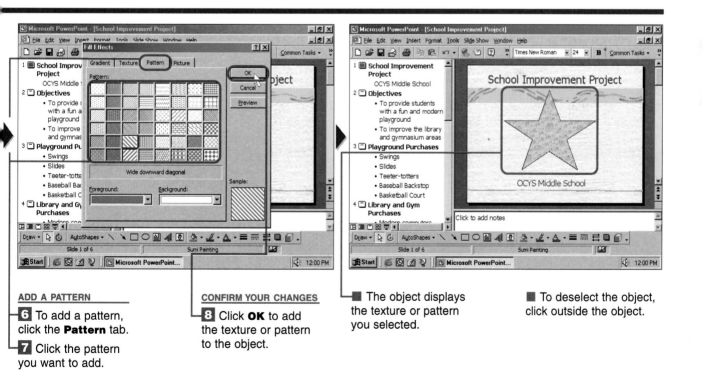

ADD A PATTERN

6 To add a pattern, click the **Pattern** tab.

7 Click the pattern you want to add.

CONFIRM YOUR CHANGES

8 Click **OK** to add the texture or pattern to the object.

■ The object displays the texture or pattern you selected.

■ To deselect the object, click outside the object.

ROTATE AN OBJECT

You can rotate an
object on a slide.

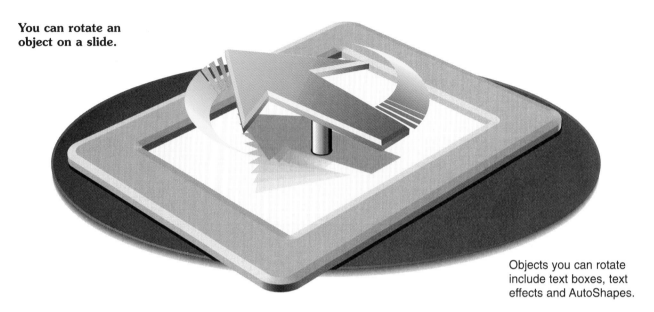

Objects you can rotate
include text boxes, text
effects and AutoShapes.

ROTATE AN OBJECT

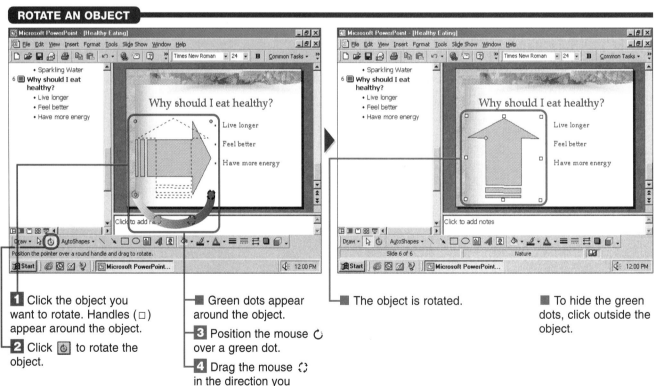

1 Click the object you
want to rotate. Handles (□)
appear around the object.

2 Click 🔄 to rotate the
object.

■ Green dots appear
around the object.

3 Position the mouse ↺
over a green dot.

4 Drag the mouse ↻
in the direction you
want to rotate the object.

■ The object is rotated.

■ To hide the green
dots, click outside the
object.

180

You can make an
object on a slide appear
three-dimensional.

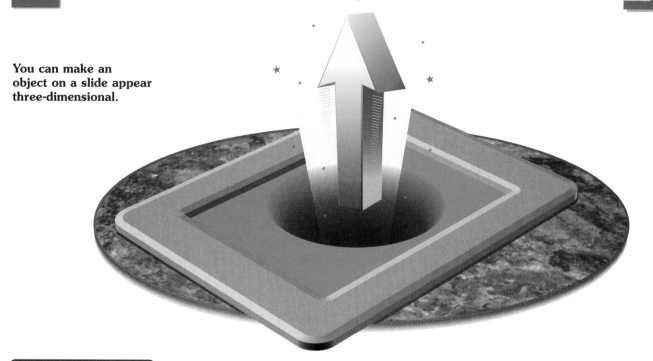

MAKE AN OBJECT 3-D

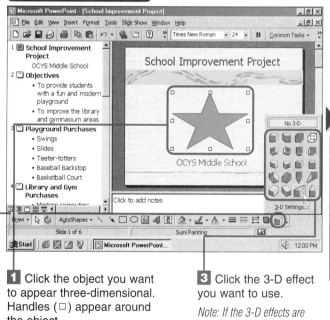

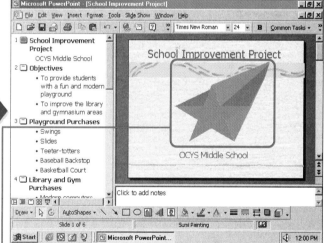

1 Click the object you want
to appear three-dimensional.
Handles (□) appear around
the object.

2 Click 🔲 to select a 3-D
effect.

3 Click the 3-D effect
you want to use.

*Note: If the 3-D effects are
dimmed, you cannot make
the object you selected
three-dimensional.*

■ The object displays
the 3-D effect.

■ To deselect the object,
click outside the object.

■ To remove a 3-D
effect from an object,
repeat steps **1** to **3**,
except select **No 3-D**
in step **3**.

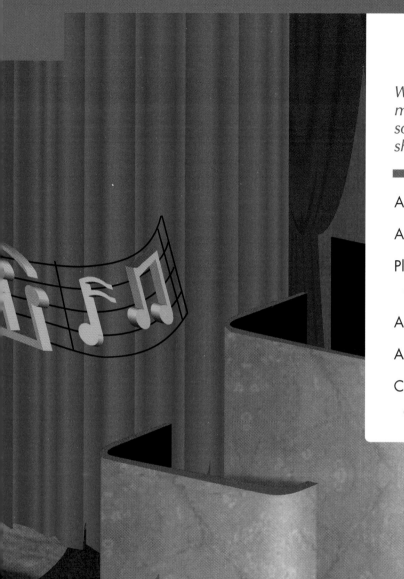

CHAPTER 10

Add Multimedia

Would you like to learn how to add multimedia, such as movies and sounds, to your slides? This chapter shows you how.

COMPACT DISC PLAYER CD-390

disc

POWER

ADD A SOUND

You can add a sound to a slide in your presentation. This can help make your presentation more interesting and entertaining.

PowerPoint comes with many sounds that you can choose from.

ADD A SOUND FROM THE GALLERY

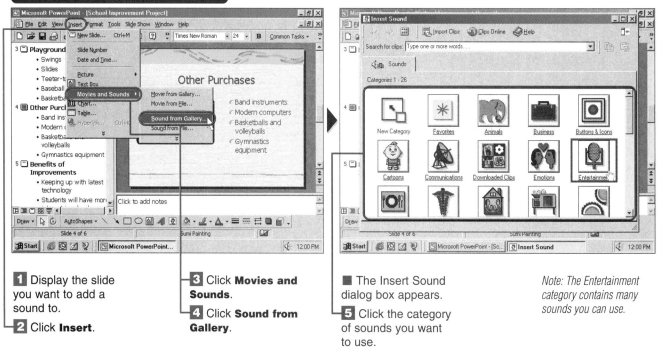

1 Display the slide you want to add a sound to.

2 Click **Insert**.

3 Click **Movies and Sounds**.

4 Click **Sound from Gallery**.

■ The Insert Sound dialog box appears.

5 Click the category of sounds you want to use.

Note: The Entertainment category contains many sounds you can use.

Where can I find more sounds?

If you are connected to the Internet, you can visit Microsoft's Clip Gallery Live Web site to find additional sounds. In the Insert Sound dialog box, click **Clips Online**. In the dialog box that appears, click **OK** to connect to the Web site.

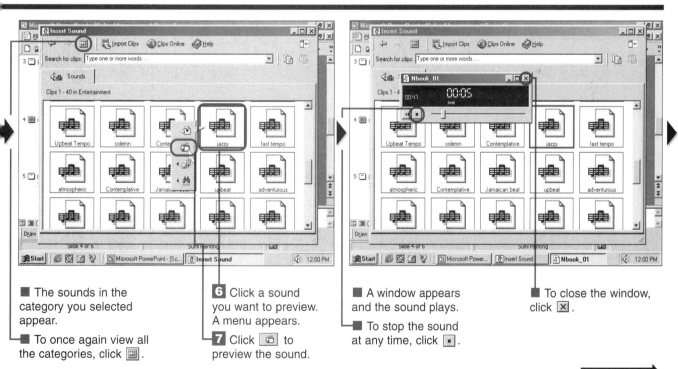

■ The sounds in the category you selected appear.

■ To once again view all the categories, click ▦.

6 Click a sound you want to preview. A menu appears.

7 Click 🔊 to preview the sound.

■ A window appears and the sound plays.

■ To stop the sound at any time, click ■.

■ To close the window, click ☒.

CONTINUED ▶

ADD A SOUND

When you add a sound to a slide, you can specify how you want the sound to play during a slide show.

You can have a sound play automatically when the slide is displayed or only when you click the speaker icon on the slide.

ADD A SOUND FROM THE GALLERY (CONTINUED)

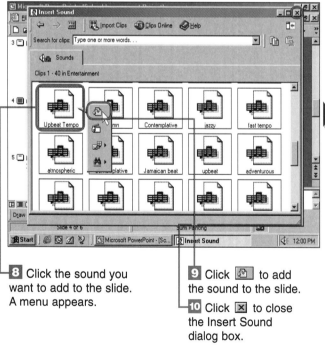

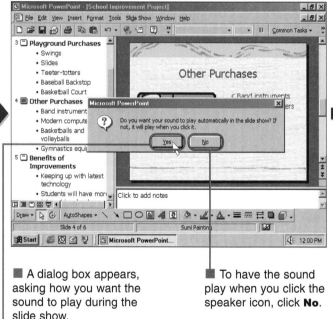

8 Click the sound you want to add to the slide. A menu appears.

9 Click 🖼 to add the sound to the slide.

10 Click ☒ to close the Insert Sound dialog box.

■ A dialog box appears, asking how you want the sound to play during the slide show.

11 To have the sound play automatically when the slide is displayed, click **Yes**.

■ To have the sound play when you click the speaker icon, click **No**.

How do I remove a sound I added to a slide in my presentation?

To remove a sound from a slide, you must delete the speaker icon (🔊) from the slide. Display the slide in the Normal view and then click the speaker icon. Press the `Delete` key to remove the sound from the slide. For information on the views, see page 40.

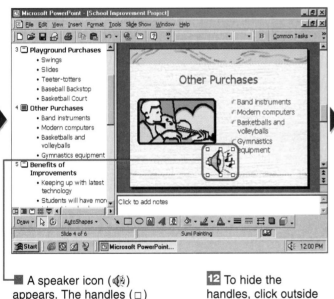

■ A speaker icon (🔊) appears. The handles (□) around the speaker icon let you change the size of the icon. To move or size the speaker icon, see page 170.

12 To hide the handles, click outside the speaker icon.

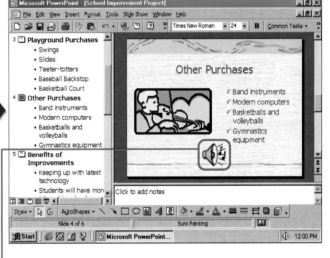

■ To play the sound in the Normal view, double-click the speaker icon (🔊).

Note: To view a slide show, see page 260.

ADD A SOUND

You can add a
sound stored on
your computer
to a slide in your
presentation.

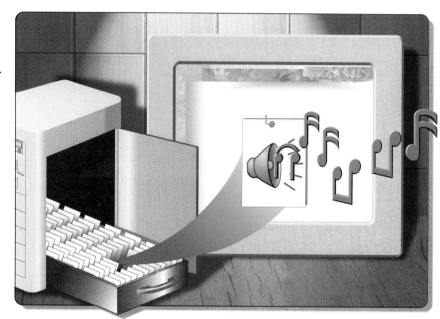

Adding a sound is
useful if you want to
add a theme song,
advertising jingle or
clip from a famous
speech.

ADD A SOUND FROM A FILE

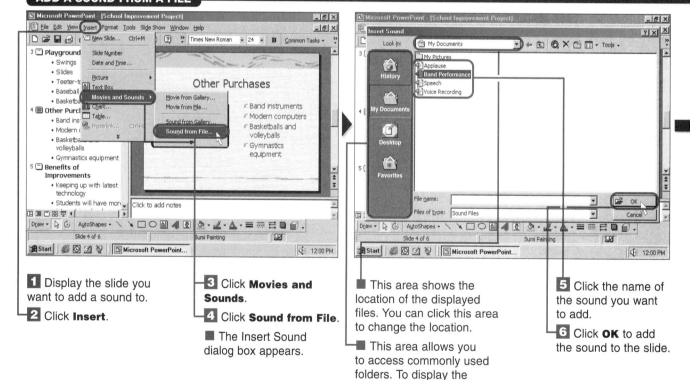

1 Display the slide you
want to add a sound to.

2 Click **Insert**.

3 Click **Movies and
Sounds**.

4 Click **Sound from File**.

■ The Insert Sound
dialog box appears.

■ This area shows the
location of the displayed
files. You can click this area
to change the location.

■ This area allows you
to access commonly used
folders. To display the
contents of a folder, click
the folder.

5 Click the name of
the sound you want
to add.

6 Click **OK** to add
the sound to the slide.

Where can I get sounds that I can use in my presentation?

Many computer stores sell CD-ROM discs that contain collections of sounds. There are also Web sites on the Internet that offer free sounds. You can find sounds at the following Web sites:

www.dailywav.com

www.soundamerica.com

www.wavcentral.com

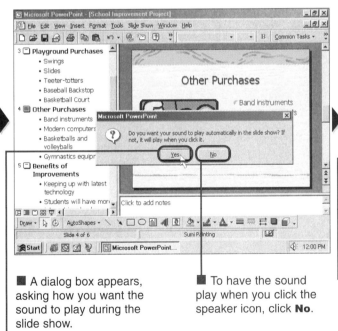

■ A dialog box appears, asking how you want the sound to play during the slide show.

7 To have the sound play automatically when the slide is displayed, click **Yes**.

■ To have the sound play when you click the speaker icon, click **No**.

■ A speaker icon (📢) appears.

8 To hide the handles (□) around the speaker icon, click outside the speaker icon.

■ To play the sound in the Normal view, double-click the speaker icon.

■ To move or size the speaker icon, see page 170. To remove the sound from the slide, see the top of page 187.

ADD A MOVIE

You can add a
movie to a slide
to add interest to
your presentation.

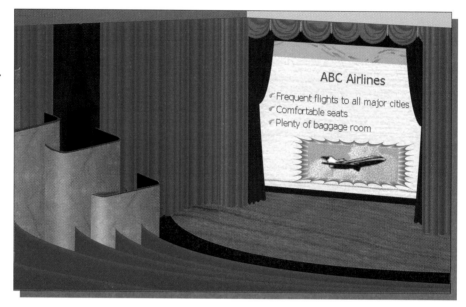

PowerPoint
provides
many movies
that you can
choose from.

ADD A MOVIE FROM THE GALLERY

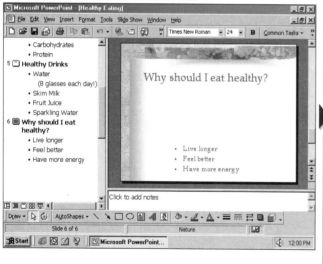

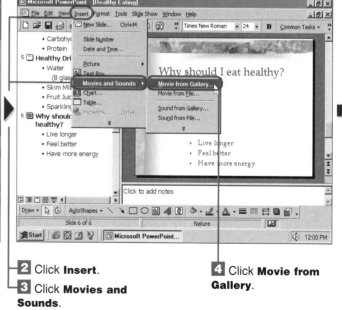

1 Display the slide you
want to add a movie to.

2 Click **Insert**.

3 Click **Movies and
Sounds**.

4 Click **Movie from
Gallery**.

Where can I find more movies?

If you are connected to the Internet, you can visit Microsoft's Clip Gallery Live Web site to find additional movies. In the Insert Movie dialog box, click **Clips Online**. In the dialog box that appears, click **OK** to connect to the Web site.

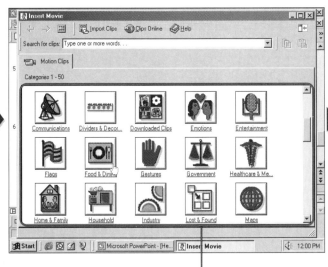

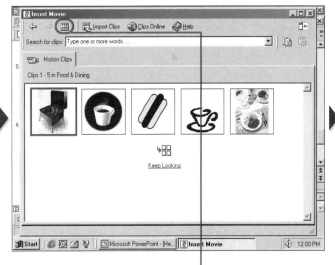

■ The Insert Movie dialog box appears.

5 Click the category of movies you want to use.

■ The movies in the category you selected appear.

■ To once again view all the categories, click 🔳.

CONTINUED ▶

ADD A MOVIE

A movie you add from the Gallery will play automatically when the slide is displayed during a slide show.

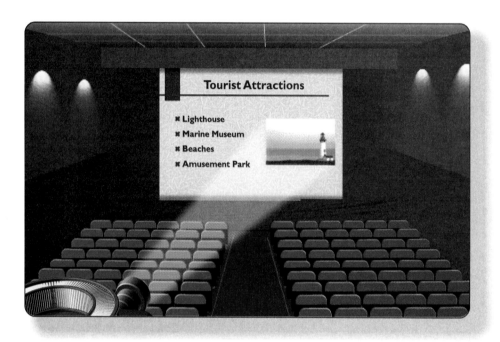

ADD A MOVIE FROM THE GALLERY (CONTINUED)

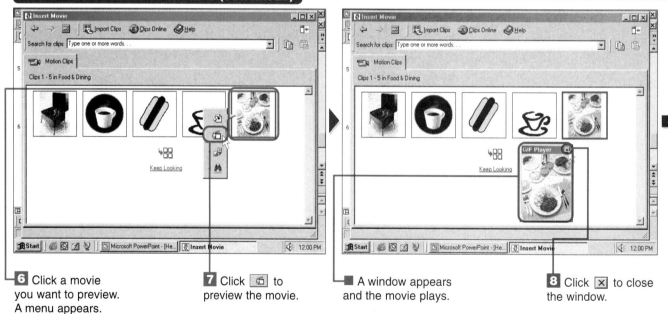

6 Click a movie you want to preview. A menu appears.

7 Click ⬛ to preview the movie.

■ A window appears and the movie plays.

8 Click ☒ to close the window.

How do I remove a movie I added to a slide in my presentation?

Display the slide in the Normal view and then click the movie. Press the `Delete` key to remove the movie from the slide. For information on the views, see page 40.

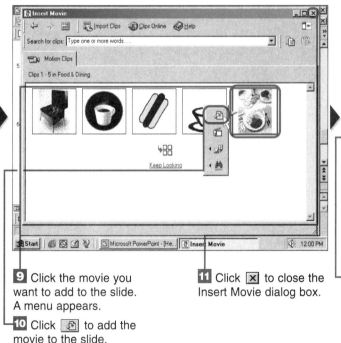

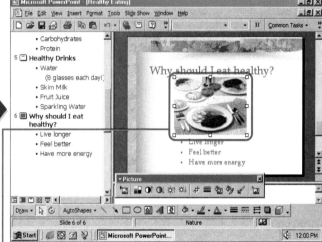

9 Click the movie you want to add to the slide. A menu appears.

10 Click 🔊 to add the movie to the slide.

11 Click ✕ to close the Insert Movie dialog box.

■ The movie appears. The handles (□) around the movie let you change the size of the movie. To move or size a movie, see page 170.

12 To hide the handles, click outside the movie.

■ The movie will play automatically when the slide is displayed during the slide show. To view a slide show, see page 260.

ADD A MOVIE

You can add a
movie stored on
your computer
to a slide in your
presentation.

Adding a movie is
useful if you want
to add a movie clip
from a television
commercial, news
event, sporting
event or film.

ADD A MOVIE FROM A FILE

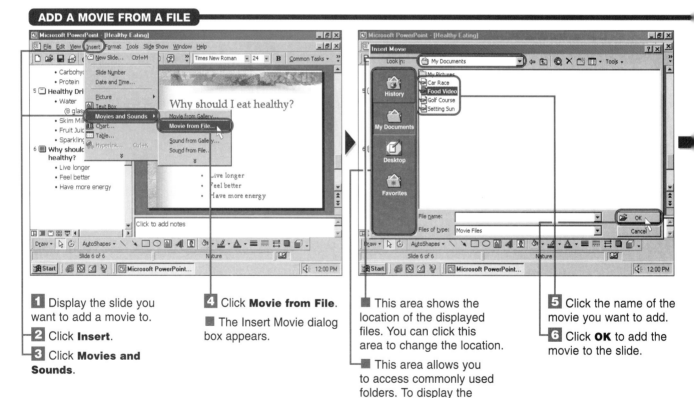

1 Display the slide you
want to add a movie to.

2 Click **Insert**.

3 Click **Movies and
Sounds**.

4 Click **Movie from File**.

■ The Insert Movie dialog
box appears.

■ This area shows the
location of the displayed
files. You can click this
area to change the location.

■ This area allows you
to access commonly used
folders. To display the
contents of a folder, click
the folder.

5 Click the name of the
movie you want to add.

6 Click **OK** to add the
movie to the slide.

Can I change the size of a movie I added to my slide?

Most movies are designed to play best at their original size. If you increase the size of a movie you added from a file, the movie may become jerky, appear grainy or display other visual distortions.

You can increase the size of a movie you added from the Gallery without distorting the movie. To add a movie from the Gallery, see page 190.

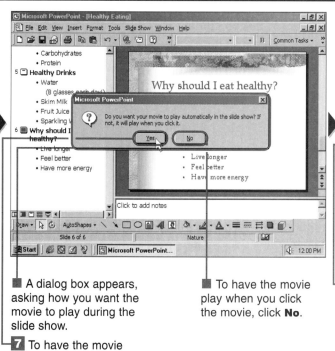

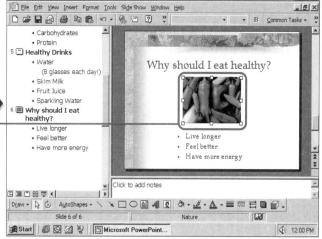

■ A dialog box appears, asking how you want the movie to play during the slide show.

7 To have the movie play automatically when the slide is displayed, click **Yes**.

■ To have the movie play when you click the movie, click **No**.

■ The first frame of the movie appears.

8 To hide the handles (□) around the movie, click outside the movie.

■ To play the movie in the Normal view, double-click the movie.

■ To move or size the movie, see page 170. To remove the movie from the slide, see the top of page 193.

PLAY A MUSIC CD
DURING A SLIDE SHOW

You can play tracks
from a music CD
during a slide show
to add background
music to your slides.

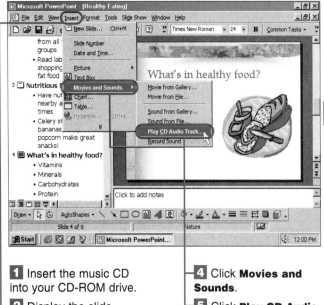

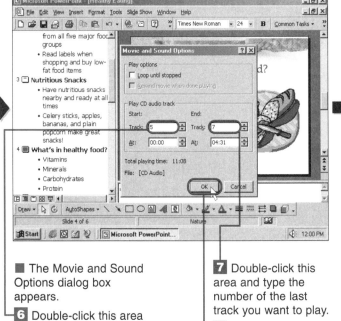

1 Insert the music CD
into your CD-ROM drive.

2 Display the slide
where you want to
play the music CD.

3 Click **Insert**.

4 Click **Movies and
Sounds**.

5 Click **Play CD Audio
Track**.

*Note: If Play CD Audio Track
does not appear on the menu,
position the mouse ⟍ over the
bottom of the menu to display
all the menu commands.*

■ The Movie and Sound
Options dialog box
appears.

6 Double-click this area
and type the number of
the first track you want
to play on the music CD.

7 Double-click this
area and type the
number of the last
track you want to play.

8 Click **OK** to confirm
your changes.

How do I stop my music CD from playing automatically when I insert it into the CD-ROM drive?

When you insert a music CD into a CD-ROM drive, the CD may automatically begin playing. To stop the CD from playing automatically, press and hold down the `Shift` key as you insert the CD into the drive.

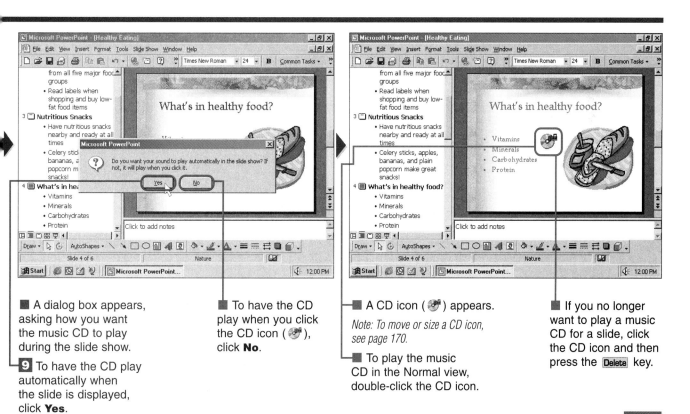

■ A dialog box appears, asking how you want the music CD to play during the slide show.

9 To have the CD play automatically when the slide is displayed, click **Yes**.

■ To have the CD play when you click the CD icon (🎵), click **No**.

■ A CD icon (🎵) appears.

Note: To move or size a CD icon, see page 170.

■ To play the music CD in the Normal view, double-click the CD icon.

■ If you no longer want to play a music CD for a slide, click the CD icon and then press the `Delete` key.

PLAY A MUSIC CD DURING A SLIDE SHOW

The music CD tracks you add to a slide will automatically stop playing when you display the next slide in a slide show. You can choose to have the music CD play for several slides.

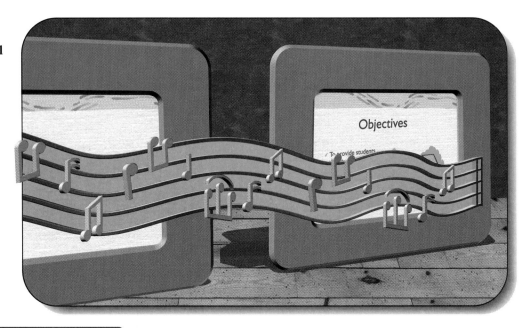

PLAY A MUSIC CD FOR MULTIPLE SLIDES

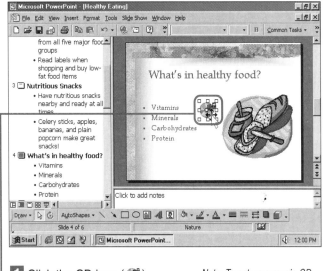

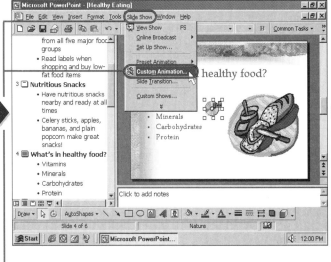

1 Click the CD icon (💿) for the music CD you want to play for multiple slides. Handles (□) appear around the icon.

Note: To set up a music CD to play during a slide show, perform steps 1 to 9 starting on page 196.

2 Click **Slide Show**.

3 Click **Custom Animation**.

■ The Custom Animation dialog box appears.

? Why doesn't the music CD I set to play for multiple slides begin playing as soon as I click a blank area on the slide?

To play as soon as you click a blank area on the slide, the music CD must be set as the first animation. To change the animation order of objects on a slide, see page 222.

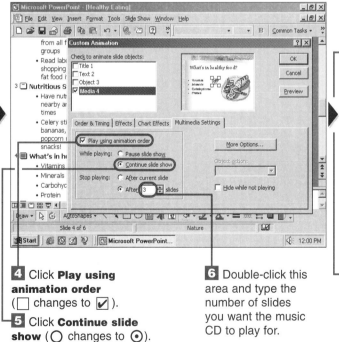

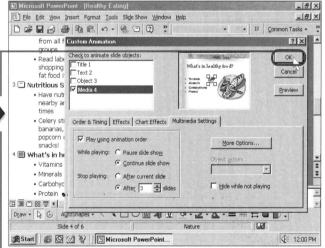

4 Click **Play using animation order** (☐ changes to ☑).

5 Click **Continue slide show** (○ changes to ⊙).

6 Double-click this area and type the number of slides you want the music CD to play for.

7 Click **OK** to confirm your changes.

■ To start playing the CD during a slide show, click a blank area on the slide containing the CD icon (🎵). To view a slide show, see page 260.

*Note: If you selected **Yes** in step **9** on page 197, the CD will play automatically when the slide is displayed.*

ADD A RECORDED SOUND

You can record your own sound and then add it to a slide. This is useful if you need to include a statement from a colleague who is unable to attend your presentation.

ADD A RECORDED SOUND

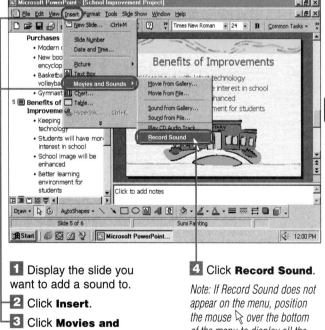

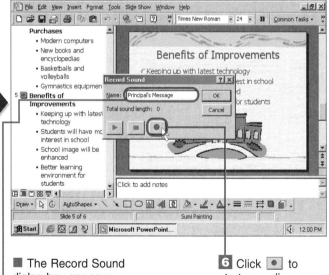

1 Display the slide you want to add a sound to.

2 Click **Insert**.

3 Click **Movies and Sounds**.

4 Click **Record Sound**.

Note: If Record Sound does not appear on the menu, position the mouse ℞ over the bottom of the menu to display all the menu commands.

■ The Record Sound dialog box appears.

5 To specify a name for the sound, drag the mouse I over this area and then type the name.

6 Click ● to start recording.

7 Speak into your microphone or start your sound device.

200

What devices can I record sounds from?

You can record sounds from any sound device you can connect to your computer, such as a microphone, CD player, stereo or VCR.

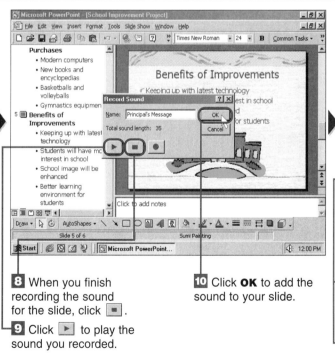

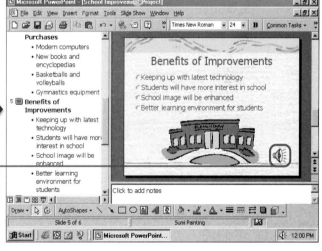

8 When you finish recording the sound for the slide, click ■.

9 Click ► to play the sound you recorded.

10 Click **OK** to add the sound to your slide.

■ A speaker icon (◄) appears. To move or size the speaker icon, see page 170.

■ To play the sound in the Normal view, double-click the speaker icon.

Note: To play the sound during a slide show, click the speaker icon on the slide. To view the slide show, see page 260.

■ To remove the sound from the slide, see the top of page 187.

ADD NARRATION TO A SLIDE SHOW

You can record voice narration and add it to a slide show. This is ideal for a self-running slide show at a kiosk. Kiosks are often found at trade shows and shopping malls.

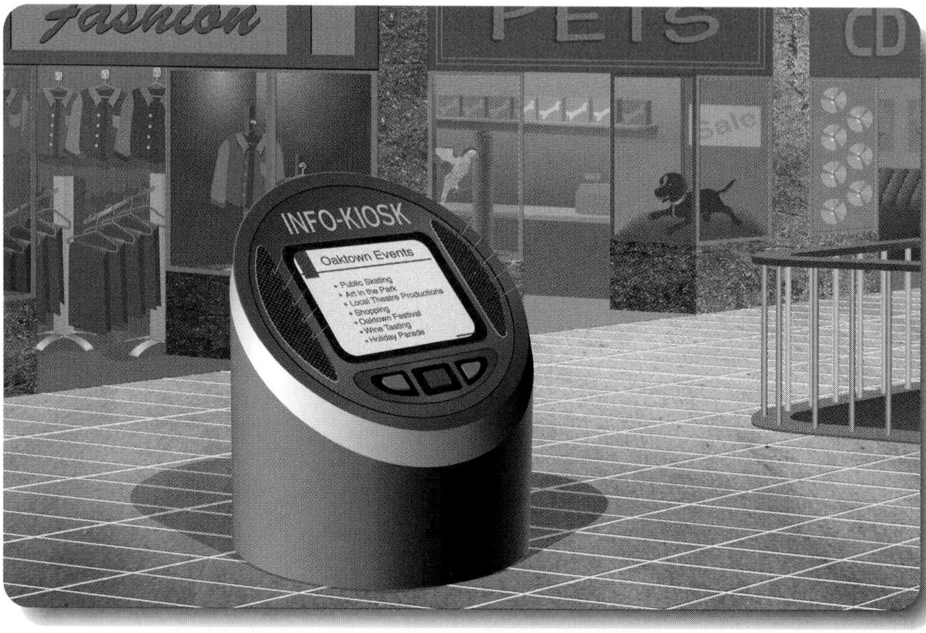

ADD NARRATION TO A SLIDE SHOW

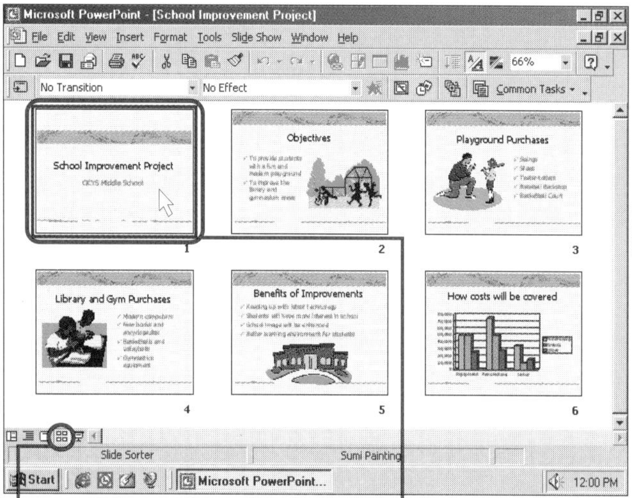

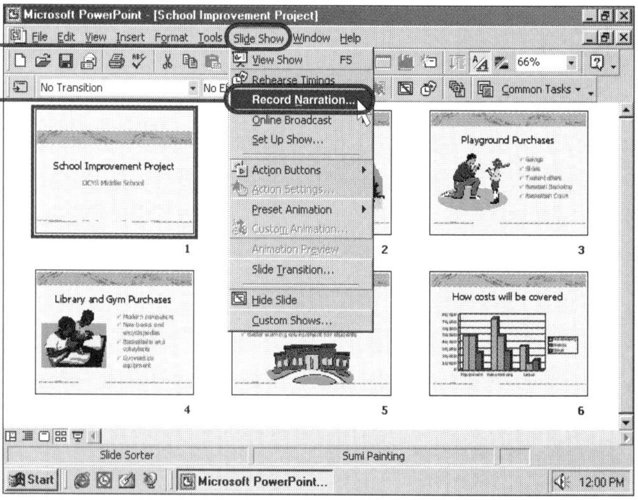

1 Click ⊞ to change to the Slide Sorter view.

2 Click the first slide in your presentation.

3 Click **Slide Show**.

4 Click **Record Narration**.

Note: If Record Narration does not appear on the menu, position the mouse ↖ over the bottom of the menu to display all the menu commands.

■ The Record Narration dialog box appears.

What should I do to prepare for recording narration?

You should prepare and rehearse a script that includes the information you want to record for each slide in your slide show. This can help you avoid awkward pauses that may distract the audience.

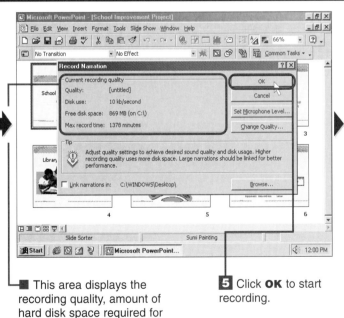

■ This area displays the recording quality, amount of hard disk space required for each second of narration, amount of free space on your hard disk and amount of recording time available.

5 Click **OK** to start recording.

■ The first slide in the slide show appears.

6 Speak into your microphone to record narration for the slide.

7 To display the next slide, click the current slide or press the **Spacebar**.

CONTINUED

ADD NARRATION TO A SLIDE SHOW

You can have PowerPoint
save the amount of time
you spent narrating each
slide. PowerPoint will
use these timings to
advance the slides
automatically during
your slide show.

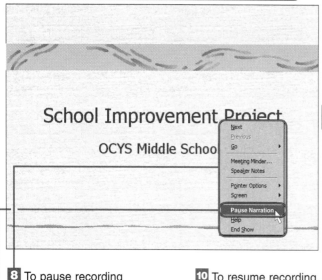

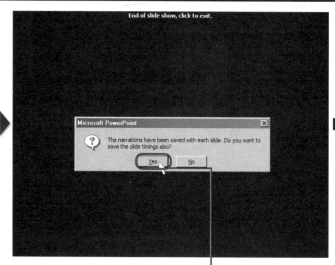

8 To pause recording
the narration at any time,
right-click the current slide.
A menu appears.

9 Click **Pause Narration**.

10 To resume recording,
repeat steps **8** and **9**,
except select **Resume
Narration** in step **9**.

■ When you finish the
slide show, a dialog box
appears, stating that the
narrations have been
saved with each slide.

11 To save the amount
of time you spent
narrating each slide
and use the timings
when you later view the
slide show, click **Yes**.

Can I turn off the narration for a slide show?

Yes. You can temporarily turn off the narration for a slide show without deleting the narration you recorded for the slides. To temporarily turn off the narration, see page 252.

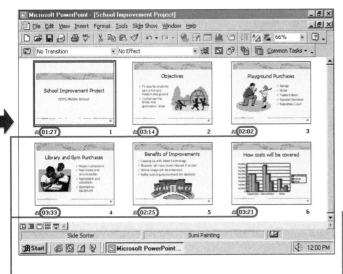

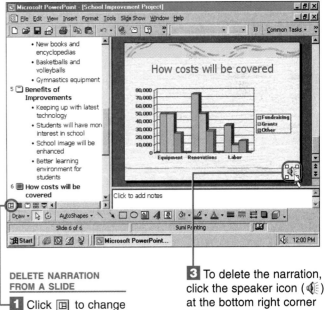

■ The time you spent narrating each slide appears below the slides.

■ When you view the slide show, you will hear the narration you recorded. To view the slide show, see page 260.

DELETE NARRATION FROM A SLIDE

1 Click 🔲 to change to the Normal view.

2 Display the slide you no longer want to play a narration.

3 To delete the narration, click the speaker icon (🔊) at the bottom right corner of the slide. Then press the Delete key.

CHANGE HOW A SOUND OR MOVIE PLAYS

You can change how you want a sound or movie to play during a slide show.

You can have a sound or movie play automatically when the slide is displayed or only when you click the left mouse button.

CHANGE HOW A SOUND OR MOVIE PLAYS

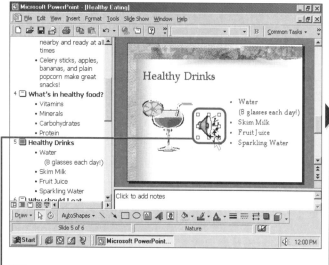

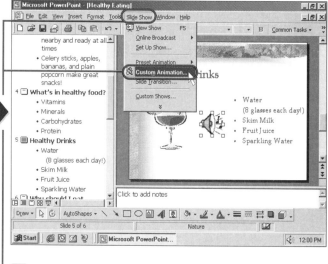

1 Click the sound or movie you want to change. Handles (□) appear around the object.

2 Click **Slide Show**.

3 Click **Custom Animation**.

■ The Custom Animation dialog box appears.

Why doesn't the sound or movie I set to play automatically begin as soon as the slide appears during the slide show?

To play as soon as the slide appears on your screen, a sound or movie must be set as the first animation. To change the animation order of objects on a slide, see page 222.

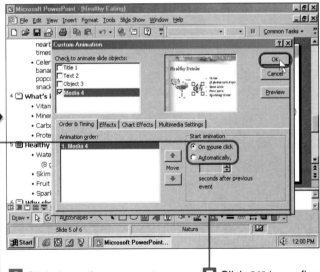

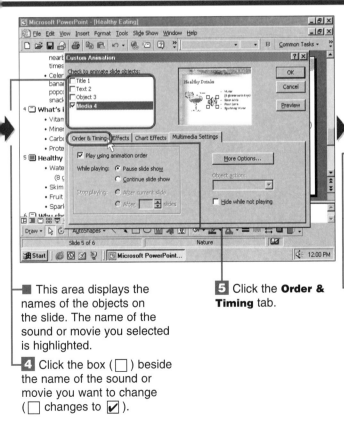

■ This area displays the names of the objects on the slide. The name of the sound or movie you selected is highlighted.

4 Click the box (□) beside the name of the sound or movie you want to change (□ changes to ☑).

5 Click the **Order & Timing** tab.

6 Click the option you want to use to play the sound or movie (○ changes to ⊙).

On mouse click - Play sound or movie after you click the left mouse button

Automatically - Play sound or movie automatically when slide is displayed

7 Click **OK** to confirm your changes.

CHAPTER 11

Add Special Effects

Are you interested in adding special effects to your presentation? This chapter teaches you how to animate objects, use interesting transitions to introduce slides and more.

ADD SLIDE TRANSITIONS

You can use effects
called transitions
to help you move
from one slide to
the next.

When you use the
AutoContent Wizard to
create a presentation,
PowerPoint may
automatically add
slide transitions to the
presentation for you.
You can change these
transitions at any time.

ADD SLIDE TRANSITIONS

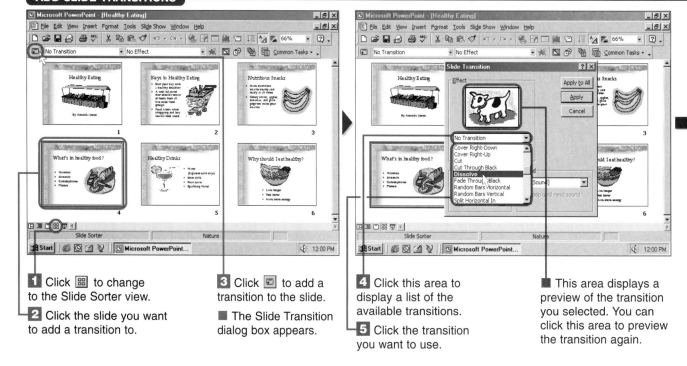

1 Click ⊞ to change
to the Slide Sorter view.

2 Click the slide you want
to add a transition to.

3 Click 🔲 to add a
transition to the slide.

■ The Slide Transition
dialog box appears.

4 Click this area to
display a list of the
available transitions.

5 Click the transition
you want to use.

■ This area displays a
preview of the transition
you selected. You can
click this area to preview
the transition again.

?

Can I add a different transition to each slide in my presentation?

Although PowerPoint allows you to add a different transition to each slide in your presentation, using too many different transitions may distract the audience. The audience may focus on how each slide is introduced, rather than the information you are presenting.

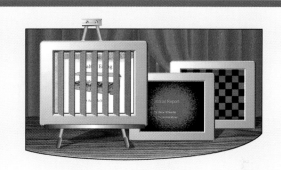

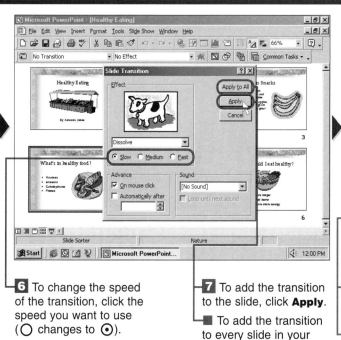

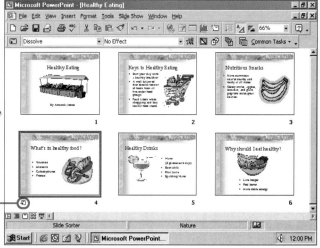

6 To change the speed of the transition, click the speed you want to use (○ changes to ⊙).

7 To add the transition to the slide, click **Apply**.

■ To add the transition to every slide in your presentation, click **Apply to All**.

■ The 🖃 symbol appears below the slide you added a transition to.

■ To preview the transition for the slide, click 🖃 below the slide.

■ To remove a transition, repeat steps **1** to **5**, except select **No Transition** in step **5**. Then perform step **7**.

ADD SIMPLE ANIMATIONS

You can add movement and sound effects to the objects on your slides. This can help keep your audience's attention throughout your presentation.

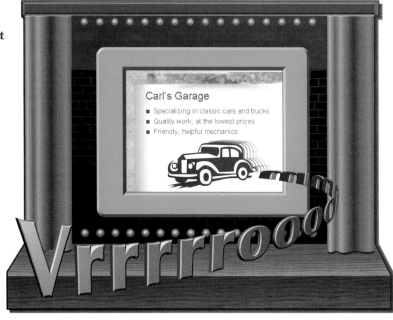

You can animate objects such as a title, list of points, AutoShape, clip art image or text effect.

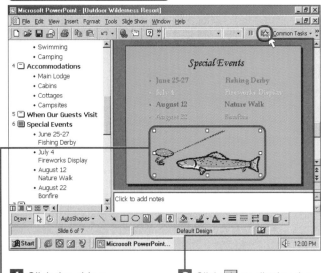

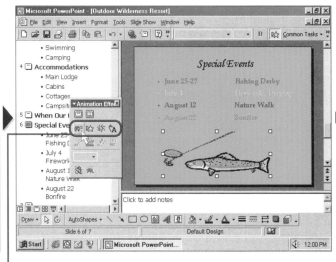

1 Click the object you want to animate. Handles (□) appear around the object.

Note: If you want to add animations to a chart, see page 218.

2 Click ☆ to display the Animation Effects toolbar.

Note: If ☆ is not displayed, click ≫ on the Formatting toolbar to display all the buttons.

■ The Animation Effects toolbar appears.

3 Click the animation effect you want to use.

Note: The available animation effects depend on the type of object you selected in step 1.

? **How do I display the animated objects in my slide show?**

When viewing your slide show, you must click the slide to display each animated object on the slide. For example, if you animated a list of points, you must click the slide each time you want a point to appear.

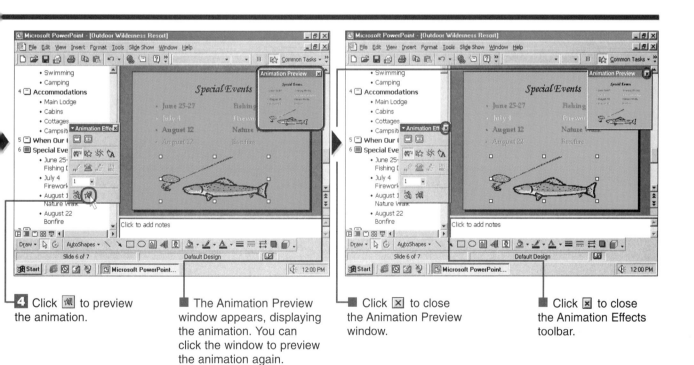

4 Click [icon] to preview the animation.

■ The Animation Preview window appears, displaying the animation. You can click the window to preview the animation again.

■ Click [X] to close the Animation Preview window.

■ Click [x] to close the Animation Effects toolbar.

ADD CUSTOM ANIMATIONS

You can add a custom animation to an object such as a clip art image, AutoShape or bulleted list.

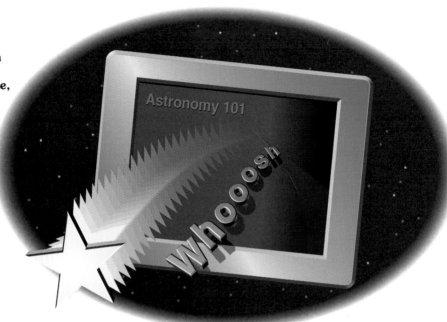

Adding a custom animation allows you to specify which movement and sound effect you want to use.

ADD CUSTOM ANIMATIONS

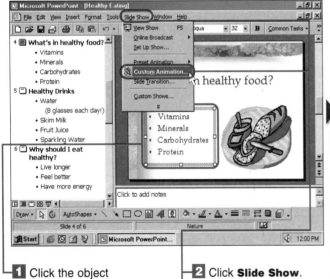

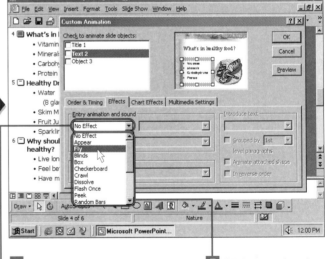

1 Click the object you want to animate. Handles (□) appear around the object.

Note: If you want to add animations to a chart, see page 218.

2 Click **Slide Show**.

3 Click **Custom Animation**.

■ The Custom Animation dialog box appears.

4 Click this area to display a list of the available animation effects.

5 Click the animation effect you want to use.

**What types of sound effects
can I add to my animation?**

Here are some examples of
the sound effects you can use.

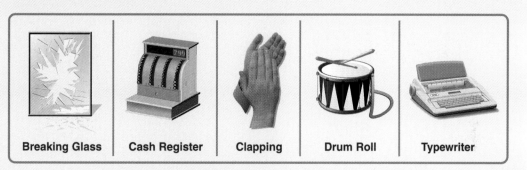

| Breaking Glass | Cash Register | Clapping | Drum Roll | Typewriter |

6 Click this area to
display a list of options
for the animation effect.

7 Click the way you
want the animation effect
to appear.

*Note: The available options
depend on the animation
effect you selected in step **5**.
You cannot choose an option
for some animation effects.*

8 Click this area to
display a list of the
available sound effects.

9 Click the sound
effect you want to use.

*Note: If you do not want to use
a sound effect, click **[No Sound]**.*

CONTINUED

ADD CUSTOM ANIMATIONS

You can specify the action you want to occur after an animation. For example, you can have PowerPoint change the color of the object after an animation.

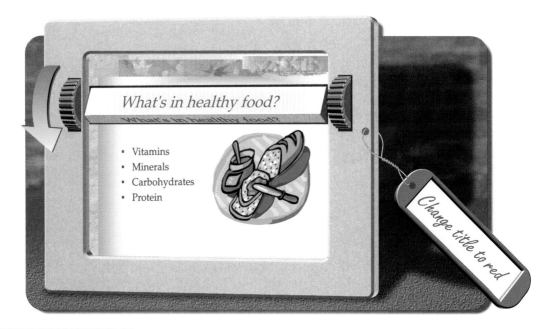

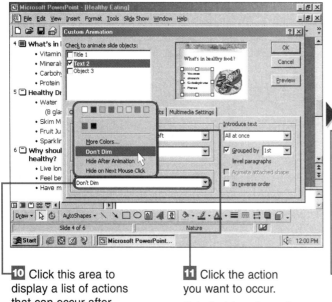

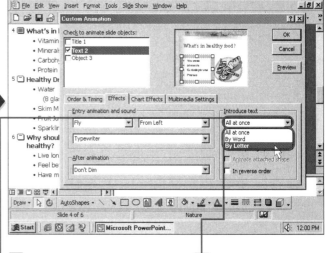

10 Click this area to display a list of actions that can occur after the animation.

11 Click the action you want to occur.

Note: For information on the actions you can select, see the top of page 217.

12 If you are adding an animation to text, click this area to display a list of ways PowerPoint can display the text on the slide.

13 Click the way you want PowerPoint to display the text.

All at once - Display entire paragraph at once

By Word - Display one word at a time

By Letter - Display one letter at a time

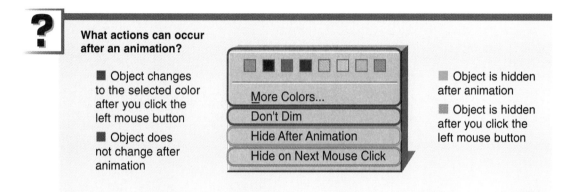

What actions can occur after an animation?

■ Object changes to the selected color after you click the left mouse button

■ Object does not change after animation

More Colors...

Don't Dim

Hide After Animation

Hide on Next Mouse Click

■ Object is hidden after animation

■ Object is hidden after you click the left mouse button

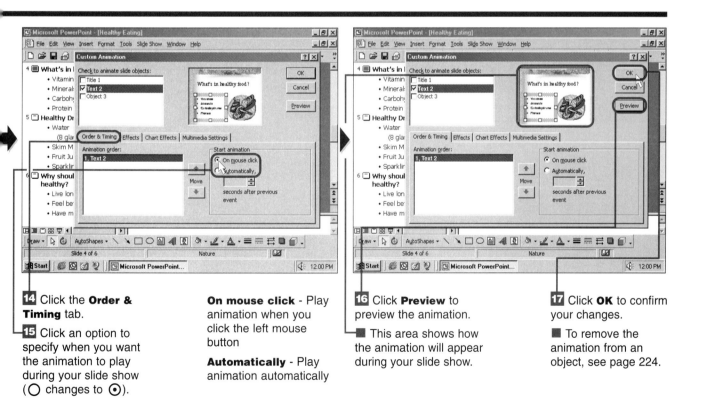

14 Click the **Order & Timing** tab.

15 Click an option to specify when you want the animation to play during your slide show (○ changes to ⊙).

On mouse click - Play animation when you click the left mouse button

Automatically - Play animation automatically

16 Click **Preview** to preview the animation.

■ This area shows how the animation will appear during your slide show.

17 Click **OK** to confirm your changes.

■ To remove the animation from an object, see page 224.

ADD ANIMATIONS TO CHARTS

You can add an animation to a chart on a slide. This allows you to introduce the chart in a dramatic way during a slide show.

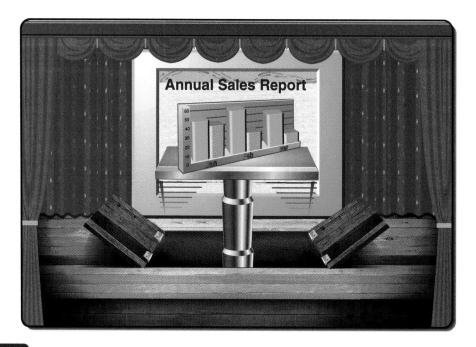

ADD ANIMATIONS TO CHARTS

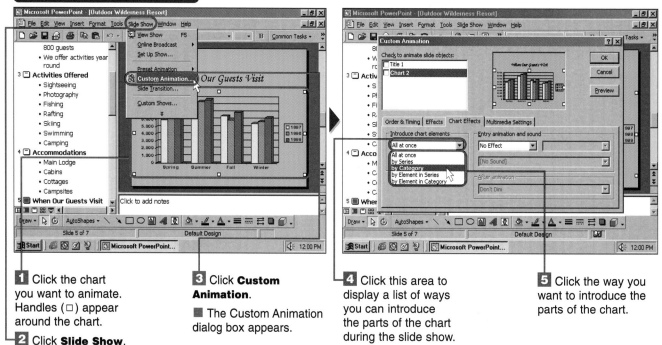

1 Click the chart you want to animate. Handles (□) appear around the chart.

2 Click **Slide Show**.

3 Click **Custom Animation**.

■ The Custom Animation dialog box appears.

4 Click this area to display a list of ways you can introduce the parts of the chart during the slide show.

5 Click the way you want to introduce the parts of the chart.

? How can I introduce the parts of a chart during a slide show?

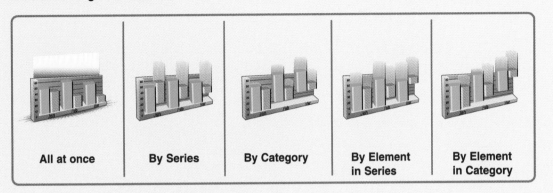

| All at once | By Series | By Category | By Element in Series | By Element in Category |

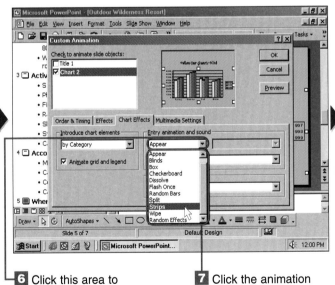

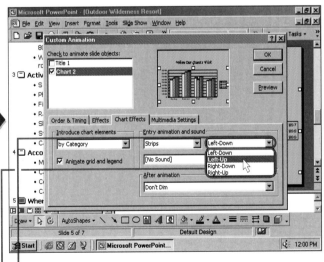

6 Click this area to display a list of the available animation effects.

7 Click the animation effect you want to use.

Note: The available animation effects depend on the option you selected in step 5.

8 Click this area to display a list of options for the animation effect.

9 Click the way you want the animation effect to appear.

Note: The available options depend on the animation effect you selected in step 7. You cannot choose an option for some animation effects.

CONTINUED ▶

ADD ANIMATIONS TO CHARTS

You can have PowerPoint play a sound effect for the chart animation, such as applause or screeching brakes.

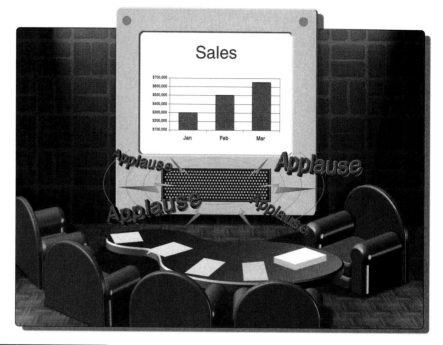

ADD ANIMATIONS TO CHARTS (CONTINUED)

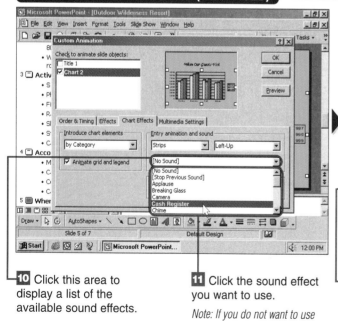

■10 Click this area to display a list of the available sound effects.

■11 Click the sound effect you want to use.

Note: If you do not want to use a sound effect, click [No Sound].

■12 Click this area to display a list of actions that can occur after the chart animation.

■13 Click the action you want to occur.

Note: For information on the actions you can select, see the top of page 221.

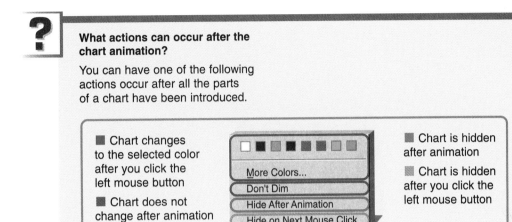

What actions can occur after the chart animation?

You can have one of the following actions occur after all the parts of a chart have been introduced.

■ Chart changes to the selected color after you click the left mouse button

■ Chart does not change after animation

More Colors...

Don't Dim

Hide After Animation

Hide on Next Mouse Click

■ Chart is hidden after animation

■ Chart is hidden after you click the left mouse button

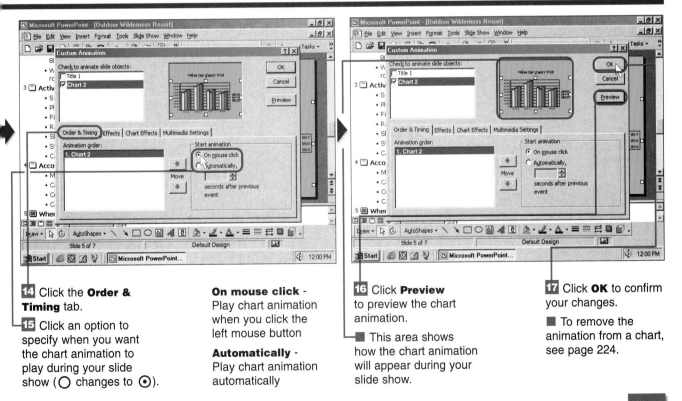

14 Click the **Order & Timing** tab.

15 Click an option to specify when you want the chart animation to play during your slide show (○ changes to ⊙).

On mouse click - Play chart animation when you click the left mouse button

Automatically - Play chart animation automatically

16 Click **Preview** to preview the chart animation.

■ This area shows how the chart animation will appear during your slide show.

17 Click **OK** to confirm your changes.

■ To remove the animation from a chart, see page 224.

CHANGE ANIMATION ORDER

If you added animations to several objects on a slide, you can change the order that the animated objects will appear during the slide show.

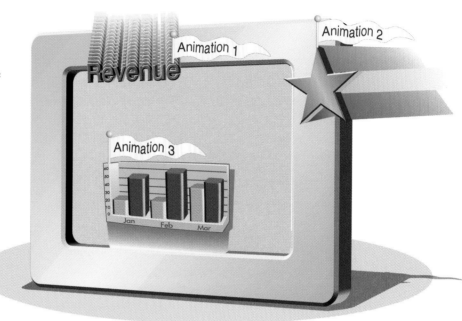

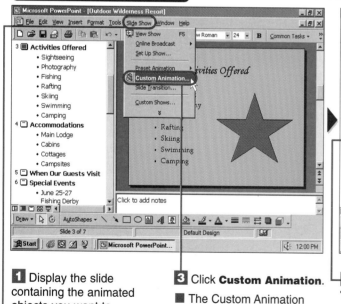

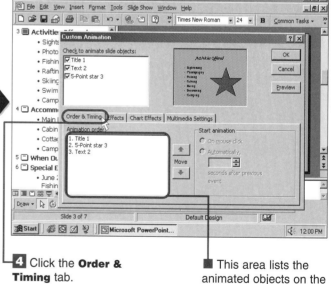

1 Display the slide containing the animated objects you want to appear in a different order.

2 Click **Slide Show**.

3 Click **Custom Animation**.

■ The Custom Animation dialog box appears.

4 Click the **Order & Timing** tab.

■ This area lists the animated objects on the slide. The objects are listed in the order they will appear during the slide show.

Why would I change the order of the animated objects on a slide?

Changing the order of animated objects gives you more control over the way you present information to the audience. For example, you can display a chart you want the audience to focus on before you introduce the text on the slide.

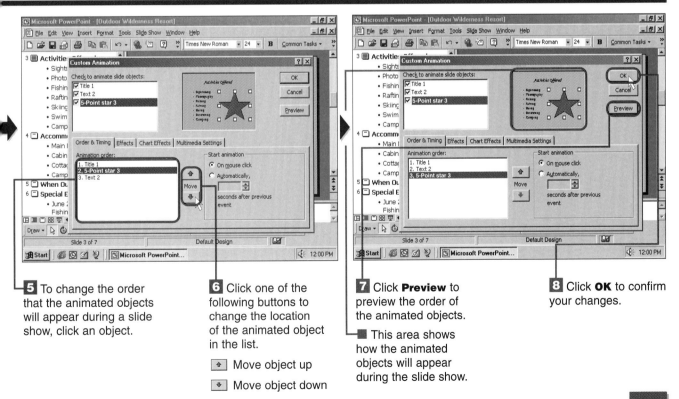

5 To change the order that the animated objects will appear during a slide show, click an object.

6 Click one of the following buttons to change the location of the animated object in the list.

⬆ Move object up

⬇ Move object down

7 Click **Preview** to preview the order of the animated objects.

■ This area shows how the animated objects will appear during the slide show.

8 Click **OK** to confirm your changes.

REMOVE ANIMATION

If you no longer want an object to appear animated on a slide, you can remove the animation from the object.

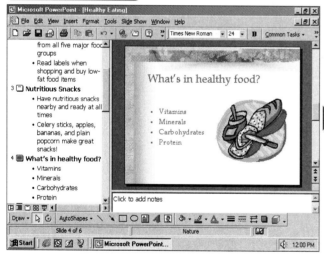

1 Display the slide containing the object you no longer want to animate.

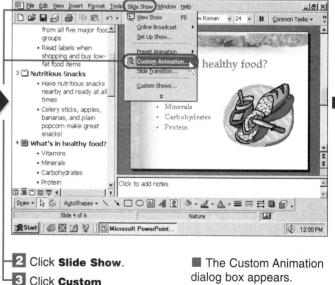

2 Click **Slide Show**.

3 Click **Custom Animation**.

■ The Custom Animation dialog box appears.

?

Can I remove an animation that PowerPoint added to an object?

When you use the AutoContent Wizard to create a presentation, PowerPoint may automatically add animations to some of the objects on your slides. You can remove these animations as you would remove any animation you added.

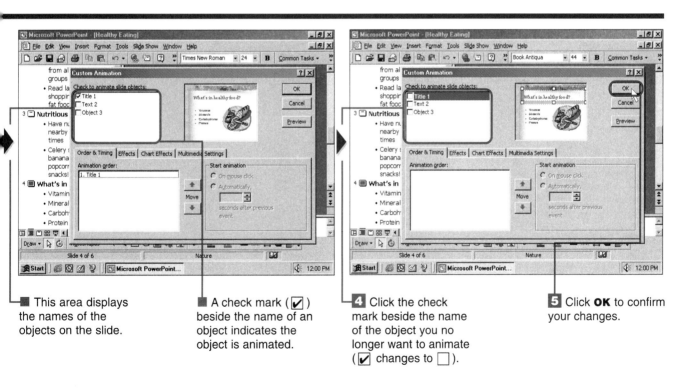

■ This area displays the names of the objects on the slide.

■ A check mark (☑) beside the name of an object indicates the object is animated.

4 Click the check mark beside the name of the object you no longer want to animate (☑ changes to ☐).

5 Click **OK** to confirm your changes.

ADD AN ACTION BUTTON

An action button allows you to jump to another slide in your presentation. This can help make your presentation easier to browse through.

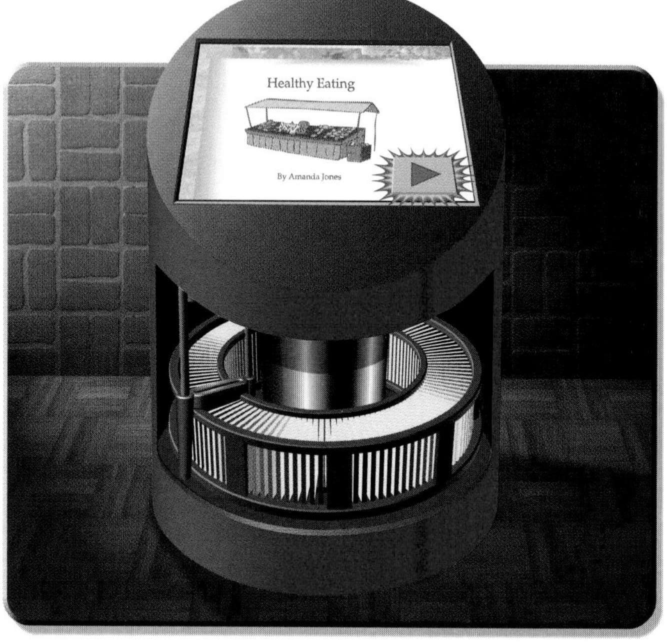

Adding action buttons to slides is useful if people will view your presentation at a kiosk. Kiosks are often found at trade shows and shopping malls.

ADD AN ACTION BUTTON

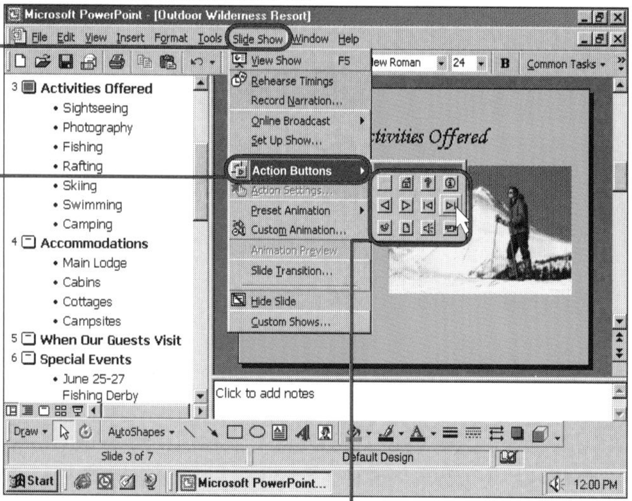

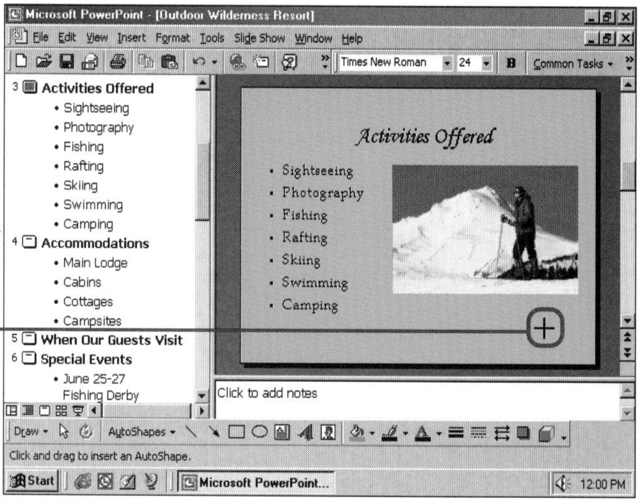

1 Display the slide you want to add an action button to.

2 Click **Slide Show**.

3 Click **Action Buttons**.

Note: If Action Buttons does not appear on the menu, position the mouse over the bottom of the menu to display all the menu commands.

4 Click the action button you want to add to the slide.

5 Click the location on the slide where you want the action button to appear.

■ The Action Settings dialog box appears.

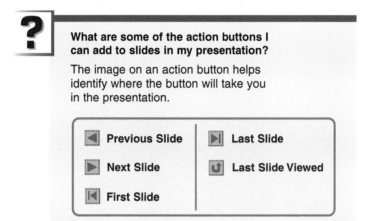

What are some of the action buttons I can add to slides in my presentation?

The image on an action button helps identify where the button will take you in the presentation.

◀	Previous Slide	▶❙	Last Slide
▶	Next Slide	↰	Last Slide Viewed
❙◀	First Slide		

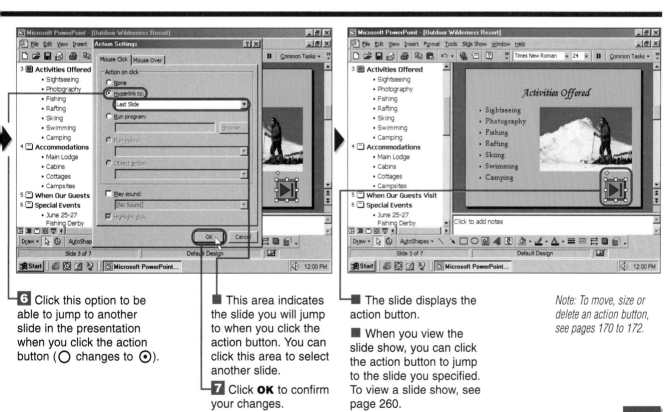

6 Click this option to be able to jump to another slide in the presentation when you click the action button (○ changes to ◉).

■ This area indicates the slide you will jump to when you click the action button. You can click this area to select another slide.

7 Click **OK** to confirm your changes.

■ The slide displays the action button.

■ When you view the slide show, you can click the action button to jump to the slide you specified. To view a slide show, see page 260.

Note: To move, size or delete an action button, see pages 170 to 172.

CHAPTER 12

Fine-Tune a Presentation

Are you ready to put the finishing touches on your presentation? This chapter shows you how to reorder slides, create speaker notes, print your presentation and more.

REORDER SLIDES

You can change the order of the slides in your presentation.

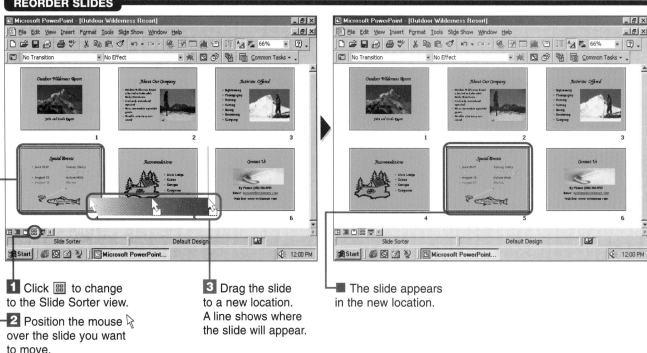

1 Click ▦ to change to the Slide Sorter view.

2 Position the mouse ↖ over the slide you want to move.

3 Drag the slide to a new location. A line shows where the slide will appear.

■ The slide appears in the new location.

You can remove
a slide you no
longer need in
your presentation.

DELETE A SLIDE

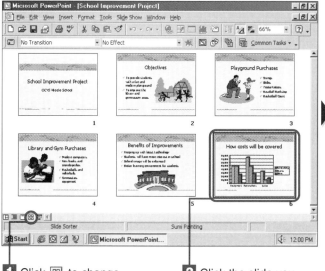

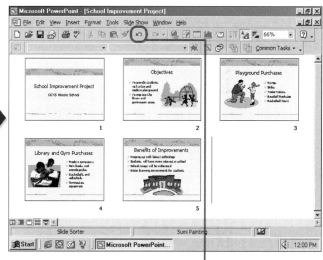

1 Click ▦ to change
to the Slide Sorter view.

2 Click the slide you
want to delete.

3 Press the Delete key
to remove the slide.

■ The slide disappears.

■ To immediately
return the slide to the
presentation, click ↶.

HIDE A SLIDE

You can hide a slide in
your presentation. This
allows you to include
supporting information
in your slide show,
but not display the
information unless
the audience requires
clarification.

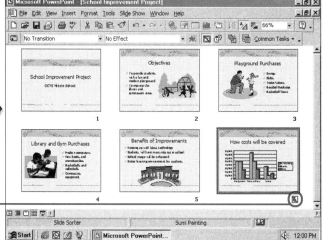

HIDE A SLIDE

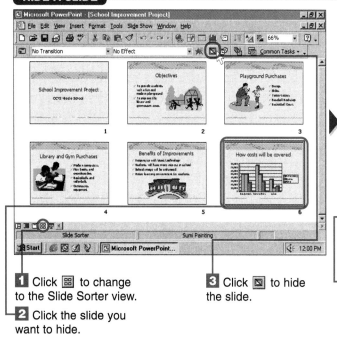

1 Click ▦ to change
to the Slide Sorter view.

2 Click the slide you
want to hide.

3 Click 🔳 to hide
the slide.

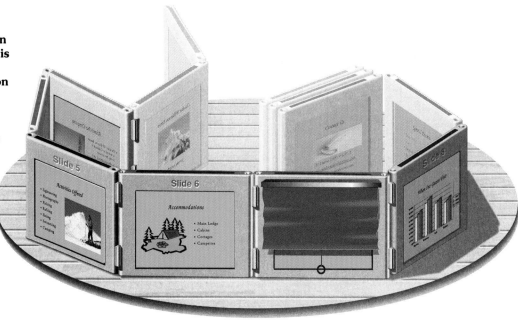

■ A symbol (🔳) appears
through the slide number.

■ If you no longer want
to hide the slide, repeat
steps **1** to **3**.

■ To display a hidden
slide during a slide show,
press the **H** key when
viewing the slide before
the hidden slide. To view a
slide show, see page 260.

VIEW SLIDES IN BLACK AND WHITE

You can preview how your slides will look when printed on a black-and-white printer.

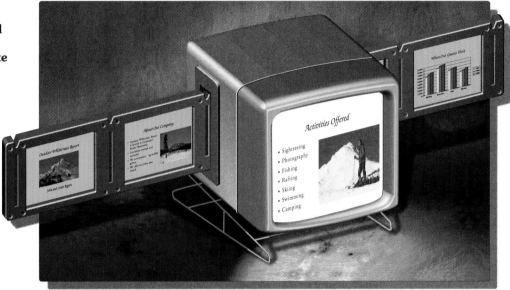

VIEW SLIDES IN BLACK AND WHITE

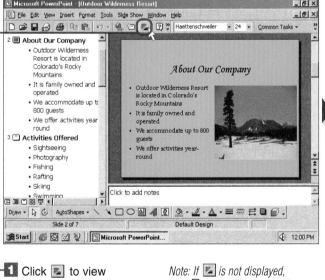

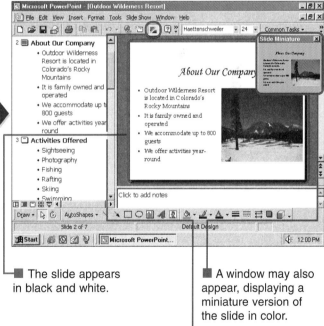

1 Click  to view your slides in black and white.

Note: If ▧ is not displayed, click ▸▸ on the Standard toolbar to display all the buttons.

■ The slide appears in black and white.

■ A window may also appear, displaying a miniature version of the slide in color.

■ Click ▧ to once again view the slides in color.

CREATE A SUMMARY SLIDE

You can create a
summary slide that lists
the titles of all the slides
in your presentation.
A summary slide is
useful for introducing
the contents of your
presentation to the
audience.

CREATE A SUMMARY SLIDE

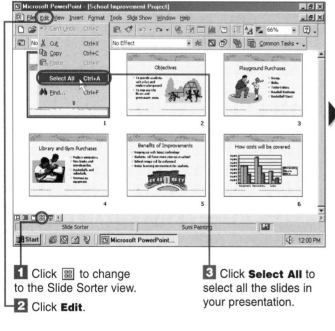

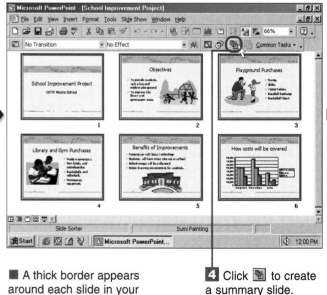

1 Click ⊞ to change
to the Slide Sorter view.

2 Click **Edit**.

3 Click **Select All** to
select all the slides in
your presentation.

■ A thick border appears
around each slide in your
presentation.

4 Click 🖼 to create
a summary slide.

Why did two summary slides appear at the beginning of my presentation?

PowerPoint can only fit a certain amount of information on each slide. If your presentation contains many slides, PowerPoint may need to create more than one summary slide to list all the titles in the presentation.

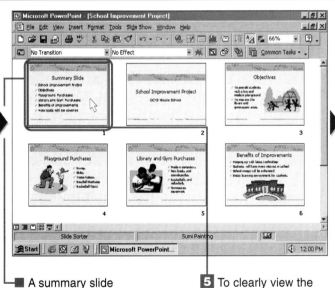

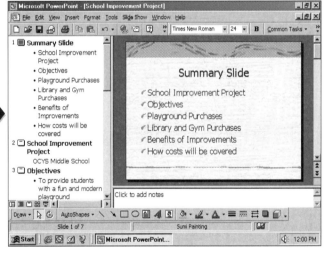

■ A summary slide appears at the beginning of your presentation, listing the title of each slide.

Note: To move the summary slide to a different location in your presentation, see page 230.

5 To clearly view the contents of the summary slide, double-click the slide.

■ The summary slide appears in the Normal view. You can edit the summary slide as you would edit any slide in your presentation.

ADD SLIDES FROM ANOTHER PRESENTATION

You can add slides
to your current
presentation from
a presentation you
previously created.

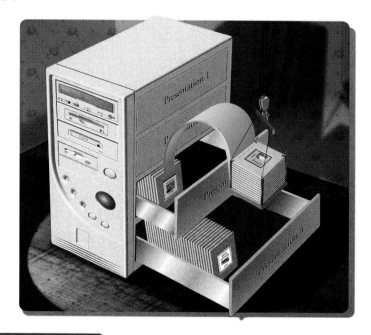

ADD SLIDES FROM ANOTHER PRESENTATION

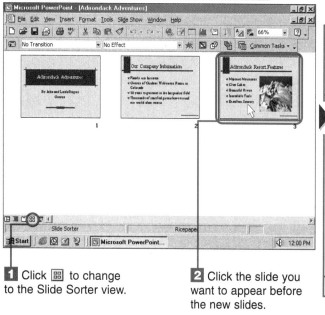

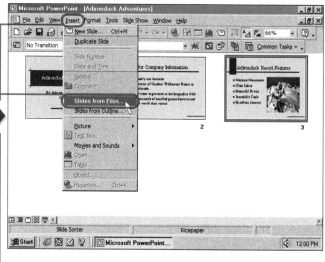

1 Click ⊞ to change
to the Slide Sorter view.

2 Click the slide you
want to appear before
the new slides.

3 Click **Insert**.

4 Click **Slides from
Files**.

*Note: If Slides from Files does
not appear on the menu, position
the mouse ₖ over the bottom of
the menu to display all the menu
commands.*

■ The Slide Finder dialog
box appears.

When I add slides from another presentation, does PowerPoint remove the slides from the other presentation?

No. PowerPoint makes a copy of the slides in the original presentation and places the copy in your current presentation. The slides in the original presentation do not change.

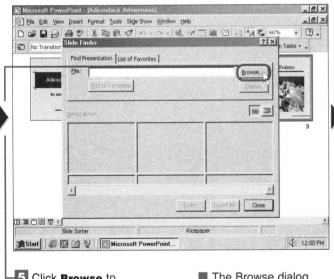

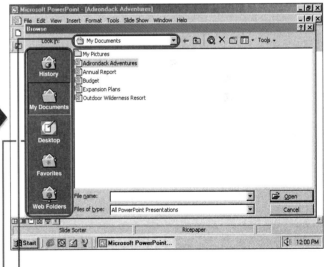

5 Click **Browse** to locate the presentation that contains the slides you want to use.

■ The Browse dialog box appears.

■ This area shows the location of the displayed presentations. You can click this area to change the location.

■ This area allows you to access commonly used folders. To display the contents of a folder, click the folder.

Note: For information on the commonly used folders, see the top of page 25.

CONTINUED

ADD SLIDES FROM ANOTHER PRESENTATION

When you add slides from
another presentation,
PowerPoint automatically
changes the design of the
slides to match the design
of the current presentation.

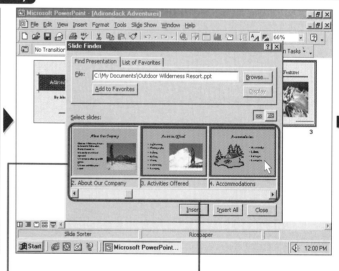

6 Click the name of
the presentation that
contains the slides
you want to add to the
current presentation.

7 Click **Open**.

■ The slides in the
presentation appear in
this area. The slide title
appears below each
slide. You can use the
scroll bar to browse
through the slides.

8 Click each slide you
want to add to the current
presentation. A blue border
appears around each slide
you select.

*Note: To deselect a slide you
accidentally selected, click the
slide again.*

238

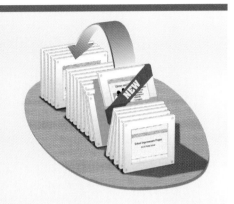

? **Can I move the slides I added to my presentation?**

After adding slides to your presentation, you can change the order of the slides. To reorder slides in a presentation, see page 230.

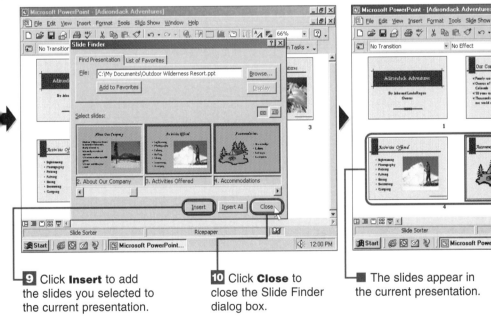

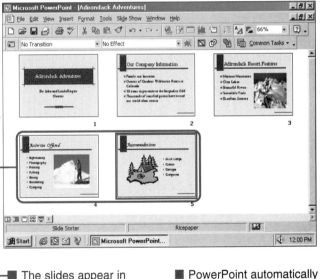

9 Click **Insert** to add the slides you selected to the current presentation.

10 Click **Close** to close the Slide Finder dialog box.

■ The slides appear in the current presentation.

■ PowerPoint automatically changes the design of the slides to match the design of the current presentation.

ADD A COMMENT

You can add a comment to a slide in your presentation. A comment can provide a reminder about a task you need to complete or a change you want to make.

Comments you add to your slides will be displayed during the slide show. You may want to hide the comments on the slides before presenting the slide show.

ADD A COMMENT

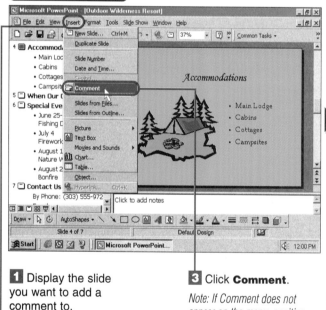

1 Display the slide you want to add a comment to.

2 Click **Insert**.

3 Click **Comment**.

Note: If Comment does not appear on the menu, position the mouse ⬚ over the bottom of the menu to display all the menu commands.

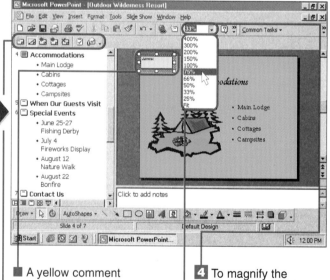

■ A yellow comment box appears, displaying your name.

■ The Reviewing toolbar also appears. To hide the toolbar, see page 50.

4 To magnify the slide so you can clearly view the comment box, click ⬚ in this area.

Note: If the Zoom area is not displayed, click ⬚ on the Standard toolbar to display all the buttons.

5 Click the zoom setting you want to use.

How can I delete a comment I no longer need?

Click the comment you want to delete. Then click an edge of the comment box and press the Delete key.

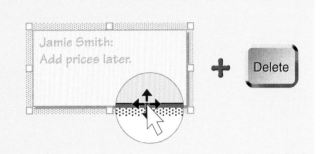

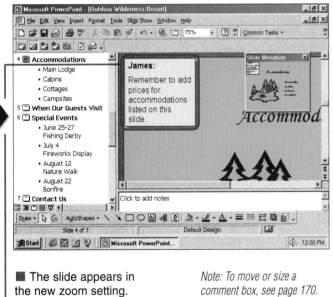

■ The slide appears in the new zoom setting.

6 Type your comment.

7 When you finish typing your comment, click outside the comment box.

Note: To move or size a comment box, see page 170.

■ To once again display the entire slide, repeat steps **4** and **5**, except select **Fit** in step **5**.

HIDE OR DISPLAY COMMENTS

1 Click **View**.

2 Click **Comments**.

Note: If Comments does not appear on the menu, position the mouse over the bottom of the menu to display all the menu commands.

■ PowerPoint hides or displays the comments in your presentation.

CREATE SPEAKER NOTES

You can create speaker notes that contain copies of your slides with all the ideas you want to discuss. You can use these notes as a guide when delivering your presentation.

Speaker notes can include statistics or additional information that you may need to answer questions from the audience.

CREATE SPEAKER NOTES

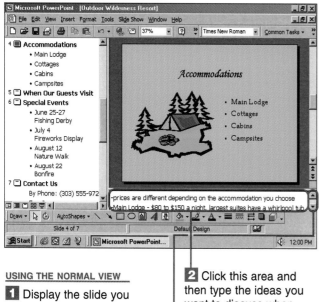

USING THE NORMAL VIEW

1 Display the slide you want to create speaker notes for.

2 Click this area and then type the ideas you want to discuss when you display the slide during the presentation.

■ If you type more than one line of text, you can use the scroll bar to browse through the text.

USING THE NOTES PAGE VIEW

1 Click **View**.

2 Click **Notes Page** to display the presentation in the Notes Page view.

Note: If Notes Page does not appear on the menu, position the mouse ⬚ over the bottom of the menu to display all the menu commands.

Can I print my speaker notes?

Yes. When you have finished creating your speaker notes, you can print the notes pages so you will have a paper copy of your notes to refer to while delivering your presentation. For information on printing notes pages, see page 246.

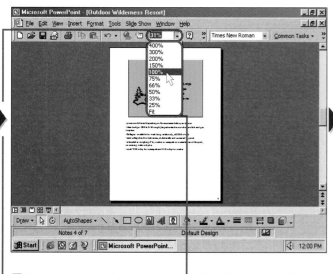

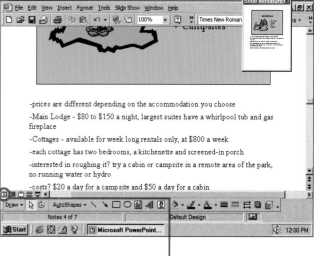

■ The notes page for the current slide appears.

Note: You can use the scroll bar to view the notes pages for other slides.

3 To magnify the notes page so you can clearly view the notes, click ▾ in this area.

Note: If the Zoom area is not displayed, click ▸ on the Standard toolbar to display all the buttons.

4 Click the zoom setting you want to use.

■ The notes page appears in the new zoom setting.

■ You can edit the text on the notes page as you would edit any text in your presentation.

Note: To once again display the entire notes page, repeat steps 3 and 4, except select Fit in step 4.

■ When you finish reviewing the notes pages, click ▣ to return to the Normal view.

SET UP A PRESENTATION FOR PRINTING

Before printing your presentation, you can specify how you want to output the presentation, such as on paper, 35mm slides or overheads.

You can also specify the orientation you want to use when printing your presentation.

SET UP A PRESENTATION FOR PRINTING

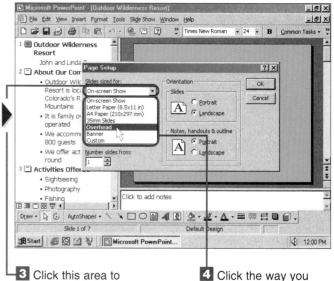

1 Click **File**.

2 Click **Page Setup**.

■ The Page Setup dialog box appears.

3 Click this area to display the ways you can output the slides.

4 Click the way you want to output the slides.

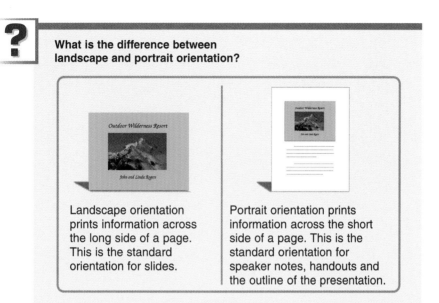

? What is the difference between landscape and portrait orientation?

Landscape orientation prints information across the long side of a page. This is the standard orientation for slides.

Portrait orientation prints information across the short side of a page. This is the standard orientation for speaker notes, handouts and the outline of the presentation.

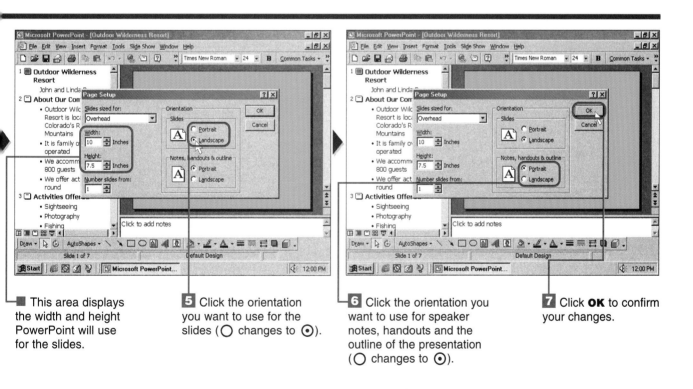

■ This area displays the width and height PowerPoint will use for the slides.

5 Click the orientation you want to use for the slides (○ changes to ◉).

6 Click the orientation you want to use for speaker notes, handouts and the outline of the presentation (○ changes to ◉).

7 Click **OK** to confirm your changes.

PRINT A PRESENTATION

You can produce a paper copy of a presentation for your own use or to hand out to the audience.

PRINT A PRESENTATION

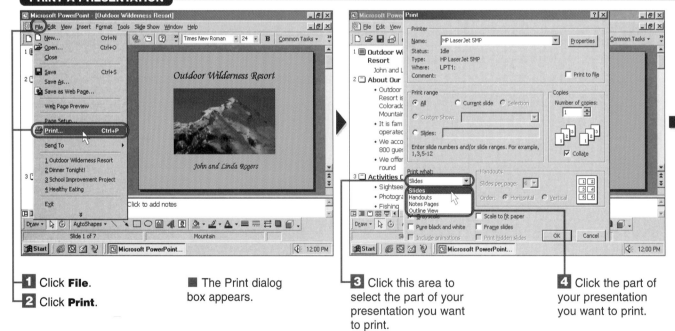

1 Click **File**.

2 Click **Print**.

■ The Print dialog box appears.

3 Click this area to select the part of your presentation you want to print.

4 Click the part of your presentation you want to print.

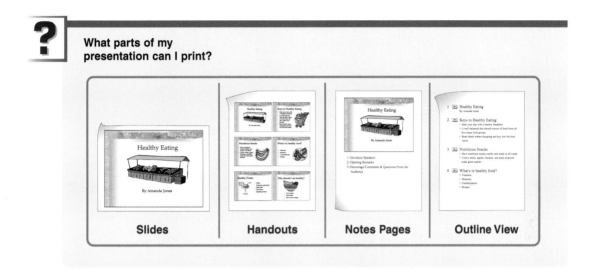

What parts of my presentation can I print?

Slides   Handouts   Notes Pages   Outline View

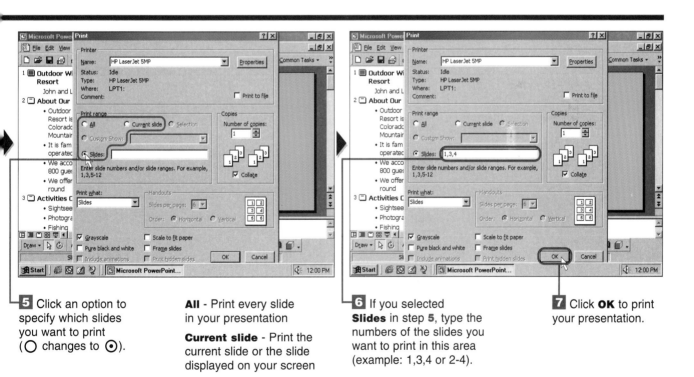

5 Click an option to specify which slides you want to print (○ changes to ⊙).

All - Print every slide in your presentation

Current slide - Print the current slide or the slide displayed on your screen

Slides - Print the slides you specify

6 If you selected **Slides** in step **5**, type the numbers of the slides you want to print in this area (example: 1,3,4 or 2-4).

7 Click **OK** to print your presentation.

WORK WITH A PRESENTATION IN MICROSOFT WORD

You can work with your presentation as a Microsoft Word document. This gives you more flexibility when creating and printing handouts or speaker notes for your presentation.

To work with a presentation in Microsoft Word, you need Microsoft Word installed on your computer.

WORK WITH A PRESENTATION IN MICROSOFT WORD

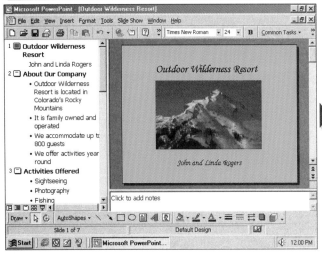

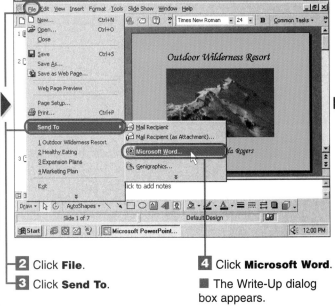

1 Open the presentation you want to work with in Microsoft Word. To open a presentation, see page 28.

■ If you plan to print the Microsoft Word document on a black-and-white printer, you should display the slides in the presentation in black and white before performing step **2**. To display slides in black and white, see page 233.

2 Click **File**.

3 Click **Send To**.

4 Click **Microsoft Word**.

■ The Write-Up dialog box appears.

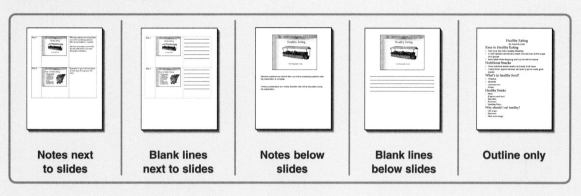

? What page layouts can I use for my presentation in Microsoft Word?

| Notes next to slides | Blank lines next to slides | Notes below slides | Blank lines below slides | Outline only |

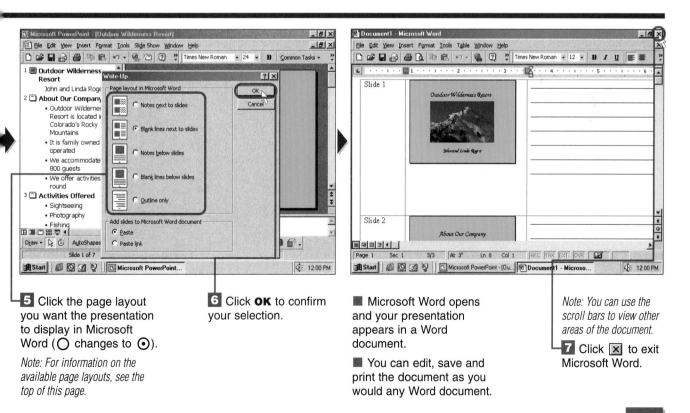

5 Click the page layout you want the presentation to display in Microsoft Word (○ changes to ●).

Note: For information on the available page layouts, see the top of this page.

6 Click **OK** to confirm your selection.

■ Microsoft Word opens and your presentation appears in a Word document.

■ You can edit, save and print the document as you would any Word document.

Note: You can use the scroll bars to view other areas of the document.

7 Click ⊠ to exit Microsoft Word.

CHAPTER 13

Deliver a Presentation

Are you ready to deliver your presentation? This chapter shows you how to set up, rehearse and deliver your presentation.

SET UP A SLIDE SHOW

You can specify how you want to present a slide show on a computer. For example, you can deliver the slide show yourself or allow other people to browse through the slide show on their own.

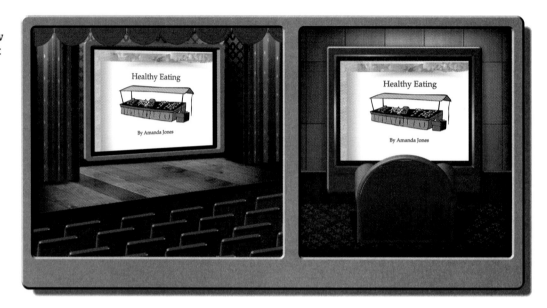

SET UP A SLIDE SHOW

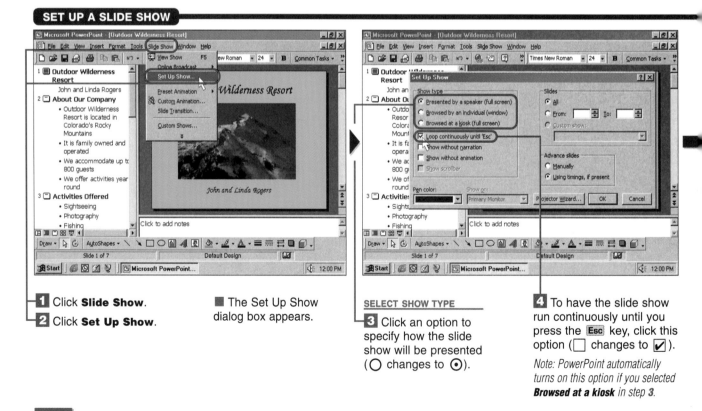

1 Click **Slide Show**.

2 Click **Set Up Show**.

■ The Set Up Show dialog box appears.

SELECT SHOW TYPE

3 Click an option to specify how the slide show will be presented (○ changes to ⊙).

4 To have the slide show run continuously until you press the **Esc** key, click this option (☐ changes to ☑).

Note: PowerPoint automatically turns on this option if you selected ***Browsed at a kiosk*** *in step 3.*

How can I present my slide show?

Presented by a speaker

Select this option if you plan to deliver the slide show to an audience.

Browsed by an individual

Select this option if a person will view the slide show on their own.

Browsed at a kiosk

Select this option if you plan to present a self-running slide show at a kiosk. Kiosks are often found at trade shows and shopping malls.

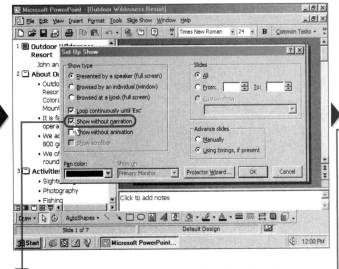

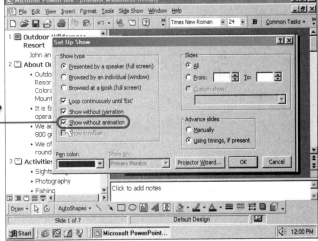

5 If you added narration to the slides, you can click this option to run the slide show without the narration (☐ changes to ☑).

Note: To add narration to slides, see page 202.

6 If you added animations to the slides, you can click this option to run the slide show without the animations (☐ changes to ☑).

Note: To add animations to slides, see pages 212 to 221.

CONTINUED

SET UP A SLIDE SHOW

You can select
which slides you
want to display
during the slide
show.

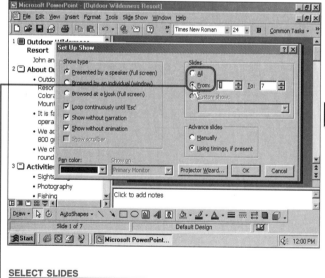

SELECT SLIDES

7 Click an option to
specify which slides you
want to include in the slide
show (○ changes to ◉).

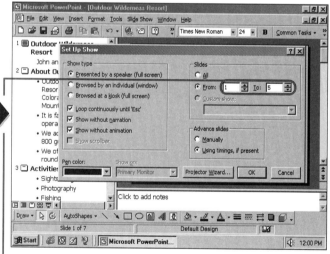

8 If you selected **From**
in step **7**, type the number
of the first slide you want
to display. Then press
the `Tab` key and type
the number of the last
slide you want to display.

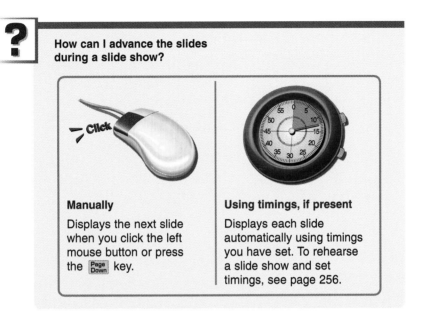

?

How can I advance the slides during a slide show?

Manually

Displays the next slide when you click the left mouse button or press the Page Down key.

Using timings, if present

Displays each slide automatically using timings you have set. To rehearse a slide show and set timings, see page 256.

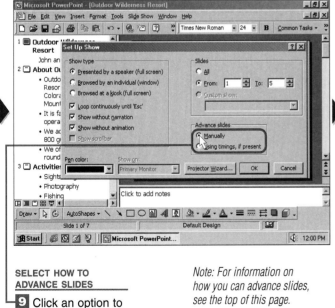

SELECT HOW TO ADVANCE SLIDES

9 Click an option to specify how you want to advance the slides (○ changes to ⊙).

Note: For information on how you can advance slides, see the top of this page.

CONFIRM YOUR CHANGES

10 Click **OK** to confirm your changes.

■ PowerPoint will use the settings you specified when you view the slide show.

Note: To view a slide show, see page 260.

REHEARSE A SLIDE SHOW

You can rehearse your slide show and have PowerPoint record the amount of time you spend on each slide.

REHEARSE A SLIDE SHOW

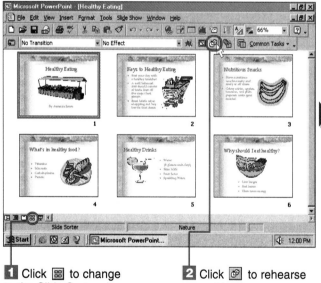

1 Click 🔳 to change to the Slide Sorter view.

2 Click 🔲 to rehearse your slide show.

■ The first slide in the slide show appears.

■ The Rehearsal dialog box displays the time spent on the current slide and the total time spent on the slide show.

How does PowerPoint use the timings I record?

PowerPoint can use the recorded timings to advance your slides automatically during a slide show. This is useful if you want to set up a self-running slide show for a kiosk. Kiosks are often found at trade shows and shopping malls.

If you do not want PowerPoint to advance your slides automatically, see page 252.

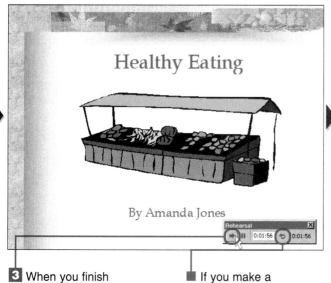

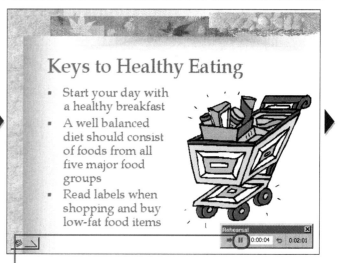

3 When you finish rehearsing the current slide, click ➡ to display the next slide.

■ If you make a mistake and want to reset the timer for the current slide, click ↩.

■ To pause the slide show at any time, click ‖. To continue the slide show, click ‖ again.

CONTINUED

REHEARSE A SLIDE SHOW

When you finish rehearsing your slide show, you can review the time you spent on each slide to determine if you have set an appropriate pace for your presentation.

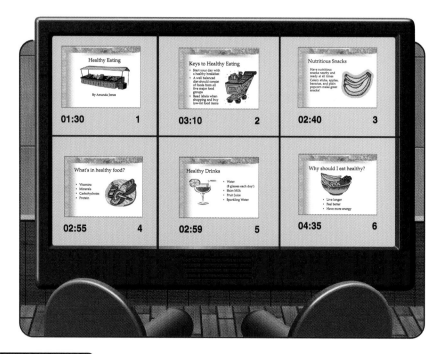

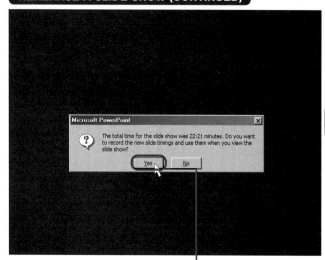

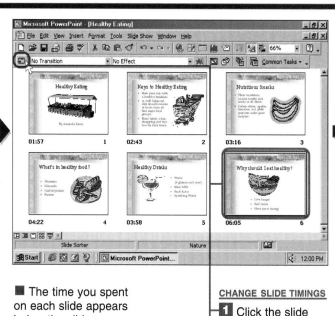

■ When you finish rehearsing the slide show, a dialog box appears, displaying the total time for the slide show.

4 To record the time you spent on each slide and use the timings when you later view the slide show, click **Yes**.

■ The time you spent on each slide appears below the slides.

CHANGE SLIDE TIMINGS

1 Click the slide you want to change the timing for.

2 Click ▣.

Why would I want to change the slide timings?

Changing the slide timings is useful when you want a slide to appear during a slide show for a longer or shorter time than you originally rehearsed. You may also want to change the slide timings to ensure your presentation runs for a specific length of time.

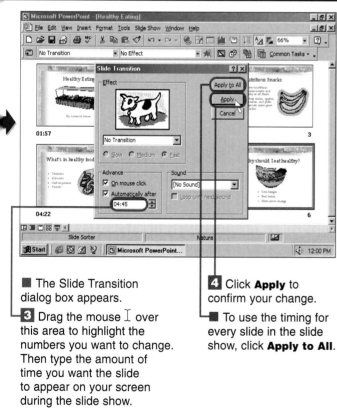

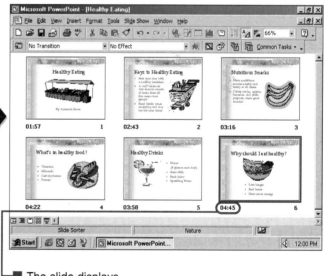

■ The Slide Transition dialog box appears.

3 Drag the mouse I over this area to highlight the numbers you want to change. Then type the amount of time you want the slide to appear on your screen during the slide show.

4 Click **Apply** to confirm your change.

■ To use the timing for every slide in the slide show, click **Apply to All**.

■ The slide displays the new timing.

VIEW A SLIDE SHOW

You can view a slide show of your presentation on a computer screen.

VIEW A SLIDE SHOW

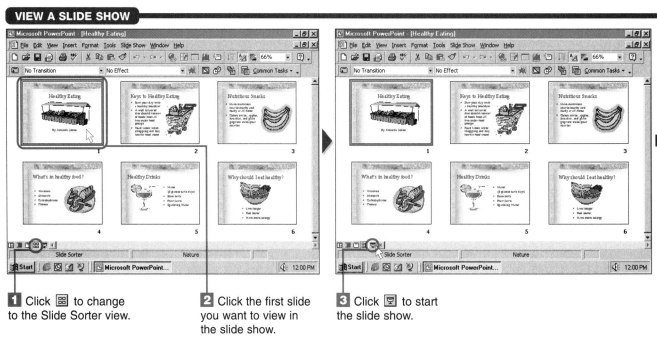

1 Click ⊞ to change to the Slide Sorter view.

2 Click the first slide you want to view in the slide show.

3 Click 🖵 to start the slide show.

How can I use my keyboard to move through a slide show?

Task	Press this key
Display the next slide	Spacebar
Display the previous slide	`◆Backspace`
Display any slide	Type the number of the slide and then press `Enter`
End the slide show	`Esc`
Pause the slide show and turn the screen black	`B` (Press `B` again to return to the slide show)
Pause the slide show and turn the screen white	`W` (Press `W` again to return to the slide show)

Healthy Eating

By Amanda Jones

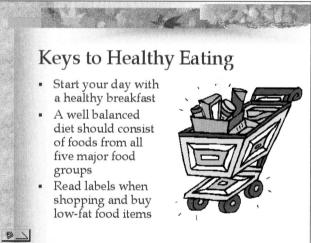

Keys to Healthy Eating

- Start your day with a healthy breakfast
- A well balanced diet should consist of foods from all five major food groups
- Read labels when shopping and buy low-fat food items

■ The first slide fills your screen.

Note: You can press the `Esc` *key to end the slide show at any time.*

4 To display the next slide, click the current slide.

■ To return to the previous slide, press the `◆Backspace` key.

■ The next slide appears.

■ Repeat step **4** until you finish viewing all the slides in the slide show.

CONTINUED

VIEW A SLIDE SHOW

During a slide show, you can instantly display any slide in your presentation. You can also draw on the slides to emphasize information you are presenting.

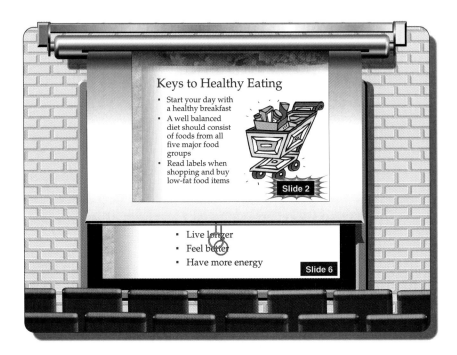

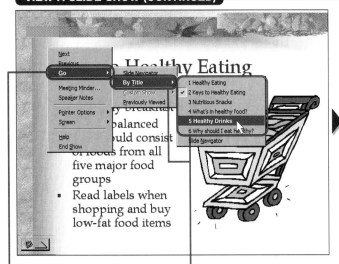

DISPLAY ANY SLIDE

1 Right-click the current slide. A menu appears.

2 Click **Go**.

3 Click **By Title**. A list of the titles of the slides in your presentation appears.

4 Click the title of the slide you want to display.

Note: A check mark (✔) appears beside the title of the current slide.

■ The slide you selected appears.

Will the lines I draw during the slide show remain on my slides?

No. Lines you draw during a slide show are temporary and will not appear when the slide show is over.

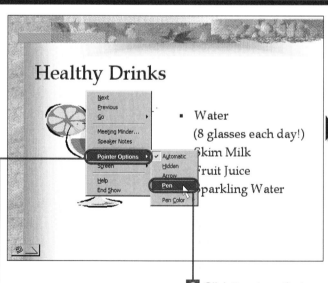

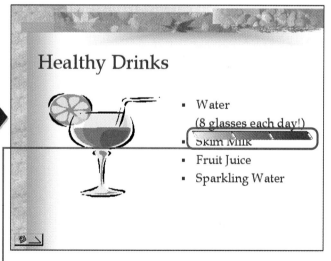

DRAW ON A SLIDE

1 Right-click the slide you want to draw on. A menu appears.

2 Click **Pointer Options**.

3 Click **Pen** to activate the pen.

Note: You can also press and hold down the `Ctrl` *key and then press the* `P` *key to activate the pen.*

4 Position the mouse where you want to start drawing on the slide.

5 Drag the mouse to draw on the slide.

■ To erase all the drawings on the slide, press the `E` key.

*Note: When drawing on a slide, you must press the **Spacebar** to display the next slide. To once again use the mouse pointer to move through slides, repeat steps 1 to 3, except select **Automatic** in step 3.*

USING MEETING MINDER

You can record meeting minutes during a slide show to take notes on important ideas discussed during your presentation. You can also assign tasks, called action items, to your colleagues during your presentation.

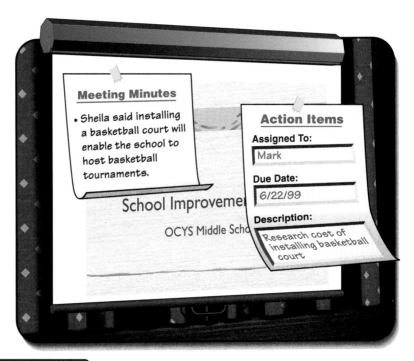

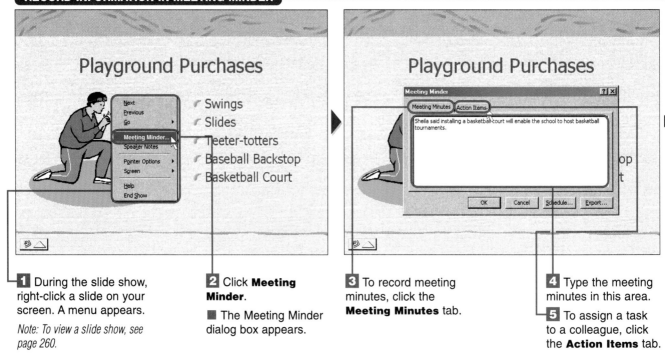

1 During the slide show, right-click a slide on your screen. A menu appears.

Note: To view a slide show, see page 260.

2 Click **Meeting Minder**.

■ The Meeting Minder dialog box appears.

3 To record meeting minutes, click the **Meeting Minutes** tab.

4 Type the meeting minutes in this area.

5 To assign a task to a colleague, click the **Action Items** tab.

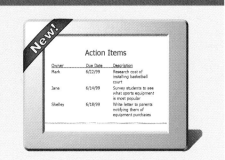

How can I view the tasks I assigned during my slide show?

PowerPoint creates a new slide at the end of the slide show listing the tasks you assigned. This lets the audience review the tasks and take note of the items that are their responsibility.

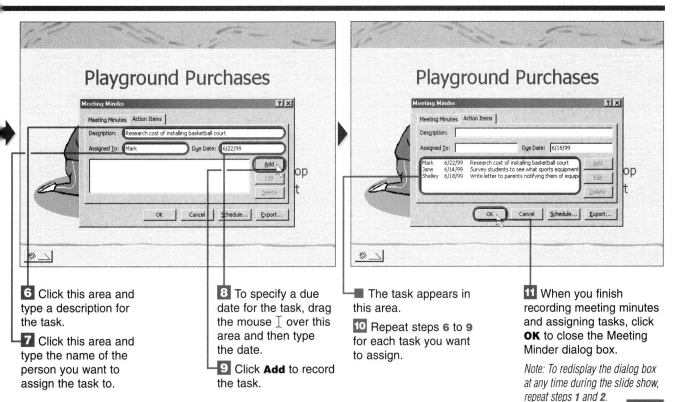

6 Click this area and type a description for the task.

7 Click this area and type the name of the person you want to assign the task to.

8 To specify a due date for the task, drag the mouse I over this area and then type the date.

9 Click **Add** to record the task.

■ The task appears in this area.

10 Repeat steps **6** to **9** for each task you want to assign.

11 When you finish recording meeting minutes and assigning tasks, click **OK** to close the Meeting Minder dialog box.

Note: To redisplay the dialog box at any time during the slide show, repeat steps 1 and 2.

USING MEETING MINDER

After you finish viewing a slide show, you can review the meeting minutes and tasks you recorded in a Microsoft Word document. You can also add your tasks to the Tasks list in Microsoft Outlook.

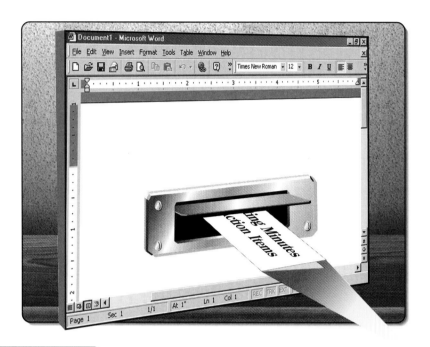

SEND INFORMATION TO MICROSOFT WORD

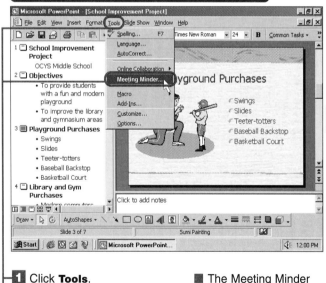

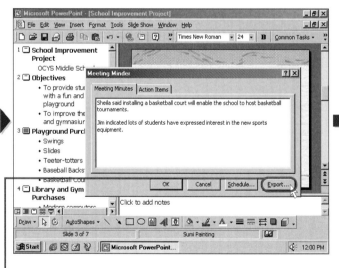

1 Click **Tools**.

2 Click **Meeting Minder**.

Note: If Meeting Minder does not appear on the menu, position the mouse ⬚ over the bottom of the menu to display all the menu commands.

■ The Meeting Minder dialog box appears.

3 Click **Export** to send the meeting minutes and tasks to Microsoft Word.

■ The Meeting Minder Export dialog box appears.

What is the Tasks list in Microsoft Outlook?

The Tasks list in Microsoft Outlook is an electronic to-do list of personal and work-related tasks you want to accomplish.

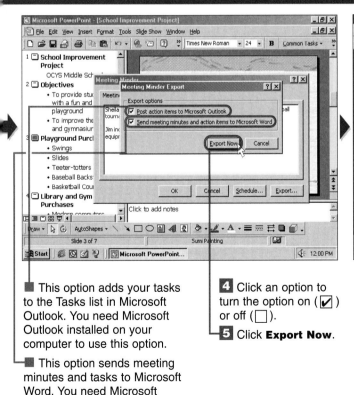

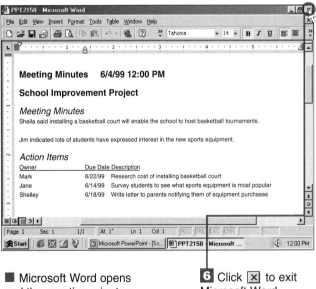

■ This option adds your tasks to the Tasks list in Microsoft Outlook. You need Microsoft Outlook installed on your computer to use this option.

■ This option sends meeting minutes and tasks to Microsoft Word. You need Microsoft Word installed on your computer to use this option.

4 Click an option to turn the option on (✔) or off (☐).

5 Click **Export Now**.

■ Microsoft Word opens and the meeting minutes and tasks appear in a Word document.

■ You can edit, save and print the document as you would any Word document.

6 Click ☒ to exit Microsoft Word.

CREATE A CUSTOM SLIDE SHOW

You can create a custom slide show that includes only some of the slides in a presentation. This is useful if you want to customize your presentation to suit specific audiences.

CREATE A CUSTOM SLIDE SHOW

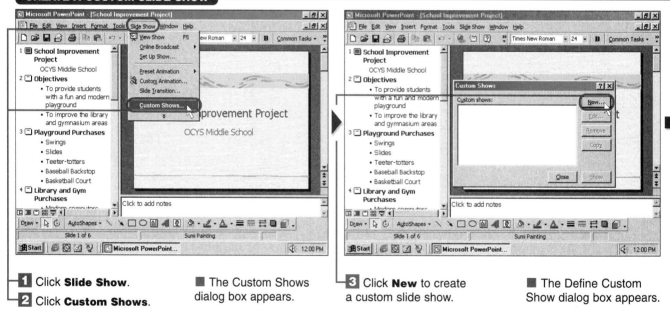

1 Click **Slide Show**.

2 Click **Custom Shows**.

■ The Custom Shows dialog box appears.

3 Click **New** to create a custom slide show.

■ The Define Custom Show dialog box appears.

?

Can I create several custom slide shows from one presentation?

You can create several custom slide shows from a presentation containing all your ideas and information. For example, you may want to use a presentation about a new product to create a detailed custom slide show for the sales department and a shorter custom slide show for the executive committee.

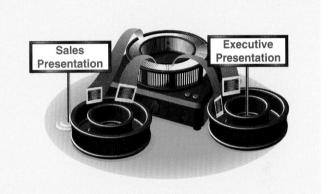

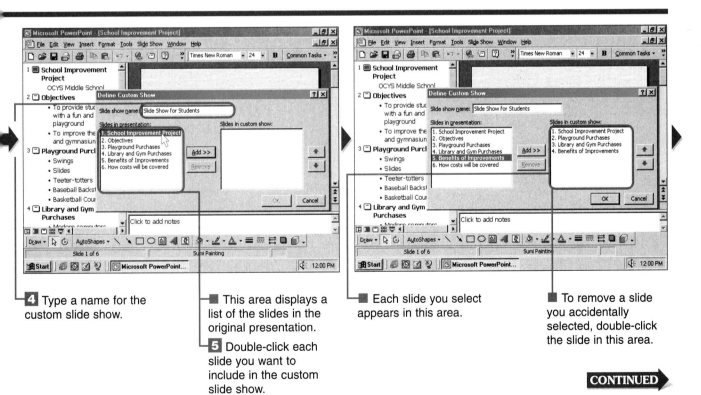

■ **4** Type a name for the custom slide show.

■ This area displays a list of the slides in the original presentation.

5 Double-click each slide you want to include in the custom slide show.

■ Each slide you select appears in this area.

■ To remove a slide you accidentally selected, double-click the slide in this area.

CONTINUED▶

CREATE A CUSTOM SLIDE SHOW

You can rearrange
the order of the
slides in a custom
slide show to suit
your needs.

Changing the order of
the slides in a custom
slide show does not
affect the order of the
slides in the original
presentation.

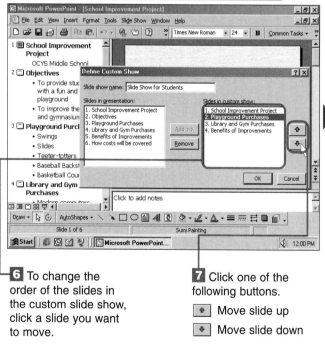

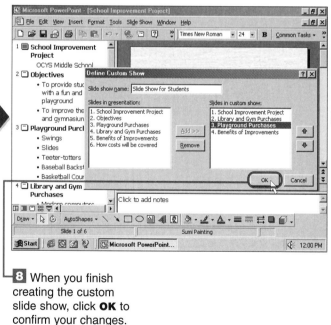

6 To change the
order of the slides in
the custom slide show,
click a slide you want
to move.

7 Click one of the
following buttons.

⬆ Move slide up

⬇ Move slide down

8 When you finish
creating the custom
slide show, click **OK** to
confirm your changes.

How do I make changes to the slides in a custom slide show?

When you make changes to the slides in the original presentation, the slides in the custom slide show automatically display the changes.

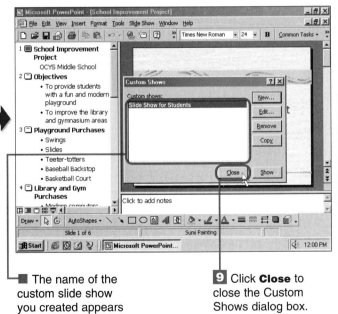

■ The name of the custom slide show you created appears in this area.

9 Click **Close** to close the Custom Shows dialog box.

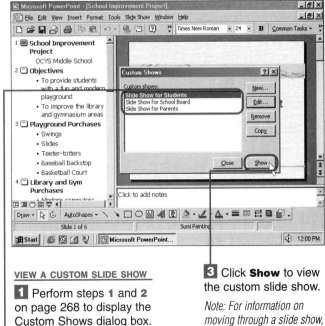

VIEW A CUSTOM SLIDE SHOW

1 Perform steps 1 and 2 on page 268 to display the Custom Shows dialog box.

2 Click the custom slide show you want to view.

3 Click **Show** to view the custom slide show.

Note: For information on moving through a slide show, see the top of page 261.

PRESENT A SLIDE SHOW USING TWO MONITORS

You can present
a slide show to
an audience using
one monitor while
you view the
presentation on
another monitor.

Presenting a slide
show using two
monitors allows you
to see your speaker
notes and the outline
of your presentation
while the audience
views only the slides.

PRESENT A SLIDE SHOW USING TWO MONITORS

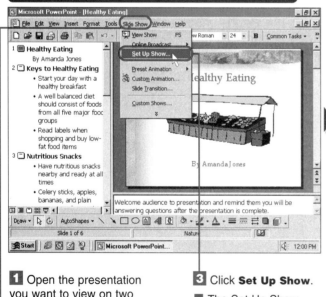

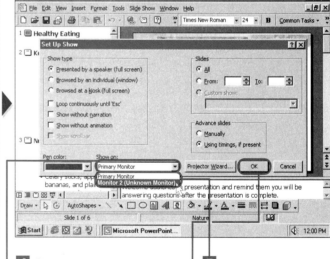

1 Open the presentation
you want to view on two
monitors. To open a
presentation, see page 28.

2 Click **Slide Show**.

3 Click **Set Up Show**.

■ The Set Up Show
dialog box appears.

4 Click this area to
display a list of monitors
set up on your computer.

*Note: If this area is not
available, your computer is
not set up to use two monitors.
For more information, see the
top of page 273.*

5 Click the monitor you
want to use to present
the slide show to the
audience.

6 Click **OK** to confirm
your change.

How can I set up my computer to use two monitors?

To set up your computer to use two monitors, your computer must be running Windows 98 and have dual-monitor hardware installed. For more information on setting up your computer to use two monitors, refer to your Windows 98 manual.

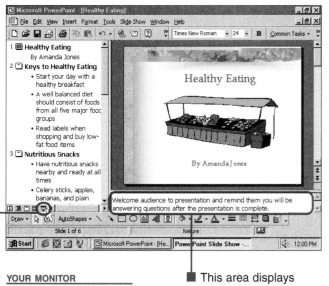

YOUR MONITOR

1 Click 🖵 to begin the slide show.

■ Your monitor displays the presentation in the Normal view. The slide show appears on the audience's monitor.

■ This area displays the speaker notes for the current slide.

AUDIENCE'S MONITOR

■ The audience's monitor displays the slide show.

■ You can click the current slide to display the next slide in the slide show.

Note: For more information on viewing a slide show, see page 260.

USING THE PACK AND GO WIZARD

You can use the Pack and Go Wizard to package your presentation onto a floppy disk and transport it to another computer.

The Pack and Go Wizard efficiently packages your presentation and all the files associated with the presentation, such as sound or image files.

PACKAGE A PRESENTATION

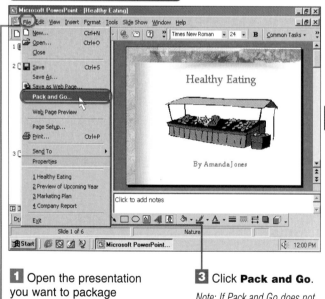

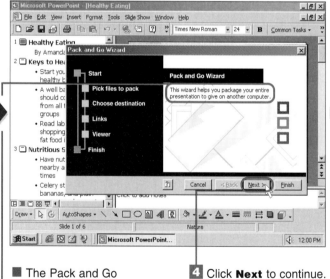

1 Open the presentation you want to package and transport to another computer. To open a presentation, see page 28.

2 Click **File**.

3 Click **Pack and Go**.

Note: If Pack and Go does not appear on the menu, position the mouse over the bottom of the menu to display all the menu commands.

■ The Pack and Go Wizard appears.

■ This area describes the wizard.

4 Click **Next** to continue.

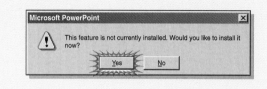

Why does this dialog box appear when I try to use the Pack and Go Wizard?

This dialog box appears if the Pack and Go Wizard is not installed on your computer. Insert the CD-ROM disc you used to install PowerPoint into your CD-ROM drive and then click **Yes** to install the wizard.

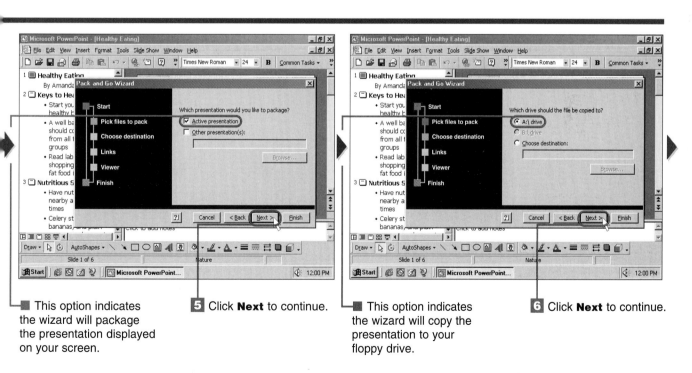

■ This option indicates the wizard will package the presentation displayed on your screen.

5 Click **Next** to continue.

■ This option indicates the wizard will copy the presentation to your floppy drive.

6 Click **Next** to continue.

CONTINUED

USING THE PACK AND GO WIZARD

The Pack and Go Wizard compresses, or squeezes, your presentation so you can easily transfer the presentation from one computer to another.

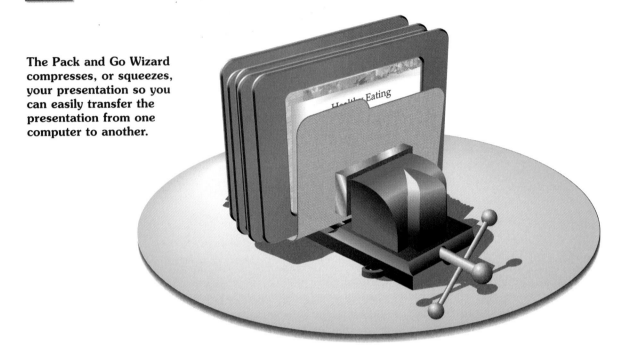

PACKAGE A PRESENTATION (CONTINUED)

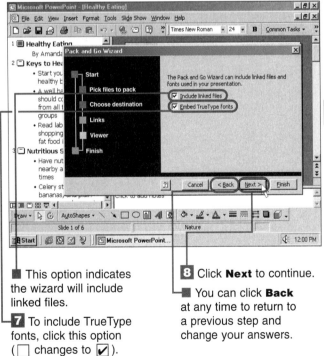

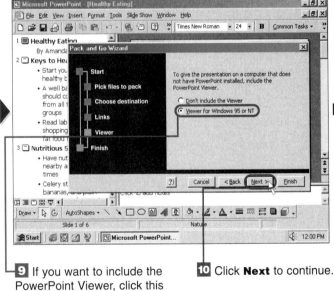

■ This option indicates the wizard will include linked files.

7 To include TrueType fonts, click this option (☐ changes to ☑).

8 Click **Next** to continue.

■ You can click **Back** at any time to return to a previous step and change your answers.

9 If you want to include the PowerPoint Viewer, click this option (○ changes to ◉).

Note: If you chose to include the PowerPoint Viewer, insert the CD-ROM disc you used to install PowerPoint into your CD-ROM drive.

10 Click **Next** to continue.

What can I include when packaging my presentation?

Linked Files

Allows you to open files included in your presentation, such as sounds and movies, on the other computer.

TrueType Fonts

Ensures that the text in your presentation will be displayed correctly, even if the other computer does not have the same fonts installed.

PowerPoint Viewer

Allows you to deliver your presentation on a computer that does not have PowerPoint installed.

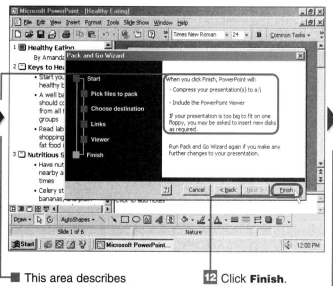

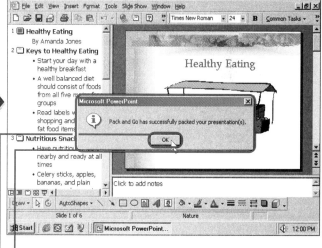

■ This area describes the tasks PowerPoint will perform to package the presentation.

11 Insert a floppy disk into your floppy drive.

12 Click **Finish**.

Note: If your presentation is too large to fit on one floppy disk, a dialog box will appear, asking you to insert another disk.

■ This dialog box appears when the wizard has successfully packaged the presentation.

13 Click **OK** to close the dialog box.

■ If you make changes to the presentation after using the Pack and Go Wizard, you will need to run the wizard again to update the package.

USING THE PACK AND GO WIZARD

When you arrive at your destination, you can unpack your presentation on the computer you will use to deliver the presentation.

UNPACK A PRESENTATION

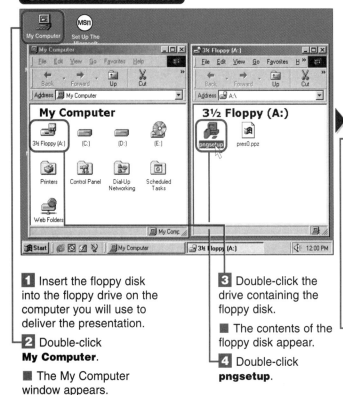

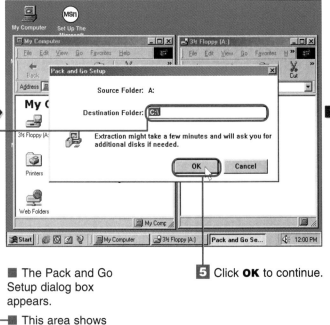

1 Insert the floppy disk into the floppy drive on the computer you will use to deliver the presentation.

2 Double-click **My Computer**.

■ The My Computer window appears.

3 Double-click the drive containing the floppy disk.

■ The contents of the floppy disk appear.

4 Double-click **pngsetup**.

■ The Pack and Go Setup dialog box appears.

■ This area shows the location where the wizard will save the presentation.

5 Click **OK** to continue.

Can I view the slide show again later?

By default, the Pack and Go Wizard saves the presentation you unpacked on drive C. You can open the presentation and view the slide show again at any time.

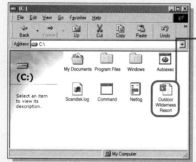

2 Double-click the presentation you want to open. PowerPoint presentations display the icon.

■ To view the slide show, see page 260.

1 To display the contents of drive C, perform steps **2** and **3** below, except double-click drive C in step **3**.

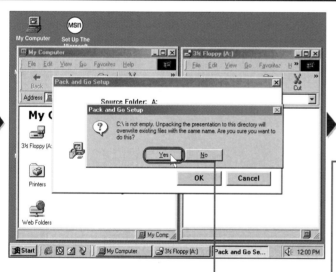

■ A warning dialog box appears, stating that the location where the wizard will save the presentation contains files. Saving the presentation to this location will replace any existing files with the same name.

6 Click **Yes** to continue.

Note: If you used more than one disk to package the presentation, a dialog box will appear, asking you to insert the next disk.

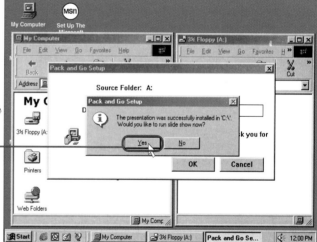

■ A dialog box appears, stating that the presentation was successfully installed.

7 Click **Yes** to view the slide show.

■ The slide show begins. For information on viewing a slide show, see page 260.

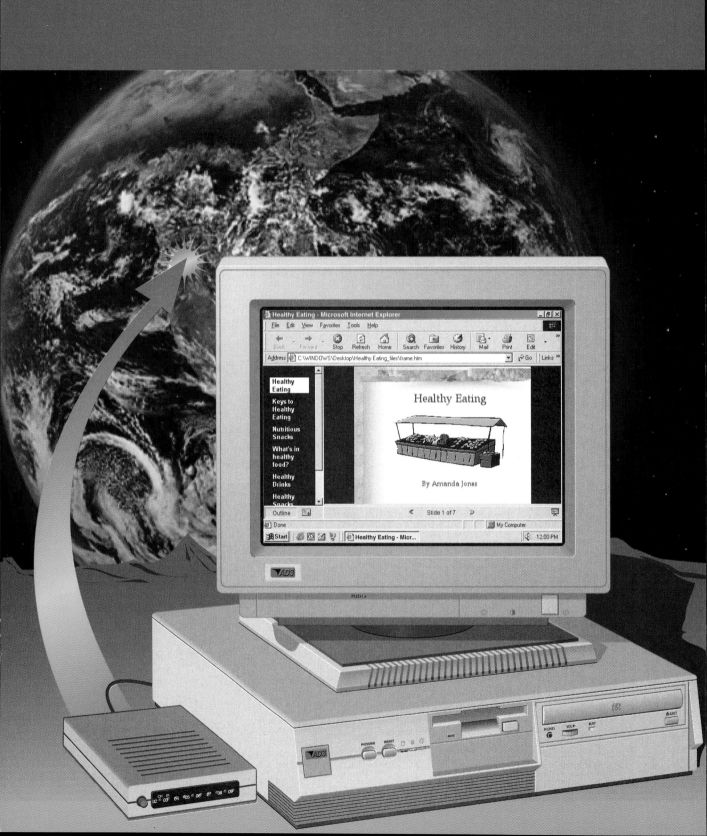

CHAPTER 14

PowerPoint and the Internet

Are you wondering how you can use PowerPoint to share information with other people on the Internet? In this chapter you will learn how to e-mail a presentation, save a presentation as a Web page and more.

Keys to Healthy Eating
- Start your day with a healthy breakfast
- A well balanced diet should consist of foods from all five major food groups
- Read labels when shopping and buy low-fat food items

You can e-mail
a presentation
to a friend,
family member
or colleague.

Before you can e-mail a
presentation, Microsoft
Outlook must be set up on
your computer. Microsoft
Outlook is a program that
allows you to send and
receive e-mail messages.

E-MAIL A PRESENTATION

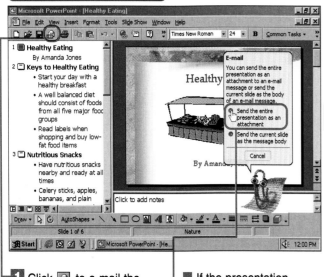

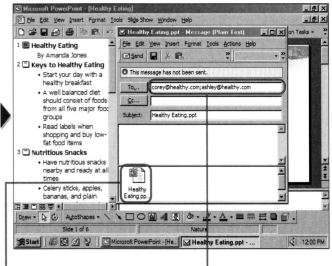

1 Click 🖃 to e-mail the
current presentation.

*Note: If 🖃 is not displayed,
click 🔧 on the Standard toolbar
to display all the buttons.*

■ If the presentation
contains more than one
slide, a message appears,
asking if you want to send
the entire presentation or
just the current slide.

2 Click this option to send
the entire presentation.

■ A window appears
for the e-mail message.

■ An icon for the
presentation appears
in the message.

3 Click this area and
type the e-mail address
of each person you want
to receive the message.
Separate each address
with a semicolon (;).

How do I e-mail one slide in my presentation?

To e-mail the slide currently displayed on your screen, perform steps **1** to **5** below, except select **Send the current slide as the message body** in step **2**. Then click **Send this Slide** to send the message.

When you e-mail one slide, the slide appears in the body of the message.

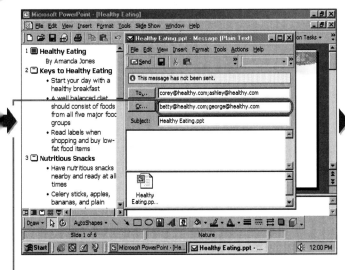

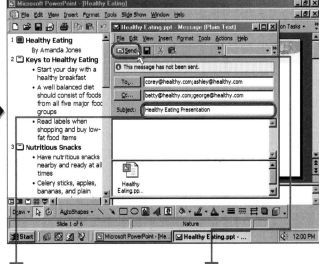

4 To send a copy of the message, click this area and type the e-mail address of each person you want to receive a copy. Separate each address with a semicolon (;).

Note: You may want to send a copy of the message to people who are not directly involved but would be interested in the message.

5 Click this area and type a subject for the message.

Note: If a subject already exists, you can drag the mouse I over the existing subject and then type a new subject.

6 Click **Send** to send the message.

CREATE A HYPERLINK

You can create a hyperlink to connect a word or phrase in your presentation to another document on your computer, network, corporate intranet or the Internet.

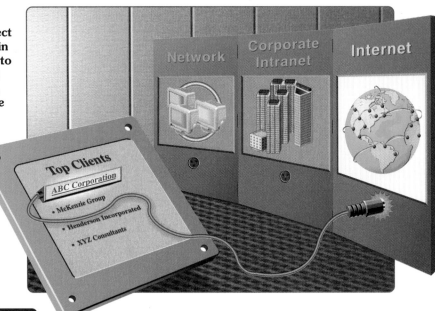

An intranet is a small version of the Internet within a company or organization.

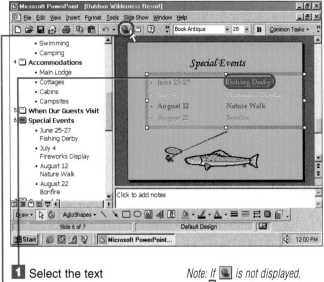

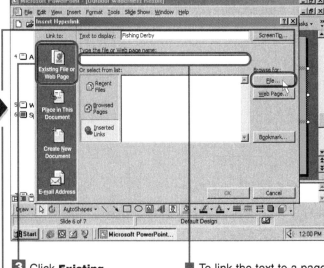

1 Select the text you want to make a hyperlink. To select text, see page 56.

2 Click 🔗 to create a hyperlink.

Note: If 🔗 is not displayed, click ❯ on the Standard toolbar to display all the buttons.

■ The Insert Hyperlink dialog box appears.

3 Click **Existing File or Web Page**.

4 To link the text to a document on your computer or network, click **File**.

■ To link the text to a page on the Web, click this area and then type the address of the Web page (example: www.maran.com). Then skip to step **7** on page 286.

Can I make an object a hyperlink?

Yes. If your presentation includes an object, such as an AutoShape or clip art image, you can make the object a hyperlink. To make an object a hyperlink, click the object and then perform steps **2** to **7**, starting on page 284.

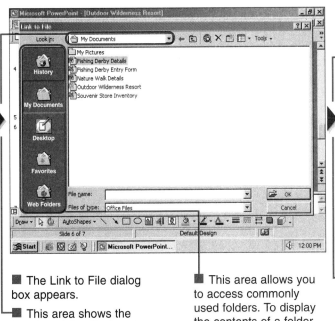

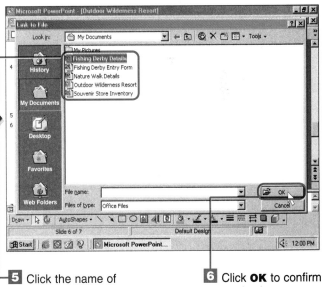

■ The Link to File dialog box appears.

■ This area shows the location of the displayed documents. You can click this area to change the location.

■ This area allows you to access commonly used folders. To display the contents of a folder, click the folder.

Note: For information on the commonly used folders, see the top of page 25.

5 Click the name of the document you want to link the text to.

6 Click **OK** to confirm your selection.

CONTINUED

CREATE A HYPERLINK

When you select a hyperlink during a slide show, the document or Web page connected to the hyperlink will appear on your screen.

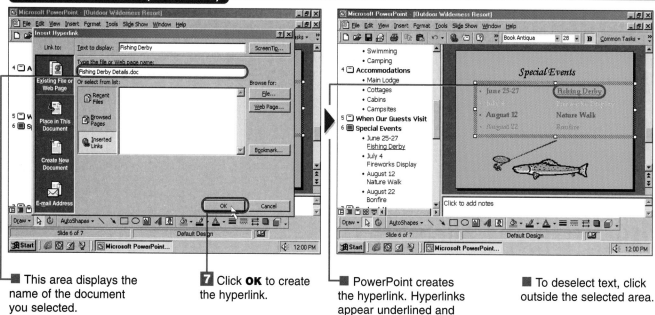

■ This area displays the name of the document you selected.

7 Click **OK** to create the hyperlink.

■ PowerPoint creates the hyperlink. Hyperlinks appear underlined and in color.

■ To deselect text, click outside the selected area.

? **Can PowerPoint automatically create a hyperlink for me?**

When you type the address of a document located on your network or the Internet, PowerPoint will automatically change the address to a hyperlink for you.

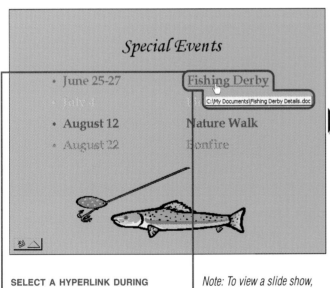

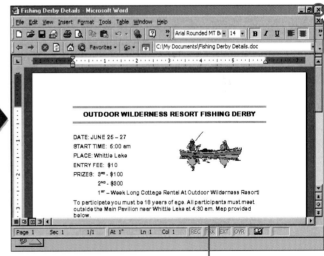

SELECT A HYPERLINK DURING A SLIDE SHOW

■ When you position the mouse 🖑 over a hyperlink during a slide show, a yellow box appears, displaying where the hyperlink will take you.

Note: To view a slide show, see page 260.

1 Click a hyperlink to display the document or Web page connected to the hyperlink.

■ The document or Web page connected to the hyperlink appears.

2 When you finish reviewing the document or Web page, click ☒ to close the window.

PREVIEW A PRESENTATION AS A WEB PAGE

You can preview how your presentation will look as a Web page. This allows you to see how the presentation will appear on the Internet or your company's intranet.

An intranet is a small version of the Internet within a company or organization.

PREVIEW A PRESENTATION AS A WEB PAGE

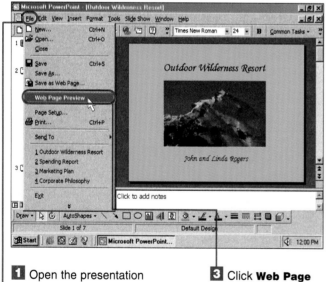

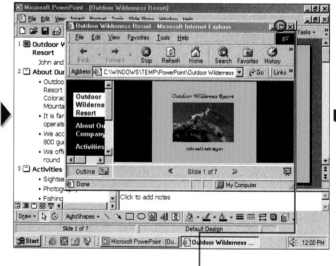

1 Open the presentation you want to view as a Web page. To open a presentation, see page 28.

2 Click **File**.

3 Click **Web Page Preview** to preview your presentation as a Web page.

■ Your Web browser window opens, displaying your presentation as a Web page.

■ To maximize the Web browser window to fill your screen, click □.

? **Will my Web page look the same to everyone who views the Web page?**

Different Web browsers may display your Web page differently. There are many Web browsers used on the Web. The two most popular Web browsers are Microsoft Internet Explorer and Netscape Navigator.

Microsoft Internet Explorer

Netscape Navigator

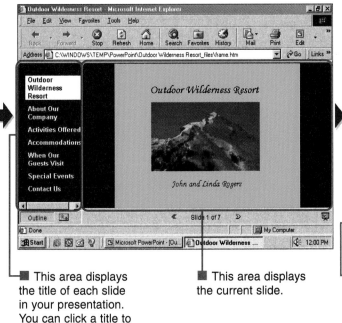

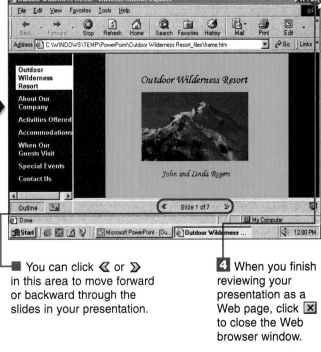

■ This area displays the title of each slide in your presentation. You can click a title to display a different slide.

■ This area displays the current slide.

■ You can click « or » in this area to move forward or backward through the slides in your presentation.

4 When you finish reviewing your presentation as a Web page, click ☒ to close the Web browser window.

SAVE A PRESENTATION AS A WEB PAGE

You can save a
presentation as a
Web page. This
lets you place the
presentation on
the Internet or your
company's intranet.

An intranet is a small
version of the Internet
within a company or
organization.

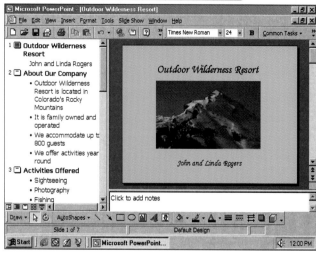

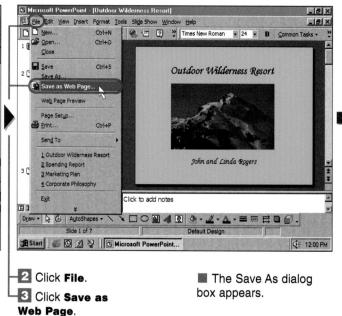

1 Open the presentation
you want to save as a
Web page. To open a
presentation, see page 28.

2 Click **File**.

3 Click **Save as
Web Page**.

■ The Save As dialog
box appears.

How do I make my Web page available for other people to view?

After you save a presentation as a Web page, you can transfer the page to a computer that stores Web pages, called a Web server. Once you publish a Web page on a Web server, the page will be available for other people to view. For more information on publishing a Web page, contact your network administrator or Internet service provider.

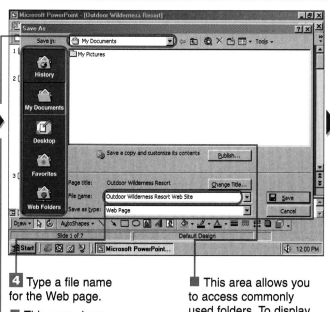

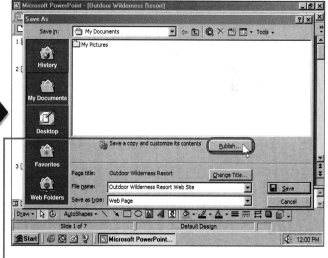

4 Type a file name for the Web page.

■ This area shows the location where PowerPoint will store the Web page. You can click this area to change the location.

■ This area allows you to access commonly used folders. To display the contents of a folder, click the folder.

Note: For information on the commonly used folders, see the top of page 25.

5 Click **Publish**.

■ The Publish as Web Page dialog box appears.

CONTINUED

SAVE A PRESENTATION AS A WEB PAGE

You can customize your Web page to display only specific slides. You can also choose not to display your speaker notes on the Web page.

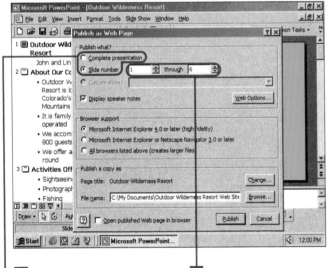

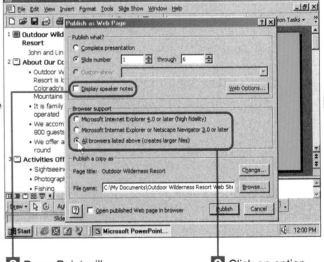

6 Click an option to specify whether you want to save the entire presentation or only specific slides as a Web page (○ changes to ◉).

7 If you selected **Slide number** in step **6**, double-click this area and type the number of the first slide you want to save. Press the `Tab` key and type the number of the last slide you want to save.

8 PowerPoint will display your speaker notes on each Web page. If you do not want to display your speaker notes, click this option (☑ changes to ☐).

9 Click an option to specify which Web browser(s) you want to be able to display your Web page (○ changes to ◉).

?

Which Web browser(s) should I choose to display my Web page?

You should choose the Web browser that most people will use to view your Web page. The most popular browsers on the Web are currently Microsoft Internet Explorer and Netscape Navigator.

Older versions of Web browsers will not be able to display objects such as sound and movies in your presentation. To ensure that most people will be able to view your Web page, select the **All browsers listed above** option in step **9** below.

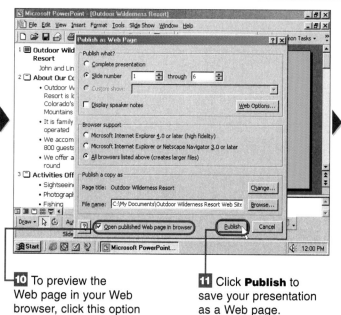

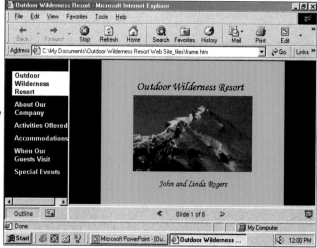

10 To preview the Web page in your Web browser, click this option (☐ changes to ☑).

11 Click **Publish** to save your presentation as a Web page.

■ Your Web browser opens and displays the Web page. For information on viewing a Web page in the Web browser, see page 288.

INDEX

INDEX

H

handles on objects, 171
handouts
    footers or headers, change, 116-117
    orientation, change, 244-245
    print, 246-247
headers, change, 116-117
height, change
    of objects, 171
    of rows, in tables, 157
help
    using help index, 36-37
    using Office Assistant, 34-35
hide
    comments, 241
    datasheets, 142
    Office Assistant, 35
    ruler, 101, 103
    slide text, 63
    slides, 232
    Tables and Borders toolbar, 162
    text formatting, 93
    toolbars, 50-51
History folder, 25
hyperlinks
    create, 284-287
    select during slide shows, 287
    use objects as, 285

I

ignore spelling errors, 77
images. See graphics; objects
importance of text, change, 68
indent text, 100-101
index, help, use, 36-37
insert
    action buttons, 226-227
    AutoCorrect entries, 81
    AutoShapes, 124-125
    boxes in organization charts, 149
    bullets, 99
    characters, 60
    charts, 136-137
    clip art, 130-131
    columns in tables, 158-159
    comments, 240-241
    data tables, in charts, 140

    decimal places, 143
    hyperlinks, 284-287
    movies, 190-193, 194-195
    numbers, 99
    organization charts, 146-151
    pictures, 132-133
    points, 61
    rows in tables, 158-159
    slides
        from another presentation, 236-239
        new, 46-47
    sounds, 184-187, 188-189
        recorded, 200-201
    summary slides, 234-235
    symbols, 70-71
    tables, 154-155
    tabs, 102-103
    text, 60-61
    text boxes, 126-127
    text effects, 128-129
Internet
    overview, 9
    and PowerPoint, 282-293
intranets, 284, 288, 290
italicize, text, 84, 90-91

K

keyboards, move through slide shows using, 261
kiosks, 9
    set up slide shows to present at, 252-255

L

landscape orientation, 245
layout of slides, change, 44-45
LCD (Liquid Crystal Display) panels, 9
left
    align text, 88
    tabs, 102-103
light bulbs displayed on slides, 19
lines
    on objects
        color, change, 175
        dash style, change, 177
        remove, 175
        thickness, change, 176
    in tables, thickness for borders, change, 166-167
linked files, 277
links. See hyperlinks
Liquid Crystal Display (LCD) panels, 9

INDEX

INDEX

INDEX

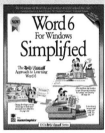

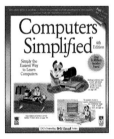

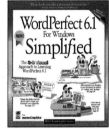

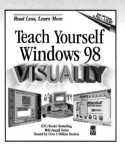

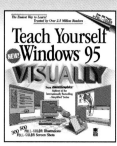
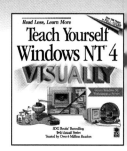

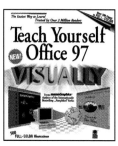
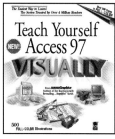